# Becoming
# Laura Ingalls Wilder

✧

MISSOURI BIOGRAPHY SERIES

*William E. Foley, Editor*

# Becoming Laura Ingalls Wilder

## The Woman behind the Legend

✣

John E. Miller

UNIVERSITY OF MISSOURI PRESS
COLUMBIA AND LONDON

Copyright © 1998 by
The Curators of the University of Missouri
University of Missouri Press, Columbia, Missouri 65201
Printed and bound in the United States of America
All rights reserved
5   4   3   2   1      02   01   00   99   98

Library of Congress Cataloging-in-Publication Data

Miller, John E., 1945–
    Becoming Laura Ingalls Wilder : the woman behind the legend / John
E. Miller.
        p.   cm.—(Missouri biography series)
    Includes index.
    ISBN 0-8262-1167-4 (alk. paper)
    1. Wilder, Laura Ingalls, 1867–1957—Biography.   2. Women authors,
American—20th century—Biography.   3. Women pioneers—United
States—Biography.   4. Frontier and pioneer life—Missouri.
5. Missouri—Biography.   I. Title.   II. Series.
PS3545.I342Z769   1998
813'.52—dc21
    [B]                                                                97-51348
                                                                         CIP

⊗™ This paper meets the requirements of the
American National Standard for Permanence of Paper
for Printed Library Materials, Z39.48, 1984.

Designer: Kristie Lee
Typesetter: BOOKCOMP
Printer and Binder: Thomson-Shore, Inc.
Typefaces: Berkeley Book and Nuptual Script

*For Ann*

# Contents

# Acknowledgments

❦

*I*n researching and writing this biography, I have benefited from the assistance and ideas of many people, and I want to thank them all for their generosity and enthusiasm. Dwight M. Miller, senior archivist at the Herbert Hoover Library, was a fount of information and advice. I would like to thank the other staff at the Hoover Library, as well as those at the State Historical Societies of South Dakota, Missouri, Wisconsin, Iowa, Minnesota, and Kansas, the Detroit Public Library, and the National Archives. Vivian Glover and Craig Munger at the Laura Ingalls Wilder Museum in De Smet were always courteous and helpful, and Jo Ann Gray and her staff at the Laura Ingalls Wilder/Rose Wilder Lane Home and Museum in Mansfield likewise made my job much easier. The guides and personnel at the Ingalls and Wilder home sites in Pepin, Independence, Walnut Grove, Burr Oak, and Spring Valley were also quite helpful. Connie Potter at the National Archives steered me in the right direction and went out of her way to answer my questions. Dozens of people who knew Laura Ingalls Wilder and her family or who have read her books talked to me and passed on their knowledge and thoughts. I especially want to acknowledge those who granted me formal interviews, including Nava Austin, Joan Cooley, Clifford Cooper, Peggy Dennis, Carl Hartley, Virginia Hartley, Clyde Rowan, Neta Seal, Aubrey Sherwood, and Amon Short.

Many other people too numerous to mention have provided information and encouraged me in this project. A special word of thanks goes to Bill Anderson, who read the manuscript and answered many of my questions and who has prevented at least some of the kinds of errors that inevitably

creep into a work such as this. Thanks also goes to Bill Holtz, who was instrumental in getting me started on this project and who read the manuscript and made pointed suggestions regarding it. Beverly Jarrett, Bill Foley, Jane Lago, and Annette Wenda, my editors at the University of Missouri Press, have been great to work with and made the work even more pleasurable than it otherwise would have been.

I am grateful to Roger MacBride and his heirs for granting permission to use the Rose Wilder Lane Papers, and I also want to thank the State Historical Society of Missouri, the South Dakota State Historical Society, the Herbert Hoover Presidential Library, the Laura Ingalls Wilder/Rose Wilder Lane Home and Museum, Bill Anderson, and Phyllis Bell for permission to reproduce photographs.

This biography is dedicated to my daughter, Ann, who dressed up like Laura as a little girl and who helped kindle my enthusiasm for the books. I have to admit that it was my wife, Kathy, who first read the books to Ann, and I want to thank her for going along with all my wanderings to sites and archives and for listening to endless reports of my findings. Finally, without my son, Tom, this book would have taken a lot longer to turn out. He has been the computer expert in the house, and now that he is off to college I'm going to have to solicit his advice long-distance.

# Becoming
## Laura Ingalls Wilder

# Introduction

*ॐ*

he books of Laura Ingalls Wilder, one of America's best-known and most widely read authors of children's literature, continue to fascinate children and adults alike. They provide an appealing picture of life on the agricultural frontier during the 1870s and 1880s. The eight novels that she published between 1932 and 1943 are prominently displayed in many bookstores, often in their own special section that includes other books written by and about her, not to mention a growing proliferation of Laura Ingalls Wilder cookbooks, songbooks, date books, trivia books, calendars, and other spin-offs. Recently, several new fictional series have appeared, extending the stories of her daughter Rose's life after the family moved to Mansfield, Missouri, in 1894, and of her mother Caroline Ingalls's childhood near Brookfield, Wisconsin.

Wilder's books gained instant popularity upon their publication during the 1930s and 1940s and continue to enjoy strong sales. They acquired additional readers and fans between 1974 and 1983 with the airing of the television series *Little House on the Prairie,* starring Michael Landon as Pa, Karen Grassle as Ma, and Melissa Gilbert as Laura. The episodes possessed only the most tenuous relation to historical fact, but they continue to be rerun today, to the delight of Wilder fans everywhere. One of the most intriguing aspects of the Wilder phenomenon is the huge popularity she enjoys in many foreign countries, especially Japan. Her novels have been translated into more than forty languages and dialects.

When people today think about Laura Ingalls Wilder, they usually conjure up one of two images: either a young girl and adolescent named

Laura, whom they have come to know and love through the novels, or a sweet old lady who lived in the Missouri Ozarks and waited until her mid-sixties to start writing stories about her childhood. They are less likely to think about what happened to her between the ages of eighteen, when she married Almanzo Wilder, and sixty-five, when she emerged as an author whose books, published every year or two, stirred eager anticipation among her growing number of fans.

The most interesting question that we can ask about this remarkable woman is how the little girl who is described in the books finally emerged as the skillful author who rendered stories so beautifully and evocatively that enthusiasts today—both young and old—continue to reread them. (True Wilder fans differ among themselves only in how many times they have read the entire series.) Some people consider it a kind of miracle that this "untutored genius" suddenly became an accomplished writer with no apparent previous experience. Others simply take it for granted that Wilder sat down in her house at Rocky Ridge to draw upon an astonishingly accurate memory to write as honestly and straightforwardly as possible the stories about her childhood that stood out foremost in her mind.

My primary purpose in writing this biography is to confront the question of how "Laura," the girl depicted in the "Little House" books, *became* "Laura Ingalls Wilder," the author of these classics of children's literature. To write her "autobiographical" novels, Wilder needed to undergo a process of *becoming,* which depended heavily upon the inheritance that she had received both from her family and, across the years, from the various environments in which she lived.

In my earlier book, *Laura Ingalls Wilder's Little Town: Where History and Literature Meet,* I described how Wilder during her sixties and seventies in a sense "became" the Laura of the novels: a dutiful and obedient but also strong-willed and independent-minded girl and then young woman who married Almanzo Wilder at the end and drove off with him to make a family and a living on the open spaces of the Dakota countryside. To some readers, the presumed reality of the fictional Laura can become so compelling that it overwhelms their ability to imagine that the actual Laura Ingalls—upon whose life the stories are based—may have been something other than the way she depicted herself in the novels. Reviewers from the outset noted the autobiographical nature of the books, and many readers, with good reason, came to assume that the stories describe things as "they

really happened." What needs to be understood, however, is that the novels, while based in fact, are fiction, and the author relied on the tools that fiction writers normally employ. While we can assume that many of the episodes happened roughly the way they are described, we should not equate the fictional Laura with the real person who wrote the stories and upon whom they are based.

Wilder first attempted to tell her life story, as her daughter had been urging, in 1930. The autobiography was titled "Pioneer Girl" and covered the same period of time later described in her novels, from before she could remember anything as a child (in the novels her age was elevated in the beginning to make the stories plausible) until her marriage at eighteen in 1885. While some book editors were interested in the manuscript, Wilder ultimately failed to find a publisher. Instead, the manuscript became the basis for the much expanded and fictionalized accounts that Wilder's readers later came to know and love. By failing to publish her autobiography, which would have gained her some instant but relatively modest recognition, she opened up an opportunity for herself: the chance to write a third-person fictional account, taking the elements of her own remembered childhood from the hindsight of six decades and conforming them to the dictates of fictional literature.

In some measure, therefore, this book is about how the real Laura Ingalls Wilder became, to her readers, the fictional Laura. More important, however, it is about how the young Laura Ingalls became a successful and popular author recognized far and wide as Laura Ingalls Wilder. In that process of "becoming" she would be addressed by several different names: "Laura," "little half-pint" and "flutterbudget" (by her father, if we believe the descriptions in her novels), "Laura Ingalls," "Laura Wilder," "Mrs. A. J. Wilder" (by the newspaper and townspeople in Mansfield), "Mama Bess" (by her daughter), "Bessie" (by her husband), "Bessie Wilder," and, last, "Laura Ingalls Wilder" (by her fans). The latter, with only a couple of exceptions, did not come into use until the last twenty-five years of her life. It was Wilder's pen name, but it was not the name she most commonly used. Getting to know Laura Ingalls Wilder, therefore, partly involves discovering how her personality evolved coincident to a variety of name changes over time.

At the heart of any analysis of Laura Ingalls Wilder lies a paradox: How did this seemingly ordinary woman come to produce such extraordinary

work? To answer that question, several different approaches might be taken. One would be to deny the latter premise and to argue that, while interesting, Wilder's work was amateurish at best and appealed only to readers addicted to sentimentality, simplicity, and naive characterizations of life on the frontier. Another possible tack would be to admit the excellence of her books but to argue that her daughter Rose's contribution to them was decisive or even primary. Or, one can believe the premise that Laura Ingalls Wilder was, in fact, an extraordinary woman who had something significant to impart to her readers.

The obvious obstacle to making this last claim is that, outside of her writing career, she appeared on the surface to be an ordinary woman in so many respects. Whether operating in the guise of pioneer girl, student, schoolteacher, wife, mother, chicken farmer, churchgoer, lodge member, bridge player, club member, or citizen, Wilder acted out many of the same kinds of scripts that her peers did. To many residents of Mansfield, however, she did seem to project an aura of being "a cut above" other people. In her books, too, she portrayed herself as a leader and unwilling, at times, to accept conventional norms and routines.

Several of Wilder's accomplishments stand out. She was a charter member of and a leading participant in a women's discussion club, the Athenians, established in 1916. She helped found and then served as secretary-treasurer of the local branch of the National Farm Loan Association from the late teens through early 1928. She also ran, unsuccessfully, for public office (as collector of Pleasant Valley Township) in 1925. However, the accomplishments of her daughter, Rose, probably set her apart the most. Rose had been a precocious child. After leaving home at the age of seventeen to become a telegraph operator, she sold real estate in California and then made a name for herself as a newspaperwoman, serial writer, novelist, and short story writer. Her wanderings and adventures in Greenwich Village, Paris, Albania, and elsewhere provided a lively counterpoint to the seemingly prosaic lives of her parents back at Rocky Ridge Farm in the Missouri Ozarks. Rose eventually became a successful and widely recognized figure on the American literary scene during the 1920s and 1930s.

To have produced such an extraordinary child might suggest something beyond the ordinary in the parents. I believe that Laura's own writing career, which included more than a decade of journalism work for the *Missouri Ruralist* before her twelve-year stint as a novelist, indicates her own

unusual intelligence and sensibility. Only recently have her farm-journalism efforts become widely available or noticed. While scholars and critics might not be much impressed by the articles' literary quality, my interest in Wilder's columns, written between 1911 and 1924, lies not so much in their literary distinction (they are competently written and largely direct and straightforward in style) as in the psychological and moral insight they exhibit. In Chapter 5, I identify the major themes that Wilder developed in her biweekly columns and suggest that they demonstrate a sophistication and a subtlety of treatment that carried over into her fiction. Thus, the paradox of how an ordinary woman could produce such extraordinary work evaporates; Wilder becomes extraordinary in her own right. We can then explain the continued popularity and indeed the enduring excellence of her work.

The question of Rose Wilder Lane's role in producing her mother's novels is an important one. In his biography of Lane, William Holtz paints a fascinating portrait of Rose's mercurial and contradictory personality and argues that she transformed her mother's relatively rough, unfinished notes and drafts, which lacked any real literary value, into the polished gems that continue to delight us. The daughter, in his estimate, rewrote, reconstructed, embellished, and expanded upon her mother's amateurish scribblings to such an extent that she became, in effect, the "ghostwriter."[1]

From my reading of the evidence, however, Wilder demonstrated a high degree of writing competence from the beginning, and her daughter's contribution to the finished products, while important, was less significant than has been asserted. Other researchers, including Rosa Ann Moore, William T. Anderson, and Caroline Fraser, have written about the collaborative writing process that occurred between mother and daughter in the manufacture of the novels.[2] Rose often did expand or embellish scenes, and she sometimes rearranged the order of her mother's material to make the narrative more coherent and to emphasize high points. After taking the handwritten drafts and "running them through her typewriter," she went over them with a pen before retyping them and sending them to the publisher. In several instances Rose spent just days or weeks at the task; in others it took months. Rose and her mother talked or wrote to each other about how to tackle the revisions, and they sometimes vehemently disagreed with each other about how to deal with particular problems. Evidence that has been preserved tracing this process is only partial, so we know much more about some of

the novels (especially *On the Banks of Plum Creek* and *By the Shores of Silver Lake*) than we do about others.

*Little House in the Big Woods* and *These Happy Golden Years* received the lightest editing from Rose; *The Long Winter* and *Little Town on the Prairie* probably were edited the most. Significantly, Rose spent less than a week working on the first book. The first pages that Wilder wrote, and other large sections of the book, stand largely intact, indicating that from the start she possessed a talent for narrative description. What is most surprising in considering the work that Rose did on her mother's manuscripts is not that she had to do so much to get them into shape but that she had to do so little.

An example of how this mother-daughter collaboration worked can be found in pages 2 and 3 of *The Long Winter.* The handwritten draft (see Figure 1) that Wilder sent to Rose would have been a second (or possibly a third) version, as is indicated by how clean the copy is (there are few changes or crossed-out words). Rose then typed it, making changes as she went along. On page 2 of the typed manuscript (see Figure 2), Wilder penciled in several changes before mailing it back to Rose, who incorporated them on her copy. (Wilder's change in her story from having Pa walk behind the mowing machine to having him ride on its seat illustrates how fact and fiction intermingled in her writing.) Rose then made substantial further modifications of her own (see Figure 3) before typing the final copy to send to the publisher. A glance at the published version of the book indicates that further changes in wording were made either when Rose retyped the manuscript or by the copy editors in New York. We can presume that Wilder, too, may have had something to say about these final revisions. Another example of how she communicated with Rose during the writing process can be seen in her comments on page 89 of Rose's typed manuscript (see Figure 4), which emerged as page 106 in the printed version of the book.

There certainly is room for scholars to make a systematic study of the manuscripts and to describe in detail where changes were made and—to the degree that it can be ascertained—determine who was responsible for what in the final outcome. My own reading of the evidence credits Laura with responsibility for almost all of the story lines of the novels and most of the language. Rose deserves major credit for helping shape the material into publishable form and for making revisions that usually—but not always—improved the final product.

the little house in the Big Woods.

"A man works better when he's warmed up, anyway," Pa said as he chirruped to start the horses.

It was so pleasant in the hay-field that Laura sat down in the uncut grass to watch Pa go once around. She sat so still that little brown and yellow striped gophers hurried about their affairs all around her. A tiny bird flew from one tall grass stem to another where it balanced lightly. A striped garter-snake wriggled through the grass near her foot, but Laura did not move. She knew garter-snakes were not poisonous and they ate grasshoppers.

Laura sat so still in the grass that Pa did not see her when he came back, with the mowing-machine whirring and the horses nodding their heads slowly, keeping time with their feet. David jumped when she spoke from almost under his nose and Pa looked up startled. He said "Whoa!" and the horses stopped. "I thought you were gone. Why are you hiding in the grass lik

Figure 1

2

covered it with an armful of the wilting, cut grass.

"This sun almost makes a fellow wish for a bunch of sprouts to make a shade," he said to Laura. But his teeth gleamed out between his mustache and his beard as he smiled. Laura knew that he didn't want any sprouts; he had grubbed out so many from the little cleared field in the Big Woods, and they always grew again and he had to grub them out again, every summer.

Here on the Dakota prairies there~~were~~ were no sprouts/ There was not~~because~~ a single tree, ~~nothing~~ Nothing made the smallest bit of shade from the burning sun, nothing gave any coolness to the scorching wind.

"Well, well. A man works better when ~~she~~ he's warmed up, anyway!" Pa said cheerfully. He chirruped to start the horses.

Laura sat down in the uncut grass, to watch Pa go once around, ~~the sunshine~~ *the stubble-field.* Sam and David, the Christmas horses, plodded solemnly, pulling the ~~hanging~~ *light mowing machine. The long, thin whirring* ~~blades~~ blades, notched with/steel teeth, went steadily against the waving tall grass and laid it down in a wide swath. Pa ~~walked behind~~, *sat on the high mowing machine seat* watching and guiding.

Where Laura sat in the grass the heat was pleasant, ~~like~~ *It smelled as good as the* ~~the~~ heat in an oven when bread is baking. She sat so still that little brown-and-yellow striped gophers came out of their holes and hurried about their affairs all around her. Tiny birds flew from grass stem to grass stem, ~~They gripped~~ *gripping* the bending stems with wee claws and balanced lightly. A striped gopher snake ~~something~~ *came flowing over the ground,* curving and rippling through the forest of grass. It came to Laura, where she sat hunched with her chin on her drawn-up knees and the sunshine burning on her back. She felt suddenly very big, as big as a mountain, when the snake lifted up its head with a curving of its neck and stared at the high, high wall

Figure 2

2

covered it with an armful of ~~the wilting~~ cut grass.

"This sun almost makes a fellow wish for a bunch of sprouts to

make a shade," he said, *joking.* ~~to Laura. But his teeth gleamed~~ ~~and~~ between

~~his mustache and his beard as he smiled. Laura knew that he didn't~~
*He was really glad there were no trees on the prairies. He had grubbed so*
~~want any sprouts. he had grubbed out so many~~ from the little cleared
*many, sprouts.*
fields/in the Big Woods; ~~and~~ they always grew again and he had to *every summer*

grub them out again ~~every summer.~~ ~~because~~

Here on the Dakota prairies there ~~were no sprouts. There~~ was not

a single tree, ~~anyhow.~~ ~~Nothing made the smallest bit of shade from~~
~~not one bit of shade from~~
the burning sun, ~~nothing gave any coolness to the scorching wind.~~

~~Well, well.~~ " A man works better when ~~ahm~~ he's warmed up, anyway!"
*and*
Pa said cheerfully, ~~he~~ chirruped to ~~start~~ the horses.

~~Laura sat down in the uncut grass, to watch Pa go once~~

~~around. Shambonam~~ Sam and David ~~, the Christmas horses,~~
*away.* light mowing machine. The long,
plodded ~~slowly,~~ pulling the ~~hampomhommummhomming~~
*thin* whirring
~~hampumhumming~~ blades, notched with/steel teeth, went steadily
*flat, while*
against the waving tall grass and laid it down ~~in a wide~~
*Pa rode on the open iron seat, watching, with his hand on the*
~~swath. Pa walked behind, watching and guiding.~~
*long iron lever.*
~~There Laura sat down in the tall grass.~~ ~~The heat was pleasant, more~~ ~~it~~ smelled
as good as the
~~the~~ heat *to* an oven when bread is baking. She sat so still

that little brown-and-yellow striped gophers came out of

their holes and hurried about their affairs all around her.
*gripping*
Tiny birds flew from grass stem to grass stem. ~~They gripped~~

the bending stems with wee claws and balanced lightly. A
*garter* *came flowing*
striped ~~gopher~~ snake ~~unnugumummflowinmmosumly.~~ curving ~~and~~
*toward Laura,*
~~rippling~~ through the forest of grass. ~~It came to Laura,~~

~~where~~ She sat hunched with her chin on her ~~drawn-up~~ knees
*and*
and the sunshine burning on her back, She felt suddenly ~~very~~
*curved*
~~big,~~ as big as a mountain, when the snake ~~lifted~~ up its
*her tiny calico*
head ~~with a curving of its neck~~ and stared at ~~the high, high~~

Figure 3

89

(Note: you say) " a crowd was going to take the hand-car.
Do you mean they volunteered and worked for nothing? If
so, make it read:)

the Tracy cut, but it was still stopped by the snow beyond
~~Brookins~~ *Brookings* and some of the men in town were going out to
clear the ~~maximum~~ tracks from this end.

"I don't know why they need do that, Charles," Ma said
in surprise.

"Well, we might as well be doing something," Pa replied
uneasily. "I've been in one place so long I'd like to do
a little traveling. We're going to take the hand-car and we
ought to make it to Volga by nightfall. It's only ~~fifty~~ *about forty* miles

Ma was even more surprised. "Are you going, Charles?"

"I might as well," Pa said again. "Foster's agreed to
for me tonight, and ~~nhm~~ tomorrow morning. I'll
do the chores, ~~friidmkenbacky/rahhmthnntmainudiraperomafm~~
be back on the train tomorrow."

"But what--" Ma began, and stopped. Then she said,
"Are you sure you can get to Volga before night?"

"We think so," said Pa. "The cuts are small, and there's
not so many of them. The worst stretch is beyond, from Volga
to Brookins."

~~(Your sentence is not clear: "The ten miles from Brookins
to Volga is the last bad bit of road until the cut west of
here." "Last bad bit" from which end? Pa is looking from
west to east. If Brookins is east of Volga, and he is going
only to Volga, he thinks of the bad bit of road as beyond
Volga, to the eastward. He does not think of it as "last
bad bit" unless it is the last bit he intends to do himself.
Later you have, in Volga, "the train came in from Brookins."
So I deduce that Brookins is east of Volga.)~~

*[left margin handwritten notes:]*

*East bad bit the train will have to get over until it comes to the cut west of town Brookings in east of Volga*

*Volga was ten mi. west of Brookings*

*I remember we used to say it was 60 mi. to Brookings. Mostly don't remember the oxen as I can figure by highway map. Let it be 50 mi. To be sure I'll have to write to Lily. Am I... want for an answer. Let's not be so definite of worst do to have it wrong.*

Figure 4

While the question of authorship has provoked the most interest in Laura Ingalls Wilder of late, there is a perennial problem in approaching her work: readers who find her stories to be so convincing that it becomes impossible for them to distinguish between the Laura they have read about in the books and the real Laura who actually lived and grew up on the western frontier. This obviously presents problems for readers of her biography if they are unprepared to inquire into and find out what really happened to her and her family. The myths that have endured about the "nice old lady" who lived and wrote in the farmhouse up on the hill at Rocky Ridge may stand in the way of our looking at her with open eyes. Although it would make for an interesting analysis (and it has already been done to some degree), a point-by-point comparison of the fictional Laura as described in her books with the real-life Laura whose memory served as the basis for these stories has not been my goal. Rather, I have written a biography describing and explaining the lived life, and I leave for others the task of showing wherein the fictional character she created may have departed from her actual experiences.

The greatest difficulty confronting a biographer of Laura Ingalls Wilder, interestingly enough, is the paucity of sources that speak directly to the questions of what kind of person she was and what kind of life she lived. In contrast with her daughter, Rose, who compiled and saved copious and highly revealing diaries, journals, and caches of letters, Laura did not leave behind much in the way of personal revelation. There are letters between mother and daughter and some written by Wilder to her husband during several trips away from home. There is a trip diary that she kept when the family moved to Missouri in 1894, and a few scraps of other written materials are extant. Of course, we can examine the novels and Wilder's unpublished autobiography, but they take her story only up to 1889 (through the first four years of her marriage). Consequently, biographers must piece together materials from letters, newspaper stories, local histories, land records, interviews of people who remember her, and other scattered evidence. Otherwise, the most important sources of information are Rose's letters, diaries, and journals. A good deal of what we know about Wilder, then, is colored by the perspective of her daughter. Another especially illuminating source is Wilder's *Missouri Ruralist* columns, which described some of her daily activities and, at times, dredged up memories of her childhood. More important, however, these columns illustrated her

thoughts and laid bare her basic values and beliefs. Thus, while many gaps remain in our knowledge of her and in our understanding of her motives and aspirations, there is much that can be gained by a careful reading and comparison of the sources.

In the end, what stands out most strikingly about Wilder is her perseverance. Her readers know how her family withstood the challenges of poverty, crop failures, blizzards, grasshoppers, prairie fires, and other setbacks. Throughout her life, Wilder faced similar challenges: the loss of a child, her husband's physical disability, hardscrabble economic conditions, conflicts with her daughter, a patriarchal social environment, and a long apprenticeship at the writing trade with little to show for it. Yet she persisted. Writing for the *Missouri Ruralist* provided her with an outlet for her intellectual energies—and for her ambition. For this was an ambitious woman. There was a feistiness, an independence, a willingness to go against the tide that separated the young Laura Ingalls from her peers. She received just enough feedback from adults to reinforce her feeling that somehow she was different.

This sense of uniqueness complemented and reinforced Laura's sense of self-worth and helped establish in her an identity that continually asserted itself in her daily interactions with others and in various leadership positions. In the early twentieth century there was talk of a "New Woman" on the American scene, which encouraged some women to break old patterns and assert their independence. Nevertheless, women's options remained strictly limited, especially in the Ozarks of Missouri, which remained more isolated geographically and where traditional norms and practices carried more weight than in some other regions. But Laura Wilder eventually discovered a path where she could realize her vague ambitions and fulfill that sense of destiny that she had acquired early in life. Her nonfiction writing career forced her to think seriously about the world and to express her thoughts on a wide variety of subjects. She cultivated habits of inquiry and thoughtfulness that she later used in her fiction. Few women of her generation would have bucked tradition as she did. But in so doing she transformed herself into the "Laura Ingalls Wilder" we recognize today.

# 1

## *Pioneer Girl*

### 1867–1879

⟡

he Civil War was only two years past when a baby girl was born in a cabin on the edge of the "Big Woods" in the Chippewa River valley region of Wisconsin, just a few miles from the Mississippi River. She was the second child of Charles P. and Caroline Quiner Ingalls, and they named her Laura Elizabeth after Charles's mother, Laura Louise Colby Ingalls. The young couple had moved to this remote agricultural region of western Wisconsin with Charles's parents and the rest of his family five years earlier.

Laura Ingalls was born on Thursday, February 7, 1867. The big news story of the day was the release in the nation's capital of the report of a special committee of the House of Representatives exonerating U.S. Asst. Treas. H. H. Van Dyck, who had been accused of interfering with the gold market. Meanwhile, the U.S. Senate was debating a 20 percent pay increase for Treasury Department clerks. This was the day that navigation on the Ohio River fully resumed for the season. In St. Louis former slave Frederick Douglass lectured at Fireman's Hall. Douglass County, Kansas, voters approved the issuance of three hundred thousand dollars in bonds for purchasing capital stock in the Leavenworth, Lawrence, and Galveston Railroad. Across the ocean the Pope was considering a proposal to canonize

Columbus. A new Atlantic Telegraph Company was forming, intending to lay an underwater cable from the Azores to Halifax.[1]

Such goings-on had little relevance to people so far removed from them. The Ingalls's major concern was to carve out of the wilderness a sustenance for themselves, remote from the cities and industries that were rapidly transforming the United States from a rural, agrarian society into an urban, industrial one. As the forward edge of settlement relentlessly crept forward, wilderness areas were soon transformed into populated, settled territory. By the end of the Civil War railroad tracks already connected the East Coast with the Mississippi River, and during the next several years they quickly linked the continent from coast to coast.[2]

Steamboats regularly plied the Mississippi River. Boats frequently came to shore to tie up at Pepin Landing, seven miles from the Ingalls cabin, where they took on passengers and unloaded merchandise ordered by local storekeepers. Even before the Civil War, early settlers who had entered the region were shipping out several thousand bushels of wheat every year from Pepin on steamboats bound for St. Louis and elsewhere. Potatoes and other commodities were sent in lesser quantities to points south. By the 1860s, more and more farmers drifted into the area, seeking choice locations on which to make a living from the land. In an early 1862 edition of the *Pepin County Press,* newspaper editor U. B. Shaver noted poetically—and perhaps with some degree of exaggeration—how quickly civilization was taking hold in the region. As the Indians continually were being pushed farther to the west, frontiersmen arriving from the east took their places. "Broad fields lay extended in sunlight where but a short time before wild beasts formed their coverts and hunted their prey," the editor enthusiastically announced.

> Acre after acre waved with bending wheat and rye, and gleamed with the yellow sheen of ripening corn. Cabins dotted the hill sides, and mill wheels flashed in the running streams; and ponderous rafts of pine lumber floated down our great inland sea and found a market hundreds of miles distant. Our village of Pepin at length set up its busy hum, and the air was alive with the sounds and voices of intelligent and independent industry.[3]

If the editor waxed somewhat overenthusiastic in describing the progress of the region, Laura Ingalls would be guilty seventy years later of exaggerating the primitiveness of the place where she had been born. The first lines of *Little House in the Big Woods* describe her family's cabin as virtually

isolated, far from people and civilization. "As far as a man could go to the north in a day, or a week, or a whole month, there was nothing but woods," she wrote, describing a place that had no houses, no roads, no people— just forest and the wild animals inhabiting it. Wolves and bears and other animals certainly did pose serious dangers to the settlers. As agriculturalists carved out clearings in the woods and appropriated meadows used earlier by Indians for their fields, one could listen to the busy axes of nearby lumbermen, who floated their logs down the Chippewa River into Beef Slough at its mouth, where it connected with the Mississippi on the eastern edge of the county.[4]

The lumber industry of northern Wisconsin had begun to expand rapidly during the 1840s. The Chippewa River valley, containing about one-sixth of all the pine timber west of the Appalachians, emerged as the largest and most important lumber district in the state. It was called "a logger's paradise." The depression of 1857 dealt the region a major setback, ruining many lumbermen, but the Civil War restored prosperity to the industry, and during the 1860s the number of board feet logged annually in the region ballooned from 60 million to 436 million. For several decades the region would supply logs for dozens of sawmills along the Mississippi River, which then shipped the sawed lumber by rail all over the Midwest and the northern plains.[5]

The Wisconsin frontier may have seemed remote to most Americans, but it lay in a region rapidly filling up with farmers, lumbermen, merchants, lawyers, and other go-getters. Wherever the frontier proceeded during the late nineteenth century, civilization did not lag far behind. People who moved to the edge of settlement hoped both to take advantage of the economic opportunities available in a fluid, expanding environment and to quickly establish the kinds of social relations and institutions that they had been familiar with and enjoyed farther east.[6]

Such visions of economic development and social refinement influenced Lansford and Laura Ingalls and their family to move west to Pepin County around 1862. Their second son, Charles, and his wife of two years, the former Caroline Quiner, joined a family migration that included the entire Ingalls clan. Such extended family migration to frontier regions was not uncommon after the Civil War.[7]

The Ingallses and the Quiners joined the many who migrated west from New England during the eighteenth and nineteenth centuries, through

New York and northern Pennsylvania, Ohio, Indiana, and Illinois, into and beyond Wisconsin, Minnesota, Iowa, and the Dakotas. The migrants carried with them habits, practices, values, and institutions tinged with the Puritan past. Heavily Protestant (and often Congregationalist), reformist in social orientation, Republican in politics, optimistic and hardworking, independent and self-reliant, while also cooperative and community minded, these former New Englanders impressed their values and their ways on social life wherever they went.[8]

The Ingalls family traced its roots back to the earliest Puritan migration to Massachusetts. Edmund Ingalls, born at Skirbeck in Lincolnshire in east-central England, was about thirty when he arrived in Salem, Massachusetts, in Gov. John Endecott's company in 1628. With a brother and four others Edmund started a settlement at Lynn the following year. Tragically, he drowned in the Saugus River in March 1648 while riding horseback to Boston. Lansford Whiting Ingalls, born in Canada in 1812, was an eighth-generation Ingalls in America. His family returned to the United States when the War of 1812 broke out and his father, Samuel Ingalls, enlisted in the army. After the war the family settled in western New York. Lansford married Laura Louise Colby, who was born in 1810, and, like many of their cohorts, the couple raised a large family: six boys and four girls (not counting one who died at a young age). Charles Philip was born near Cuba, New York, in the southwestern part of the state, on January 10, 1836, the third child and the second to live to adulthood. From his father, according to Donald Zochert, the blue-eyed Charles derived high-spiritedness, and from his mother, a former schoolteacher who had married at the age of eighteen, he derived a sturdy sense of self-discipline.[9]

With their family growing larger, Lansford and Laura Ingalls decided to take the five children they had at the time farther west to try their luck closer to his brothers. Charles was nine years old when they moved to the Illinois prairie about forty miles west of Chicago, which at that time was a growing boomtown of about 15,000 people. In 1853 the family moved again, this time to Jefferson County, Wisconsin, near the little village of Concord. The second county to the west of Milwaukee, which, like Chicago, was experiencing an initial growth surge, Jefferson County in 1840 had numbered just 914 free white persons, largely made up of farmers deriving from Vermont, New York, Pennsylvania, and Ohio; within a decade the population had burgeoned to 15,317. Another 15,000 were added during

the 1850s, but during the Civil War growth slowed to only 3,500. Many Indians still inhabited the area, mostly of the Winnebago tribe. During the Ingalls's stay there, the edge of the frontier moved farther west, and the country around them filled up and was settled.[10]

Growing up on a nearby farm was a young girl just three years younger than Charles. Caroline Lake Quiner was the fifth of seven children (three boys and four girls, one of whom died at just four years of age) of Henry N. and Charlotte Tucker Quiner, who had married in 1831. Originating in Connecticut, the Quiners, like the Ingallses, joined the migration to the Midwest. The family lived for a time in Ohio and Indiana before moving to the Wisconsin frontier just west of Milwaukee near the village of Brookfield, where Caroline was born on December 12, 1839.[11]

Tragedy struck in 1844 when Henry Quiner, who had engaged in trading with the Indians, drowned in a shipwreck on Lake Michigan during a violent storm. Life was hard for the fatherless family for the next several years. When Caroline was eight, her widowed mother purchased some government land bordering on the Oconomowoc River farther west in Jefferson County, two miles from Concord. The following year Charlotte married Frederick Holbrook, a Connecticut farmer, who bought some land adjoining that of his new wife, making for an enlarged farm. He became a good stepfather for the Quiner children.[12]

Education was an important value for this frontier family. Charlotte Quiner had taught school before her first marriage, and when Caroline completed her own schooling at the age of sixteen, she began teaching in the same school that she had attended as a student. Meanwhile, with her family living close to the Ingalls farm, she and her siblings became acquainted with their children. Eventually, three sets of brothers and sisters from the two families would fall in love and get married. Henry Quiner and Polly Ingalls were the first to pair off, in 1859. A year later, on February 1, 1860, Caroline Quiner married Charles Ingalls in Concord. The following year Eliza Quiner married Peter Ingalls.[13]

Meanwhile, however, things were not going well for the Ingalls family patriarch. In 1857, the year Lansford Ingalls took out a mortgage on his land, the United States slid into a sharp economic depression, the effects of which reached all the way to the Wisconsin frontier. Unable to repay all of the money that he had borrowed when it came due three years later, Lansford lost title to his land. Instead of becoming discouraged, however,

he made plans to move farther west and start over. In addition to him and his wife and their seven children still at home, their three married children decided to go with them and try their luck in the new environment. Back East, meanwhile, political events were spiraling out of control, with shots fired at Fort Sumter, South Carolina, on April 12, 1861, instigating the Civil War.[14]

At a time when many young men his age were being called to military service, Charles Ingalls managed to avoid conscription. Whether he, Henry, and Peter believed that moving to the frontier might have the effect of sparing them from military duty is uncertain. Approximately eighty thousand Wisconsinites—about one-half of all white males in the state between the ages of eighteen and forty-five—twelve thousand of whom died, served during the war. In February 1865, during the last year of the war, Charles signed a petition to hold a special town meeting to appropriate two hundred dollars for every volunteer who stepped forward to fill the local quota. Two of his brothers as well as Caroline's brother Joseph did serve in Union blue. The latter, tragically, died from wounds suffered in the Battle of Shiloh in April 1862, three months after he had enlisted. By January 3, 1865, when Hiram and James (who went by his middle name rather than his first name of Lansford) Ingalls crossed the Mississippi River and went to Lake City to enlist in the First Regiment of Heavy Artillery in the Minnesota Volunteers, the war was nearly over.[15]

Leaving Jefferson County around 1862, the Ingalls clan decided to take their chances in the Chippewa River lumbering region, at the forward edge of settlement at the time. Just as they had in Illinois and Wisconsin, they encountered other people with the same surname. One of them, Louisa Ingalls, had moved from Fort Madison, Iowa, a decade earlier to teach in the Pepin school. The village, although only several years old, had already experienced its share of ups and downs. Its location on the eastern bank of Lake Pepin, which was a widening of the Mississippi River, was strikingly beautiful, affording a panoramic view of tall bluffs on the Minnesota side. All around were stands of trees bordering on the Big Woods, with hardwood timber such as elm, oak, ash, maple, basswood, butternut, and birch. The area, while still rough and primitive, was rapidly transformed by the settlement process. The nearby *Durand Times* ran the following story in December 1865 about the killing of a big wolf: "Mr. Nathan Brown, a 'mighty hunter' in these parts, last week killed a monstrous grey wolf about a

mile above Darwin's Mill. He is supposed to be among the very few, if not the last remaining number, of this race of animals that were abundant here but a few years ago. The grey wolf never stays long on the borders of civilization but seeks the more remote and secluded portions of the country."[16]

Indian mounds dotted the county. A band of Dakotas, led by Wabasha, had roamed the region just a few years earlier, clashing frequently with rival Chippewas. Although the Dakotas had relinquished their claim to the land in a treaty in 1837, war parties had continued to crisscross the valley into the 1850s. But after the Great Sioux Uprising of 1862 in Minnesota, which left hundreds of settlers dead and resulted in the hanging of thirty-eight of the alleged ringleaders, the remaining Indians in the area around Pepin all but disappeared. The earliest white settlement began in 1846, but not until 1855 was the town of Pepin (called North Pepin in the beginning) platted, followed the next year by the construction of several stores, a Methodist Episcopal church, and a scattering of houses. In 1857 a schoolhouse was erected, and the first newspaper, the *Pepin County Independent,* was started. Town boosters predicted that the nascent village would soon become a flourishing city and took to referring to it as the "Queen City of Lake Pepin" and the "Gate City of Chippewa." Located several miles upstream from the mouth of the Chippewa River, Pepin gave promise of becoming the natural outlet for the Chippewa trade. A modest economic boom commenced. Men traveling up the Mississippi on steamboats disembarked at Pepin Landing and walked or took stagecoaches to the Chippewa pineries before commencing their return journey, shepherding thousands of logs to the milling centers at Winona, La Crosse, and elsewhere. Agriculturalists were entering claims and taking up land nearby. Town lots were selling for good prices. Four dry-goods stores and three hotels were in operation. Though free-roaming hogs sometimes posed a nuisance in the streets, lodges such as the Free Masons, Good Templars, Odd Fellows, and Sons of Malta conferred on the town a tone of progressiveness. It was not long before a literary society took shape, and an agricultural society made an appearance, too, only to fizzle out. The *Pepin Independent* boasted that with approximately one hundred dwellings, the population of the town was approaching seven hundred. Even allowing for some exaggeration, the prospects of the community and the surrounding region appeared to be bright.[17]

Then the bottom fell out, with the financial panic of 1857. The economy stalled, and population growth halted. Subsequently, one observer noted

that as a result of the nationwide economic depression, along with the harmful effects of eastern land speculators, "the town was passed into a sleep from which it has never awakened." Even obtaining initial designation in 1858 as the county seat failed to turn things around, because Durand, located along the banks of the Chippewa River eighteen miles to the northeast, managed to wrest the title in a popular vote in 1861.[18]

Pepin suffered several other setbacks during the late 1850s and early 1860s. Its boat landing was inadequate, and especially when water levels were low it was difficult, if not impossible, for steamboats to unload or take on passengers and freight. In addition, shallow-draft steamboats that began plying the Chippewa River soon cut heavily into the stage traffic between Pepin and the pineries, which previously had brought considerable business to the town. The opening of Beef Slough several miles south of town, at the mouth of the Chippewa River, as a collecting point for logs floated down the river further diverted traffic and business away from the town. Finally, when railroads began operating on the Minnesota side of the Mississippi River after 1870, the market potential of the town was reduced even further, destroying any chance for the town to become a major center of business and trade.[19]

Nevertheless, even while the Civil War continued to rage, new settlers continued to drift into the hills and valleys extending from the Mississippi River around Pepin. The county's population doubled during the 1860s, from 2,392 to 4,649. (The pace of growth slowed during the 1870s, the population rising to only 6,226 by 1880.) The Ingalls family made up part of this influx. It took them a while to locate the kind of land they were looking for and to arrange for its purchase. Charles Ingalls and his brother Peter (who was three years older) were able to earn money as harvest hands in Minnesota for a while. On September 22, 1863, Charles teamed up with Caroline's brother Henry to purchase a quarter-section of land from an Englishman named Charles Nunn, who worked as a druggist in the village of Reed's Landing on the other side of Lake Pepin. They paid him $335 for the property, advancing only $35 in cash and taking out a mortgage on the rest. The parcel was on high ground, seven miles mainly north and a little west of Pepin. It was largely covered with trees but also contained some clearings where they could begin planting crops. Henry agreed to work the north eighty acres, with Charles taking the south half of the property.[20]

The two brothers-in-law were only a year apart in age (Henry being the older of the two), and they made a good team. They frequently traded work, helping each other clear the land and harvest their crops as well as going out together to hunt and trap and fish. Earlier arrivals were already shipping small amounts of wheat and potatoes and other commodities down the Mississippi River by the time the Ingalls clan arrived. While Charles and Henry may have participated to some degree in these markets, they, like most of the other settlers in the area, remained largely self-sufficient. They planted gardens, milked their own cows, butchered hogs that roamed more or less freely in the woods, and hunted and trapped wild game. Everyone participated actively in the fall butchering process, which was vividly described many years later by Laura Ingalls Wilder in *Little House in the Big Woods*. She also wrote about hickory-smoking meat, converting deer hides into leather, churning butter, making cheese, baking bread, gathering honey, molding bullets, and manufacturing maple sugar. Charles bundled up furs that he had trapped and carried them on his back to Pepin. For Caroline there was a constant round of cooking, tending garden, sewing, and keeping house. The work for both of them was never-ending and energy draining.[21]

And then the household became larger. On January 10, 1865, on Charles's twenty-ninth birthday and just short of their fifth wedding anniversary, the couple had their first child, a girl they named Mary Amelia. A little more than two years later, on February 7, 1867, a second daughter arrived. They named her Laura Elizabeth. She had blue eyes, like her father, and brown hair. There was nothing about her to lead her parents to suspect that some day she would become a celebrated personality.

A new baby meant that now there would be four mouths to feed. Meanwhile, depressed economic conditions afflicted Wisconsin and the rest of the country between 1867 and 1871, leading Charles and Caroline to begin thinking seriously about moving someplace else to try their luck under new conditions. If we believe Laura's rendition of the story sixty years later, it was Charles—not Caroline—who pushed for venturing out again. On the frontier, talk abounded about land deals and economic opportunities that were open to people who were adventurous and willing to take advantage of them. In November 1867, Charles Ingalls and Henry Quiner signed legal papers dividing up their quarter-section of land, allowing either to sell his half and move if he desired. Five months later each family sold their half of

the property for $1,012.50 to a Swedish settler named Gustaf Gustafson, who arranged to pay them for it in installments.[22]

In the meantime, apparently, the brothers-in-law either had seen an advertisement or had talked to a land agent from Chariton County, Missouri, prompting them to try their luck in the rolling hills of central Missouri, just north of the Missouri River. Charles and Henry agreed to pay Adamantine Johnson, a big Missouri land dealer, for their plots in installments. At the end of May 1868 each signed promissory notes of $900 for eighty acres of fertile, partially wooded land.[23]

It is not entirely clear whether the two families actually moved to Missouri during the summer of 1868. Laura did not write about this episode later in her autobiography or in her novels, nor did she leave behind any record of it. If, in fact, the families did attempt to start farming in Chariton County, things must not have worked out. Within a year's time, the Ingallses were living on the treeless prairies of southeastern Kansas, which were quickly filling up during the late 1860s. It is likely that the Ingallses never set eyes on the mortgaged land they had purchased in Missouri, and on February 25, 1870, while they were living in Kansas, Charles Ingalls legally returned title to the land to Adamantine Johnson.[24]

Northeastern Kansas had been the scene of bloody skirmishes between Yankee abolitionists and Southern slaveholders after it was opened up for settlement by the Kansas-Nebraska Act of 1854. The ensuing war between the states had temporarily slowed migration to Kansas, but by 1868 and 1869 settlers were rushing into the southeastern part of the state in response to invitations and advertisements of land speculators and town boosters who stood to gain from an influx of people.[25]

Once again, just as back in Wisconsin, the Ingallses were moving into a new region that was rapidly filling up, arriving just ahead of the bulk of newcomers. In September 1869, shortly after crossing the Verdigris River, Charles and Caroline Ingalls and their two daughters came to the new town of Independence, just a few weeks after the first crude buildings had been erected. That same month there appeared the first issue of the *Independence Pioneer,* which was published for several weeks in Oswego, a town several miles farther east, until a printing press could be brought to Independence. This rawest of frontier towns was referred to as "Hayhouse Town" or "Haytown" by local Indians, because the roofs of many of the houses were made of hay. Montgomery County had been split off from

Wilson County just two years earlier. Verdigris City, on the banks of the river after which it was named, and Montgomery City, both of which were also founded in 1869, shared county-seat aspirations with Independence. But they conceded the title to the latter after an election and a subsequent district-court decision handed down in May 1870.[26]

After no doubt inquiring about available land in the area and after stocking up on provisions, the Ingallses proceeded southwesterly from Independence, halting at a spot in Rutland Township on the western side of Walnut Creek, about thirteen miles from town. This was largely treeless land, flat to gently rolling in terrain, cut through by creeks and streams. In the distance to the northwest, a line of bluffs were etched against the sky. With immigrants pouring into the area and the town of Independence growing rapidly, Charles may have found sporadic employment as a carpenter, just as he would in other places later. His occupation was listed as "carpenter"—not "farmer"—in the 1870 census.[27]

First, however, there was plenty of work to be done in getting settled before winter, once they had decided on a location. How they intended to obtain title to the land or whether they actually realized what their legal status was there is uncertain. They should have known that they had moved into the fifty-mile-wide Osage Indian Reserve that ran east to west across two-thirds of the southern part of the state. As such, they were intruders illegally squatting on the land, but they had plenty of company in what they were doing. When the census taker made his rounds the following year, among the neighbors listed on the forms were A. K. Johnson, a thirty-six-year-old farmer from Illinois with his twenty-eight-year-old Ohio-born wife and their four children; G. L. Rowles, a twenty-four-year-old single farmer from Maryland; an elderly black couple from Pennsylvania named Tann and their thirty-four-year-old son, George, a physician; G. N. Lucker, a twenty-seven-year-old farmer born in Iowa and his eighteen-year-old Illinois-born wife; another single farmer, Ed Mason, age twenty-five and born in England; and a Kentucky farm couple, Robert and Mary Gilmore, fifty-two and forty-four, respectively, and their five children, ranging in age from sixteen to three.[28]

Although a healthy representation of Missourians and Kentuckians were listed as living in Rutland Township in the 1870 census, Ohio and Indiana furnished by far the largest number of residents, with strong showings from Illinois and New York and smaller contributions from Virginia, Iowa,

Pennsylvania, Maryland, Michigan, and England. These were to a large de-gree the same kinds of people the Ingallses had encountered in Wisconsin, minus the heavy leavening of Scandinavian immigrants.[29]

All of them were there to get a start on the land. Whether individuals hoped to take out homestead claims after the Indians departed or whether they intended to purchase land from the railroad or acquire it in some other fashion is not entirely clear. Most likely, all the recent arrivals had been lured by advertisements and predictions that Indian control would shortly be extinguished and that white settlers would then be free to take ownership.

Not surprisingly, much of Laura's attention in her fictionalized version of the episode in *Little House on the Prairie* focused upon the family's concern about and relationships with the Osage Indians as that tribe's members tried to grapple with the difficult dilemma confronting them. The Osages were clearly in a no-win situation. Driven west, like other tribes, by the constant pressure of westward-moving white settlers and by treaties promising them that each forced move would be the last, they now faced the prospect of being pushed out one more time and having to move south to a much smaller area set aside for them in Oklahoma.[30]

Although Laura later had to rely on stories related by her parents rather than on her own childhood memories to describe the family's year on the Kansas prairie, her descriptions of frequent powwows and drums in the night, Indians walking into cabins to take settlers' food and tobacco, and other anxious moments between the settlers and the Indians conform to the historical record. The pressure of settlers entering the region caused the Osages to worry that they would be forced to move off their reserve. Although there was plenty of land in the region that could have been obtained free under the provisions of the Homestead Act of 1862 or that could have been purchased for $1.25 an acre under the Preemption Act of 1841, settlers demonstrated a "decided mania" for moving onto Indian lands. It seemed to be a kind of game for many of them.[31]

Railroads had pushed west across Kansas beginning in 1865. Some railroad buccaneers had turned their glance longingly south toward the Gulf of Mexico, a path directly traversing tribal reserves that had been set aside for the Cherokees and the Osages. Directors of the Kansas and Neosho Valley Railroad, through skillful political lobbying in Washington, negotiated a deal in 1867 to purchase the Cherokee Neutral Tract in the southeastern corner of the state for only $1.00 an acre. Realizing that

they had little choice in the matter, the Cherokees reluctantly accepted the $800,000 being offered them for the land rather than pressing for the $12,000,000 they had originally sought.[32]

The Osage lands, the last major Indian reserve in the state, contained close to 9 million acres, making it by far the largest. It is little wonder that many white settlers impatiently awaited its opening. When the Ingalls family arrived in September 1869 they found themselves in the middle of the maneuvering and contention. The Osage Treaty of September 1865 had ceded a little more than 4 million acres to the federal government, about one-fifth of it for $300,000 in cash and the other four-fifths to be held in trust and sold over time, with the proceeds going to the Indians. Three years later, however, through the use of bribes, presents, and other pressures, the Leavenworth, Lawrence, and Galveston Railroad managed to negotiate a draft treaty that would have allowed it to purchase 8 million acres of the Osage Reserve for the absurdly low price of $.20 an acre over a fifteen-year period. Angry protests and political pressures mounted by rival railroad groups and by settlers who did not want to have to purchase land from the railroad at premium prices blocked confirmation of the treaty in the U.S. Senate. Meanwhile, the Settlers' Protective Association went into operation. Its leaders estimated that between twelve and fifteen thousand settlers were already squatting on the Osage lands by 1868. Early the following year newcomers to the region could read newspaper editorials condemning the railroad's attempted land grab and encouraging them to move onto the Osage Diminished Reserve (even though it was illegal to do so) in order to guarantee that hardworking farmers—not greedy businessmen—would be the beneficiaries when the Osages finally moved to Oklahoma.[33]

Into this complex set of circumstances Charles and Caroline Ingalls brought their girls. Like the other settlers, they were squatting illegally on the land, waiting for the time—soon, they hoped—when Indian title would be relinquished so that they would be able to claim ownership for themselves.[34] Presumably, they opposed railroad acquisition of the land, which would have necessitated their paying more for the land than it would cost to buy it from the government. Undoubtedly, they welcomed the prospect of the Indians' departure, but they were somewhat ambivalent in their attitudes toward them. In Laura's version of the story, her mother was fearful of them, but her father frequently managed to put himself in their shoes and to understand their way of thinking.

It was neither the railroad nor the Indians themselves, however, who bore the brunt of criticism in *Little House on the Prairie*. Rather, the federal government played the villain's role for its alleged misleading of the settlers by encouraging them to move in and then reneging on the deal and ordering them off the land. Soldiers, in fact, did sometimes attempt to enforce the law and make the illegal squatters leave, but if anyone was encouraging the settlers to move onto the Osage Tract before 1870, it probably was the settlers' groups and the local town boosters, not the federal government.

Laura's descriptions of night-time drumbeating and of increased traffic along the trail running next to their cabin coincide with the stories told by historians about the distress and sense of crisis pervading the Osage camps. Grasshoppers, drought, and inability to follow the buffalo herds, as they customarily had done, reduced the Osages' food supplies, leaving them in "a deplorable condition." A newly formed Board of Indian Commissioners, set up in 1868 as a watchdog agency for Indian affairs, plaintively observed that even though the Osages were reconciled to their ultimate removal, "They are human beings, they have rights." The final chapter of the story was written on July 15, 1870, when Congress legislated for the survey and sale of the remaining Osage trust lands. With that, the members of the tribe bowed to the inevitable and prepared to leave for a reservation in Oklahoma.[35]

How aware the Ingallses were of all the goings-on in Washington and other places we cannot know. They were not alone on the prairie and lived only thirteen miles from the county seat. *Little House on the Prairie* leaves what they knew and why they decided to leave obscure. Was it simply pique at the government and at the soldiers who were sent to order illegal squatters off the land? Was it lack of information? A year later there was a big rush of settlers into the county. In the meantime, there had hardly been any time to try their luck at farming in Kansas. They spent only about a year in the state. What kinds of crops Charles Ingalls may have planted in that time we do not know, if he planted any at all. The stories Laura told later were about building a cabin, digging a well, getting sick with "fever and ague" (probably malaria), helping with cattle drives going past their place, and interacting with the Indians. In August 1870, shortly before the census was taken, a baby sister was born, Caroline Celestia, whom the family called Carrie.[36]

While they were considering what to do, a letter arrived from Gustaf Gustafson in Pepin saying that he was unable to make any more payments

on the land that he had bought from them and that he wanted them to take it back. The offer sounded inviting. They were discouraged with what had happened to them in Kansas, and now the opportunity to go back home to relatives and friends was welcome. So they packed their things into the wagon and headed back to Wisconsin, retracing their steps through Missouri and Iowa. There was a big welcome waiting for them from Grandpa and Grandma Ingalls, Peter and Eliza and their family, and the others.[37]

People continued to move into the area, and some of the families who once had lived near Charles and Caroline Ingalls had departed in their absence. A new family living near the Ingallses was that of Thomas Huleatt (or Hewlet), who had been born in Ireland, and his wife, Maria, a Pennsylvanian. Their house was just a mile down the road. Many years later in *Little House in the Big Woods,* Laura mentioned them and their children, Clarence, who was a year older than she, and Eva, who was three years younger. "Laura and Clarence ran and shouted and climbed trees," she wrote, "while Mary and Eva walked nicely together and talked." Even allowing for some exaggeration in the way she described the opposing temperaments of herself and her sister Mary, we can presume that Laura was essentially being truthful in identifying herself as a tomboy. The adventurous streak that led her to want to climb trees, ride ponies, go wading in creeks, and assume leadership roles among her peers no doubt showed itself early, and it would continue to set her apart later in life.[38]

Besides the Huleatts, Laura also mentioned a childless couple, the Petersons, who were Swedish. Early migration into the area had been heavily Scandinavian. Except for Pennsylvania, the most common birthplace for adults residing in Pepin Township, as recorded by the census taker in 1870, was Sweden. Almost as many had been born in the combined area of Prussia, Bavaria, and the other German states, and about a third that many came from Ireland. There were, in addition, handfuls who derived from Canada, Norway, Scotland, France, and Switzerland. New York ranked second behind Pennsylvania as an American birthplace, with about half as many coming from there. Ohio and Vermont each had about one-quarter as many as Pennsylvania, and other states, such as Connecticut, Massachusetts, Wisconsin, Indiana, Maine, and Maryland each contributed up to a half dozen of the adults residing in the township in 1870. It was a population slightly more native than foreign-born in origin and heavily

weighted toward the Middle Atlantic, New England, and Midwestern states as starting points.[39]

Laura later wrote in *Little House in the Big Woods* about some of the family gatherings and activities that she remembered. Henry Quiner and Charles Ingalls frequently traded work, helping each other during planting and harvest seasons, and they cooperated with other chores and activities, such as butchering. Agriculturalists were making some progress in carving out farms from the surrounding forests, as was indicated in a story published in the *Durand Times* in October 1871 after the reporter had made a quick trip around the county. Threshing was just about completed, the newspaper story noted. "Corn and potatoes are excellent," the article continued. "The farmers are building and otherwise improving their farms and adding to their own comforts many little things that go to make up a world of enjoyment by the many conveniences."[40]

Just before Christmas, Uncle Peter and Aunt Eliza brought cousins Peter, Alice, and Ella over to meet baby Carrie and to play with Mary and Laura. As Laura wrote later, her father's brothers George and James came to a dance at Grandpa Ingalls's house. George played his bugle for the girls. Another time Laura and Mary met more cousins when they went for a day to the home of Caroline's sister Martha and her husband, Charles Carpenter.[41]

For a short time, until the Gustafsons moved out of their cabin, Laura and her family lived with Uncle Henry and Aunt Polly Quiner and their cousins Louisa, Charley, Albert, and Lottie. The Ingalls extended family was mostly still around. Now that the family was back in home territory, the girls could see Grandma and Grandpa Ingalls and Uncle Peter and Aunt Eliza Ingalls and that group of cousins, Peter, Alice, Ella, and Edith. Uncle Tom Quiner, who would spend more than twenty years working for the Laird-Norton Lumber Company, came from Eau Claire to visit his sister and brother-in-law and nieces.[42]

Since she had turned six by the time the family returned to Wisconsin, Mary was enrolled for the summer term in the Barry Corner School. The schoolhouse was only about half a mile down the road from their cabin. The teacher, Anna Barry, lived nearby with her parents, after whom the crossroads was named. They had been among the earliest arrivals in the area, coming from near Pittsburgh, Pennsylvania, during the mid-1850s. Among the twenty students enrolled for the term besides Mary were Uncle Henry and Aunt Polly's four children as well as Clarence Huleatt.[43]

Laura was lonesome, and perhaps slightly jealous, when Mary went to school, leaving her home in the cabin with her mother and little sister while her father was often hunting or working in the fields. In October, when the fall term started, her parents allowed her to go to school with Mary, even though she was still only four years old. The experiment lasted only until Christmas, however, and after that Laura was kept home from school until she was a little older.[44]

Both of her parents, but especially her mother, were interested in obtaining a good education for Laura and her sisters. Even while living in primitive log cabins, they valued books and tried to ensure that their children would, too. Always on Sundays and often on other days, Caroline read to the family from novels such as *Norwood* or *Millbank*, church papers, magazines, newspapers, or anything else they could get their hands on. A favorite of the girls was Charles's big green-covered volume titled *A Description of Man and Nature in the Polar and Equatorial Regions of the Globe*. Most important, of course, was the "Good Book"—the Bible. Laura liked to look at the pictures in the family's big Bible, especially one of Adam giving names to the animals.[45]

Everywhere the family lived, if there was a church nearby they attended services. But there is no record of their attending while they were living in Pepin County. They were too far out in the country to easily get to the Methodist church in town, so they made do on their own by reading the Bible and saying their prayers before going to bed. There was little in the way of social events or community activity on the ridge where they lived, so families there had to entertain themselves mostly and relish occasional visits with neighbors and get-togethers with relatives. Charles Ingalls fulfilled his civic responsibilities by casting ballots in township elections and serving as treasurer of the Barry Corner school district. Township supervisors met at least once in the family's cabin. In this open, fluid frontier society, a sort of grass-roots democracy quickly emerged, reliant upon heavy personal involvement in community affairs.[46]

Within the family circle, Charles was a loving father who enjoyed romping with his girls and sharing his infectious brand of good humor. Laura remembered best his story-telling and fiddling abilities, but he also had enough of the kid in him to get down on all fours with his girls and play "Mad Dog" with them. His affectionate nature shone through in the tenderness he displayed toward his daughters and in the amount of time

he devoted to them. Much as she loved her mother, Laura always identified more closely with her father, to whom she was his "little half-pint of cider half drunk up."[47]

If the example set by Laura's father engendered spiritedness and spunkiness in her, her mother instructed her in the ways of becoming a woman in an environment that presented girls with few alternatives beyond marrying and raising a family. Laura and Mary assisted their mother with chores around the house. They helped by washing dishes, making beds, and cleaning house. They also learned about washing and ironing, mending and sewing, baking and cooking. The primary image Laura retained of her mother was one of her sitting in a rocker, sewing by lamplight, while her father played his fiddle or told a story.[48]

If her autobiography and novels are at all accurate, Laura and her sisters grew up in a warm, nurturing environment, loved by their parents and imbued with a sense of self-worth and significance. Though the family may have been financially unstable, the girls were enveloped with a sense of security and love. They understood that their parents were always there to protect and take care of them. The picture Laura later portrayed of her family was one of togetherness and warmth. Whatever dangers lurked outside, inside their little houses life was cozy and comfortable.[49]

It may have been inevitable that, having tasted prairie life in Kansas, Charles Ingalls would eventually tire of the wooded—and increasingly crowded—country around Pepin. Laura later described him as the typically restless type of frontiersman who was always looking toward the horizon where people were not crowding him and where he had ample elbowroom. Caroline, who longed for settled conditions and civilized practices, did not stand in the way of her husband when he started talking once again about moving, despite her reluctance. This time they looked directly westward toward lands that were opening up in southwestern Minnesota as rail lines were built in the region. Charles's brother Peter and his wife, Eliza, had been looking that way, too, and decided to depart with them but not go as far. Instead, they planned to find a farm near the Zumbro River in the southeastern part of the state.

It took several months for the two families to prepare for the move. Charles and Caroline obtained $1,000 for the land they had paid $167.50 for seven years earlier. They sold it to Andrew Anderson on October 28, 1873, and then went to visit Charles's parents and to stay with Peter and

Eliza and their family for several months until the weather improved. They needed to cross the Mississippi River while the ice was still thick enough to support their wagons. So they said their good-byes to friends and family one day in early February, just before Laura's eighth birthday, and set out. They soon found an empty house that the two families stayed in for several weeks until the weather was warmer. Peter had rented a farm near the Zumbro River, and when they got to it, Charles and Caroline and the girls waved good-bye and turned their eyes toward the western horizon.[50]

Along the way Laura saw her first train. Their destination now was near the end of the line of a new railroad whose tracks had just been laid the year before. The Winona and St. Peter Railroad was a branch of the great Chicago and North Western system, with headquarters in Chicago. The extension of its tracks west through Mankato and New Ulm, as with new lines everywhere, had led to the quick establishment of communities planted around the depots, which were set down every eight or twelve miles or so. New towns appeared at places such as Lamberton, Walnut Station, and Tracy, before the route turned to the northwest toward Marshall and ultimately to Lake Kampeska in Dakota Territory.

Once again, the Ingallses found themselves in the vanguard of settlement. Pepin had been only several years old when they got there, and Independence had been only a few weeks old upon their arrival. The town they settled near this time, Walnut Station (its name was later changed to Walnut Grove), had just gotten started in 1873, the year the trains started running, and it was formally platted by surveyors only a few weeks before the Ingallses arrived. Redwood County had been established in 1862, and settlement began in earnest two years later. For more than a century, it had been part of the territory of the Santee Sioux; before that, a succession of other tribal groups, including Cheyennes, Iowas, and Otoes, crisscrossed the region in search of game and fish. In 1851, in the Treaty of Traverse des Sioux, the Santees ceded their vast hunting grounds in return for annuities and a ten-mile-wide strip of land along each side of the Minnesota River. The Ingalls family's experiences with the Osages in Kansas had reinforced Caroline's wariness toward Indians. Now there was more for her to be worried about. On their journey across Minnesota, they came across several shells of buildings and other reminders of the bloody Sioux Uprising in 1862.[51]

The Indian disturbances of 1862 had driven out the first white settler in the area around the future Walnut Station, a man named Brown. He had

arrived a year earlier and squatted south of town near a grove of walnut trees straddling Plum Creek. Surveyors came through several years later, pitching their tents in the grove and marking off the townships around them. The first permanent settler, a Norwegian immigrant named Eleck Nelson, arrived with his wife, Alena, in 1870 and commenced farming. This Lutheran family, which eventually included seven children, was typical of the large Scandinavian element that settled the region.[52]

The town sprang up following the arrival of the railroad in 1873. J. H. Anderson and Gustave Sunwall owned the first store in town, which carried a general line of goods. Two brothers, Elias and Lafayette Bedal, played prominent roles in the community early on, the former going in the grain-buying business and the latter taking over as postmaster. The first school was held in Lafayette Bedal's home during the winter of 1873–1874 with fifteen students. The brothers also were responsible for having the town platted. Despite high hopes, however, Walnut Station grew slowly, its development inhibited in part by competition from Tracy, seven miles farther down the line. Nor did it have an opportunity to become a county seat like Independence or Pepin, since Redwood Falls, thirty miles to the northeast, captured the prize.[53]

Except for the unusual walnut grove south of town and other growths of trees along creeks and riverbeds and around lakes and other natural fire-breaks, the terrain that the Ingallses encountered when they arrived in Redwood County was bare of timber. The soil was fertile, a dark, rich loam, two to three feet thick and well drained by the numerous streams that fed into the Minnesota River. The field notes composed by an early surveyor named Moore hinted at why the land seemed to be so enticing: "The country is the richest quality of gently rolling prairie. It rolls in swelling billows as far as the eye can reach. Standing on a gentle eminence, one can look away to where the prairie meets the horizon in a dark blue line, resembling a belt of timber." There were few trees that needed to be cleared in preparation for planting crops, but the tough prairie grasses—thickly matted and deep rooted—resisted the plow initially and made breaking the soil a difficult task.[54]

Having traveled nearly two hundred miles across southern Minnesota, the Ingallses were looking for a place to turn the fertile prairie grassland into a producing farm. About two miles north of town along Plum Creek they found a quarter-section available for purchase. Charles paid a Norwegian settler $430.00 for the 172-acre farm, and the family moved into

the dwelling, which, like many in the area during the first few years of settlement, was a sod house. More precisely, it was a dugout, built into the bank along the creek. By now Laura was old enough to have experiences such as living in sod houses register keenly in her memory. The creek and the dugout and the surrounding terrain would provide many interesting stories for her later, as she reconstructed them in *On the Banks of Plum Creek*. She would recall the delights of wading in the creek, walking through dazzlingly colorful beds of wildflowers, and watching beautiful sunrises as well as the fears engendered by overflowing creek beds, howling blizzards, and rampaging grasshoppers.[55]

Unfortunately, the Ingallses arrived in Redwood County simultaneously with a severe invasion of locusts. The year before the county had been seriously affected by the pests, but 1874 and 1875 proved to be disastrous for farmers, as clouds of the creatures darkened the sky and then marched relentlessly across fields and anything else that stood in their way, stripping every living thing and depositing their eggs in the ground, guaranteeing that they would be back the following year. Charles Ingalls must have heard something before he moved about the previous year's infestation of locusts and grasshoppers; most likely the farmer who sold out to him left the area to escape the grasshoppers. Undaunted, Charles went to work for his closest neighbor, Eleck Nelson, in order to earn some cash and get ready for putting in a crop the following year.[56]

Meanwhile, although the two miles lying between them and the town kept the family on the farm most of the time, they did go to church services and to shop, and Mary and Laura were enrolled in the town school. For the first time in her short life Laura now had considerable opportunity to interact with other children, and she began to develop some of the personality traits that would become so prominent later in life, such as spunkiness, generosity, competitiveness, and resentment toward snobbery. Later, while working on her novel about Plum Creek, she drew a little map of the town, showing the railroad, the post office, a couple of stores and houses, the church, and the schoolhouse. Her memories of the village were fading by then, but in fact Walnut Grove *was* a slow-growing town, its population reaching only 153 by the 1880 census.

For the first time the Ingallses had a chance to attend church regularly. Both Charles and Caroline had been brought up in religious atmospheres, and they made Bible-reading and prayers an important part of their family

life. Rev. Edwin H. Alden, a thirty-eight-year-old Dartmouth-educated Congregational minister from Waseca, which lay a hundred miles east along the railroad, arrived in the community in August 1874 under the auspices of the Home Missionary Society to organize a new congregation. Charles and Caroline were among the dozen or so charter members and took advantage of the opportunity to be baptized. Another charter member, Julie Tower, became Laura's Sunday school teacher. A church building quickly materialized on the south end of the tiny town, with Charles Ingalls contributing a sacrificial $26.15 to help pay for the bell that was installed in the bell tower. Laura later noted that he had to forego a much needed pair of new boots to do it, but she wrote that the contribution had been only $3.00. She also described the gifts and the festivities that were held in the church five days before Christmas, when the building was formally dedicated. Small as it was, the little congregation was unable financially to support a full-time pastor for several years. For Laura's mother the church, in addition to what spiritual significance it possessed, stood out as a bulwark of civilization in the midst of a still forming, rough frontier culture. Her father, who was elected a trustee of the congregation, loved to sing at the services and to play gospel tunes on his fiddle. Biblical teachings and precepts became an integral part of Laura's life, all the more meaningful and significant because they were seldom called into question. If she did not always completely live up to their admonitions, she was not a doubter or a hypocrite about the teachings.[57]

The building of a schoolhouse the following year allowed instruction to move out of Lafayette Bedal's house. Besides the "Three R's," Laura now started learning some important things about getting along with others. She began to divide her peers into ones she liked, such as Nettie Kennedy, and ones she did not much like, such as Nellie Owens (later a model for Nellie Oleson in her novels). She learned something about social democracy and about being kind and fair to schoolmates. But she also learned about the sweetness of revenge and the temptation to deceive one's parents, at least until one was discovered.[58]

Most of the time, though, Laura and Mary were busy on the farm, doing things that little girls did, helping their mother around the house or playing games or running around the creek and the nearby tableland. There were many ways for eight- or ten-year-old girls to be helpful in the family. They could wash the dishes, help clean, run errands, drive the cows out to

pasture, and watch Carrie. By the end of their first summer, their little sister had turned four and was capable of getting into lots of mischief. They could play house on a flat rock on top of the creek bank, pick wildflowers, have fun with their dolls, and occasionally have a party. Their mother read them Bible stories and other things. There were prairie gophers to run after and other wildlife to examine. On the Fourth of July they all went to a picnic, where there were speeches, singing, and games for everyone.

The girls were not too young to realize that the family's financial situation was precarious. Living as close as they did to the land, they were aware that the family's well-being—perhaps even its survival—depended on how well the crops fared and on what kind of a price could be obtained for them. In the spring of 1875, with the help of Eleck Nelson, Charles built a new little wooden house for them on the other side of Plum Creek. He planted a crop of wheat that looked splendid until hordes of grasshoppers descended on it and methodically destroyed it. All over the region stores closed their doors, people moved out, and farmers who stayed behind looked for temporary employment in the harvest fields of eastern Minnesota, which had been untouched by the locusts. Charles Ingalls joined this migration, returning home at the end of the season with some much needed cash, allowing the family to hold out until another planting season.

That fall the family moved into town into a little house behind the Congregational church, so that it would be easier on Caroline when their expected baby arrived. On November 1, the three sisters got a baby brother, who was named Charles Frederick, but they called him Freddie. Charles may have found work in town during the winter, carpentering or clerking in one of the town's businesses, but he had no intention of doing so permanently.[59]

The following spring he was back in the fields, optimistically planting a new crop of wheat, hopeful that this time he would get a good harvest and be able to pay his bills. Laura and Mary walked to town to attend school for the term that went from spring into the summer. Once again clouds of grasshoppers darkened the horizon, once again they devoured everything in sight, and once again the crop was ruined. This time the parents concluded that enough was enough and they would try their luck somewhere else. Many other families were packing up and leaving, too. Friends of theirs in town, the Steadmans, who were fellow charter members of the Congregational church, indicated that they were going to buy a little

hotel in the village of Burr Oak in northeastern Iowa, and they invited the Ingallses to join them on the venture and help operate it. By now Charles was desperate enough to abandon the idea of farming temporarily and willing to try living in town.

They sold their farm for four hundred dollars in July to Abraham and Margaret Keller and headed east along the trail that had brought them to Walnut Grove little more than two years earlier.[60] First they stayed with Peter and Eliza at their farm along the Zumbro River in southeastern Minnesota until it was time to join the Steadmans in Burr Oak. The girls had fun playing with their cousins Peter, Alice, Ella, and Edith and with their baby brother, Lansford. There were chores and work to be done but time for play, too. Laura especially enjoyed going to get the cows and driving them home to be milked. Then tragedy struck. It was no less a tragedy for being so common on the frontier. Freddie took ill, and suddenly he was gone. It was Sunday, August 27, 1876; he was only nine months old.

Soon they were on their way again, to meet the Steadmans in Burr Oak and help run the hotel there, as had been planned. Grief over Freddie, along with the chilly fall rains, darkened the family's mood. It was a cold, miserable journey for the girls and their parents. They drove directly south along dirt roads and then three miles beyond the Iowa state line.

The road they were traveling merged into State Street, which ran north and south through the center of town, flanked by East and West Streets, and crossed perpendicularly by seven or eight side streets. Only about two hundred residents inhabited the several dozen houses that were scattered about the little community. The town's prospects for attracting people were minimal. It possessed no railroad connection. Despite some vague talk about building one, nothing ever came of it. In 1869 the tracks had reached Decorah, the county seat twelve miles south. Lacking such a transportation link, Burr Oak was destined to remain a small, out-of-the way farming village, largely isolated from currents of change that were transforming American life after the Civil War.[61]

Although not as new as the other places they had lived in, the little town was not so old either, having gotten its start in 1851. A rush of settlers into Winneshiek County after 1848 had occurred directly after the removal of the Winnebago Indians, who had been the predominant native presence there, sharing and sometimes contesting the territory with the Sauk and the Fox tribes. A large influx of settlement had come in 1850, with the

founding of Decorah, Bloomfield, Springfield, and several other nearby communities. Soon German, Bohemian, Swiss, Norwegian, English, and Scottish immigrants rushed in.[62]

Standing on a major route to the west during the early phase of settlement in northeastern Iowa, Burr Oak had shared for a brief time in the activity and excitement of the westward movement. However, by the time the Ingalls family arrived, life had settled into humdrum routine. On July 4, 1876, the Old Settlers' Association was organized to recognize the accomplishments of the pioneers who had been trailblazers in the country a quarter-century before. The two hotels in town still attracted a respectable amount of business, both from transients passing through the area and from permanent residents, but the long-term economic prospects of the town were severely limited. It was undoubtedly a measure of the family's financial desperation in Walnut Grove that Charles and Caroline had decided to take their chances in a partnership with the Steadmans in the Burr Oak House. The establishment was also known as the Masters Hotel, after its previous owner, William Masters, who sold it to the Steadmans when he moved from Burr Oak to Walnut Grove.[63]

To a nine-going-on-ten year old like Laura, the hotel probably seemed much grander than it actually was. Built into a hillside that sloped down toward Silver Creek, which ran through the lot behind it, the eleven-room structure occupied three levels, the middle one opening onto the street in front. Customers could enter the establishment through two doors on the front porch, the one on the right leading into the parlor and the one on the left into the barroom. A single bedroom behind the parlor and several more upstairs accommodated guests and permanent residents. A night's lodging cost twenty-five cents, as did a meal. A gallon of wine could be had for the same and a shot of liquor for one-fourth the cost. Down below on the lower level were the dining room, kitchen, and a bedroom where the Ingallses slept—father, mother, and their three girls.[64]

Laura and Mary helped with waiting on tables and doing the dishes, while their parents occupied themselves with cooking and cleaning and other duties, but the work itself in the tiny establishment could not have been very heavy. The hotel's location on a hillside, with a creek curving through its backyard and a little fishpond and springhouse, made for a picturesque setting. The girls were able to play with the older two Steadman boys, Johnny and Reuben, and often were left to look after the Steadman

baby, Tommy. Laura was beginning to observe foibles in human behavior, things that would have eluded her a year or two earlier. She noticed one reason that little Tommy cried so much was that his mother shook him and slapped him a lot. And Johnny, whose lameness should have occasioned sympathetic feelings in her, only elicited her scorn because of his nastiness. He was always pinching and pulling people's hair, breaking playthings, and generally making a nuisance of himself.

The girls' parents worried mainly about the potentially bad influence of the boarders and the men who frequented the barroom upstairs. Some of the men, such as Will Reed, who taught at the school on the hill, were admirable people. That label even applied to Mr. Bisby, who later rented a house to the Ingallses. But he annoyed Laura by fancying himself as someone who could teach her how to sing. Since the family was somewhat dependent upon his goodwill as a patron, Laura had to play along with his conceit. Their major concern, however, was with the drunks who shot holes in doors or who allegedly burned their lungs out by igniting fumes in their throats left by bouts with the bottle.[65]

When the two-room school situated on the hill two blocks east of the hotel was in session, the girls enjoyed attending it. There they made friends with the other schoolchildren and worked on their lessons. Laura found multiplication tables to be difficult at first, but she shone as a reader and enjoyed reading her lessons aloud at night. They included stories and poems such as "The Burial of Sir John Moore," "The Bison Track," "Paul Revere's Ride," "The Pied Piper," "Tubal Cain," and "The Village Blacksmith." Laura later remembered with gratitude the excellent training in reading that Will Reed, the school's principal, gave her. There were few diversions in the little town, but from time to time amateur theatricals were staged, there was a brass band, and temperance meetings and religious revivals also provided some diversions for the Ingallses and their neighbors. But except for a fire scare or a fistfight now and then, life must have been awfully dull in Burr Oak.[66]

The small amount of work that he had to do at the hotel left Charles with plenty of time to go into partnership with J. H. Porter, who ran a grinding mill. In addition, Charles did odd jobs and may have done some carpentering when opportunities arose. Worried about the hotel's bad influence on their girls, the Ingallses moved out of it and into a second-floor apartment above the grocery store just down the street to the south

in January 1877. Later that spring Charles sold his interest in the gristmill and prepared to look for jobs in the fields during spring planting. The family moved a second time, to Mr. Bisby's small red-brick house, located several blocks north up State Street and two blocks west, close to the Congregational church.[67]

Laura enjoyed living near the edge of an oak wood and once again having a cow. She was responsible for taking it out to pasture every morning and bringing it back every night. "I loved to wander along the creek and look at the flowers and wriggle my toes among the cool, lush grasses," she later wrote in "Pioneer Girl." "I was such a great girl now that I wore my shoes all day, but I always went barefoot after the cow." She also enjoyed wandering around with her chum Alice Ward in the graveyard at the other end of town, peering at the names on the gravestones and reading the inscriptions. Further enlivening the household was the arrival of a new sister, Grace Pearl, born on May 23, 1877. The new baby had golden hair like Mary's and blue eyes like their father's.[68]

It must have been somewhat disconcerting to Laura to discover that a woman living across the street wanted to adopt her. The daughters of Mrs. Starr, the wife of a doctor who also served as town clerk, had moved away to teach. The woman told Caroline that she was lonesome and wished that Laura could come live with her and her husband and keep her company and help her around the house. The thought that her parents might actually abandon her like that could have been traumatic for a ten year old. The way in which Laura related the episode in a humorous vein many years later, however, suggests how secure she felt within her family circle and how confident she was in the love and protection that encompassed her and her sisters while they were growing up. Describing the scene in her autobiography, she wrote, "But Ma smiled at me and said she couldn't possibly spare me. So Mrs. Star[r] went away looking very disappointed."[69]

With four girls to feed and take care of, the need for more income became insistent. The Ingallses had come to Burr Oak because the grasshopper invasion had driven them out of Minnesota and they had desperately needed to find something—anything—to help them get by temporarily. Now, after a year in Burr Oak and nothing but temporary jobs between them and destitution, they decided to return to Walnut Grove and give it another try. At least Charles would be with his girls again; the various jobs he had taken were keeping him away from home most of the time now.

The grasshopper infestation had receded, and the economic depression that had been going on since 1873 was beginning to lift. It was time to try farming again.

Charles was in high spirits as the family traveled along, joking and laughing and singing. In the West, where the population was sparse, even the air seemed fresher. At night by their campfire, after the sun went down, he played his fiddle. As the notes of "Yankee Doodle," "Buffalo Gals," "Arkansas Traveler," and "Marching through Georgia" wafted gently through the evening air, the girls and their parents wondered what to expect when they returned to Walnut Grove.

A warm welcome awaited them when they drove into town. The Ensign family invited the Ingallses to stay with them until Charles was able to build a new house. He took a job in a store to earn some money, and the two families split household expenses. Mary, Laura, and Carrie, meanwhile, went to school with the three Ensign children, Willard, Anna, and Howard. They all studied their grammar, geography, history, and arithmetic lessons from the same books, although some of the children were further along than the others. Laura especially enjoyed spelling, remembering later her successes in the spelling bees. At Friday night "spelling school," the entire town would come with their lamps and lanterns to witness the competitions.[70]

Now ten, almost eleven, Laura was learning something new every day about how people behaved and treated each other. Until then, most of the things she had learned had come from her parents; increasingly it would be from her peers and within the broader social context that she would pick up on instances of human greed and generosity, thoughtfulness and meanness, pride and ambition. In the schoolyard she could observe cliques forming, one around Carrie and the younger girls, the other around Mary and the older girls, leaving her in the middle. Being more independent-minded than the rest, Laura emerged as a natural leader and soon had the younger girls entering into such boys' games as Ante-I-Over, Pullaway, Prisoner's Base, and even baseball. Mary and her friends were scandalized by Laura's tomboyish behavior, and their mother apparently told her that she was getting to be too big to be playing with the boys like that.[71]

She was beginning to look at boys somewhat differently now. When Howard Ensign asked her to promise to marry him one day, she considered the proposition seriously until he got jealous and cried when she played

with another boy. That so disgusted Laura that she told Howard to forget the idea. But if puppy love was part of growing up, beginning to observe more closely and with more understanding the world of adult relationships was part of it, too. She discovered that the unhappy milliner who created such beautiful hats out of lace and ribbons and artificial flowers was gloomy all the time because she had been divorced from her husband. Laura saw farm wives come into town to take their drunken husbands home from the saloon, sisters trick each other out of inheritances, young women spite each other in competing for the affections of eligible young bachelors, and parents drive suitors away in order to prevent their grown children from getting married and abandoning them. She noticed how a male schoolteacher absentmindedly fondled young girls' hands and was disillusioned to discover that a Sunday school teacher had appropriated a lemon pie that Laura's mother had baked for a picnic and then told the other teachers that she had baked it herself.[72]

Laura went to work for Emeline Masters in the hotel during the summer of 1878. She earned fifty cents a week washing dishes, sweeping floors, dusting, making beds, setting tables, and baby-sitting the Masters's grandchild. In the hotel she only had to keep her ears and eyes open to learn about things that she not only would not have heard about at home but also sometimes did not entirely understand. Although she was still a schoolgirl, she bore a sturdy sense of responsibility. Her work contributed to the welfare of the family, and it was needed. Laura realized that her family was poor, but, looking around her, she could see that few of the other families in town were much better off.

From William Masters her father bought a lot in the pasture behind the hotel and built another little house for the family in the spring of 1878. Afterward he rented a room downtown and began operating a butcher shop in it. Most families ran out of home-butchered meat by the end of winter. Business was brisk for a time, but Charles sold the business at summer's end since people would be doing their own butchering again as soon as cold weather set in. With winter approaching, he hired out his carpentry skills to Mr. Masters, who was erecting a new store building next to his hotel, with a meeting hall on the second floor.[73]

Although he still lacked a steady source of income, Charles Ingalls was not without respect in the community. He was elected as a trustee of the Union Congregational church. In the winter of 1879, when a Good

Templars unit formed in Walnut Grove, he and Caroline joined. The following March he was elected justice of the peace in the first election ever held in the town, capturing twenty-three out of the twenty-nine votes that were cast. He used the front room of their house for an office, listening to the cases that were brought in to him. When this happened, Caroline would shoo the girls into the kitchen, but they eagerly listened through the door to hear what was going on in the next room. Laura learned something more about greed and treachery in some of these proceedings. There was, for example, the case of a woman who obtained revenge on her sister for having married the man she loved by tricking her out of property back in New York State.[74]

Even church took on a different color in the mind of the eleven year old. Religious revivals enlivened Walnut Grove as they did in towns all over America, but Laura felt uncomfortable listening to people publicly testify about their personal beliefs. It violated her sense of privacy. If she was more reticent than some people, however, she did not resist going to church and Sunday school every week at the Congregational church. When the opportunity arose, she topped that by attending Methodist services and Sunday school in the afternoon. The church was conducting a contest to see who could memorize the most Bible verses (called Golden Texts and Central Truths), and Laura tied for the top prize, winning a reference Bible for her efforts.[75]

How long the family would have stayed in Walnut Grove had not a new opportunity arisen is hard to say. People continued to move into the area, economic activity began to pick up, and the frontier pushed ever farther west. During the five years after 1875 the population of Redwood County jumped from 2,982 to 5,375. Charles Ingalls probably would have obtained another plot of land and tried his hand at farming again soon, but a new possibility emerged when his sister Ladocia unexpectedly came through town one day and made him a tempting offer.

# 2

## *Schoolgirl and Courting Days*

### 1879–1885

*I*n the spring of 1879 tragedy struck the Ingalls family. Although Mary was its immediate victim, the results affected the entire family, especially Laura. The older sister suddenly became sick with a pain in her head and a high fever. Her condition continued to deteriorate, and she suffered what later was diagnosed as a stroke. Dr. Jacob Wellcome, general surgeon for that stretch of the railroad, was called in from Sleepy Eye, forty miles to the east. He said that the stroke had affected the nerves in her eyes and that nothing could be done. Her sickness was a lingering result of an earlier case of the measles. Mary was going blind.[1]

Being closest in age to Mary, Laura naturally bore major responsibility for looking out for her. In effect, she became Mary's surrogate eyes. Just twelve years old, Laura's transition into adolescence was greatly accelerated by the new responsibility thrust upon her. Then, in short order, that duty took on a new coloration. The family would be moving once again. This was the last move they would make, for Caroline Ingalls apparently extracted a promise from her husband that in return for consenting to this relocation, she would never again be forced to move. Their prospects in Walnut Grove were none too good, and farther west in Dakota Territory government land was available for homesteading. Charles made up his mind to get some of that land.

The Chicago and North Western Railroad was extending its line west into Dakota Territory, and Charles's sister Ladocia offered an opportunity to him when she came through Walnut Grove on her way west to the railroad camp where her husband, Hiram Forbes, was a contractor for the building of the road. Forbes was looking for someone who could act as a bookkeeper and timekeeper for his employees. When Docia (as Charles called her) told Charles that her husband was willing to pay him fifty dollars a month if he wanted the job, it seemed to be too good an opportunity to ignore. In Dakota Territory, on the cutting edge of settlement, there would be government homesteads available close to the tracks. The decision quickly was made. The next day Charles told his sister that he would accept her offer. He sold the house that he had built and the lot that he had bought from William Masters and prepared to leave. Caroline and the girls would wait for him to return for them, using the time to dispose of items that they would not be able to take with them and to prepare for the move. Laura took advantage of the opportunity to play with her girlfriends Nettie, Sandy, and Christy for the last time.[2]

This final move carried the family west with hordes of other home seekers, expectant and optimistic about the opportunities awaiting them on the virgin soil of the Dakota prairie. The Ingalls family had bounced around from Wisconsin to Indian Territory, back to Wisconsin, out to Minnesota and back to Iowa, once more to Minnesota, and now all the way to Dakota Territory. Their path had not been smooth, or easy, but hope lingered in Charles Ingalls's heart, and Caroline and the girls were ready to follow him once more into the unknown.

Now they would become a part of the Great Dakota Boom, a wave of migration that swept into eastern Dakota Territory during the late 1870s and early 1880s, more than tripling the population of its southern part (which would enter the Union as the state of South Dakota in 1889) in five years' time. That statistic in fact underestimates the speed of the transition, for of the 82,000 residents enumerated in the 1880 census a large portion had arrived in 1878 and 1879 in anticipation of the boom sure to come with the extension of railroad lines into the region. By 1885 the number had swelled to 249,000. This was one of the last frontier regions in America made available to the plow, and tens of thousands of eager homesteaders scrambled to take advantage of the opportunity. More tens of thousands came with

them to set up stores, grain elevators, lumberyards, blacksmith shops, and other businesses that could profit from the patronage of the farmers.[3]

The area awaited the laying of railroad tracks, for until adequate transportation was available to ship grain and livestock to distant markets, the economic potential of the region would remain meager. Attempting to transport agricultural products long distances by wagon was impractical, and rivers such as the Big Sioux, the Vermillion, and the James were not suited for moving bulky goods. Only the Missouri River, running through the middle and along the southern border of the territory, provided adequate water transportation, but it benefited only those nearby it. Until the railroads arrived, agriculture necessarily remained predominately self-sufficient, limited to a relatively small number of farm families ranged around the few towns that managed to get started in the 1860s in the southeastern part of the territory.

The impetus for the Great Dakota Boom that changed all of this came from two great railroads headquartered in Chicago: the Chicago and North Western and the Chicago, Milwaukee, and St. Paul (generally referred to simply as the "North Western" and the "Milwaukee"). The president of the latter was the great Alexander Mitchell, a Scottish immigrant who took over as chief executive of the company in 1865, when it had only about 270 miles of track to its name. By the time of his death in 1887, the company had upped the number of miles laid to more than 5,000. No less imposing a figure was the head of the North Western, Marvin Hughitt, a New York State farm boy who started as a telegraph operator and worked his way through the ranks in the railroad business, emerging as the chief strategist of the North Western long before he was finally elevated to its presidency in 1887.[4]

The Winona and St. Peter branch line that was extended through Walnut Grove in 1873 took a northwesterly path from there all the way to Lake Kampeska in Dakota Territory in order to secure federal land grants. But the western end of that branch lay dormant for several years, awaiting a push of settlers into the region. The financial panic of 1873 and the depression that followed halted further railroad construction for half a decade, but by the end of the 1870s, as the national economy improved, renewed expansion again became possible. The Chicago and North Western system now projected two parallel lines of track into southern Dakota Territory,

one going west from Lake Kampeska, near the new town of Watertown, the other (referred to as the Dakota Central branch) extending directly west from Walnut Grove toward the Missouri River. Alexander Mitchell's Milwaukee Railroad, in the meantime, moved into the region with lines running north and south of these branch extensions. The Great Dakota Boom, which transformed the entire East River region of southern Dakota Territory, took shape directly as a result of the frenzied railroad building conducted by these two companies.[5]

In 1877, in preparation for the extension of the North Western west from Tracy, Marvin Hughitt journeyed to Minnesota and hired a buckboard wagon so that he could take a closer look at the broad Dakota prairie where the tracks would be laid. He found a gently rolling countryside covered with waist- to shoulder-high grass, and, except for the timber that grew around the many lakes and along rivers and streams and a lone tree here and there on the countryside, a region that was entirely unforested. The soil, however, proved to be rich and productive, full of potential for farmers who could understand its ways. Up to this time, the tall grass had been a feeding ground for the buffalo, which in turn had sustained the Dakota, or Sioux, Indians who had been living in the area. During the early 1700s the Dakotas had pushed out from Minnesota onto the open prairie and plains, fleeing their enemies, the Ojibwas, who possessed guns. They had followed the buffalo, which provided them with a richer diet and a generally more prosperous lifestyle than they had known in Minnesota. By midcentury, they were already pushing across the Missouri River and extending their hunting area all the way to the Big Horn Mountains. For several decades, the Dakotas enjoyed the highest degree of material wealth and political influence that they ever had attained. Almost as quickly as they reached their peak, however, white settlers began to invade the region, and the Dakotas entered into a period of conflict that undermined their power and ultimately destroyed their traditional way of life.[6]

Marvin Hughitt's 1877 wagon trip to settle on the future route of his railroad occurred just one year after the storied Battle of the Little Big Horn in eastern Montana, where Lt. Col. George Armstrong Custer and his Seventh Cavalry unit fell to the largest Native American military force ever assembled on the North American continent. News of the debacle arrived in the East just in time to dampen people's spirits as they prepared to celebrate the Fourth of July and to attend the great Centennial Exposition

in Philadelphia, commemorating one hundred years of nationhood. The drama that played itself out on a national scale during the three decades after the Civil War—the dispossession of the Native Americans by white settlers moving to the frontier—had its counterpart in Dakota Territory during the Great Dakota Boom and later. Just a few miles up the James River from the location that Marvin Hughitt had chosen for a division point (soon to be named Huron), Drifting Goose and his band of Yanktonnais (a subtribe of the Dakotas) had their largest campsite. With the push of white settlers into the area, Drifting Goose and his followers were forced onto reservations set aside for them, as the dominant white culture endeavored to transform them to the ways of the white world.[7]

As a twelve-year-old girl who possessed little inkling of these developments, Laura had only a dim understanding of her family's involvement in this displacement process. According to the books that she would write later, however, she was aware of the presence of Indians in the area, and she featured them prominently in her stories (just as she did in describing the family's experience in Kansas, but not Wisconsin). After her father returned to pick them up at Tracy, the family was overtaken along the trail by a French Indian whom Laura referred to in *By the Shores of Silver Lake* as "Big Jerry." As usual, Caroline was worried by the sight of an Indian, but Charles reassured her that he was a friendly and dependable sort, even if some men suspected him of being in cahoots with a ring of horse thieves. Laura herself seemed to take the more open-minded, sympathetic viewpoint toward the Indians that she depicted her father as having rather than the pinched, fearful attitude that she associated with her mother, if the books described their true feelings.

The farther the Ingalls's wagon pushed beyond the Big Sioux River, the fewer signs of civilization the family encountered. They observed old Indian trails and buffalo paths, but Charles indicated that they were not likely to catch a glimpse of one of the beasts. "Only a little while before the vast herds of thousands of buffaloes had grazed over this country," Laura wrote in her novel about the experience. "They had been the Indians' cattle, and white men had slaughtered them all." Her little sermonettes calling for tolerance of all kinds of people in articles she wrote later in the *Missouri Ruralist* and her Christian beliefs were further indications that, if she was not always a model of advanced opinion on Indian-white relations, she went considerably beyond many of her friends and neighbors in her

willingness to view Native Americans as a people worthy of respect and admiration. Something in her childhood—maybe her father's example—no doubt influenced her in this regard.[8]

The withdrawal of the buffalo from the area had taken almost the entire local Indian population away with them, and the arrival of white homesteaders stimulated most of the rest to leave. By 1878, upon hearing rumors that a railroad line would soon enter the region, settlers started crossing the Minnesota border and taking up residence in the eastern part of Brookings County. The following spring the rush began in earnest. The *Brookings County Press,* located in the tiny town of Fountain, reported in March, "Settlers are coming in all around so fast we cannot keep track of them." Moving beyond Lake Benton, Minnesota, in April, the surveying crew needed less than two months to reach the Big Sioux River, pausing there only briefly before proceeding westward toward the James. In early July, Marvin Hughitt traveled again from Chicago to help determine the locations of the towns along the tracks. Grading crews followed soon after the surveyors, and behind them came the tracklayers. By late August grading work was already moving into Kingsbury County, while the surveyors pushed west beyond the James.[9]

The *Lake Benton Times* described the work of the tracklaying crews, when they came through there in mid-September: "About two hundred men, five engineers are busily at work—sixty men laying track, forty building bridges, forty surfacers (those who follow and level the track), twenty tie men and twenty men employed on the spile drivers. There are two spile drivers, each run with a force of ten men." The workers moved into Dakota Territory on September 30, progressing about a mile a day. When they got to the new town of Brookings on October 18, George Hopp moved his *Brookings County Press* printing outfit the eight miles from Fountain, whose hopes that the tracks would come to it had evaporated. In the meantime, Medary and Oakwood, two other inland towns that had harbored similar dreams, folded up, too, and their residents moved what buildings they were able to into Brookings or to the towns on either side, Aurora and Volga. Some of the Ingalls's future neighbors were among these early arrivals: John H. Carroll, who was involved in real estate and the land business at Fountain, and Visscher V. Barnes, a lawyer at Oakwood.[10]

By this time homesteaders already filled up much of the land in the eastern part of Brookings County. "Here and there," Laura would later

observe in *By the Shores of Silver Lake*, "men were working in their fields, and now and then a team and wagon passed." When the family arrived at the railroad camp at Brookings, Laura had a good time riding horses and playing with her cousin Lena, who was a little older.[11]

In November cold weather began to set in, and the tracklayers stopped for the season at Volga (originally called Bandytown), staying there for the winter. Meanwhile, the Ingallses had driven to where Charles was working, at the forward camp at Silver Lake, thirty-five miles farther west. On the other side of Volga, they encountered few people. Writing about the experience many years later, Laura noted, probably with slight exaggeration, "Beyond the Big Sioux there were no more fields, no houses, no people in sight. There really was no road, only a dim wagon trail, and no railroad grade." Once again they discovered other family members when they arrived at the railroad camp. Caroline's brother Henry was working there, and the girls met their cousins Charley and Louisa again. In accordance with the policy of locating towns approximately eight to twelve miles apart along the tracks, one was platted the following spring just north of Silver Lake near the shanties of the men who were working on the grade. It was to be named De Smet, in honor of a Belgian Jesuit priest who had crossed through the region forty years earlier on his way to ministering to Indian tribes in the Bitterroot Range.[12]

Charles was the bookkeeper and timekeeper for the Dakota Central crews. He and Caroline warned their girls to keep their distance from the railroad workers with their rough ways and vulgar language. As was generally true in frontier regions, the first arrivals were predominately male, and they tended toward violent and rude behavior; several of them once threatened to ransack the company store if they were not paid on time. It was not too long, however, before the men were packing and heading east for the winter, leaving the Ingallses almost all alone at Silver Lake. Instead of following the rest, Charles accepted an offer from the railroad company to remain there for the winter, staying in the surveyors' house, so he could watch over the equipment and supplies that were stored there. There would be few other people in the area to keep them company, but the pantry was full of food that they could use in return for taking care of the place. And by staying during the winter Charles would have an excellent opportunity to get a head start on finding a good spot for a homestead and filing a claim on it in the spring.

The winter of 1879–1880 turned out to be mild. Charles was able to supplement the family's meager income by hunting and trapping. Wolves still frequented the area, a reminder that "civilization" had not quite arrived. But inside their snug, cozy house Caroline and the girls did their work every day, cooking and cleaning, sewing and talking. For diversion, the family played games and told stories. Charles whittled a little checkerboard for them, and almost every night he played his fiddle.[13]

Around Christmastime, Robert Boast, a young settler who had arrived earlier that summer and registered a claim on a quarter-section southeast of Silver Lake, returned from Iowa with his wife, Ella, and appropriated an empty cabin not far from the Ingalls's. Along with the Boasts, a bachelor named Walter Ogden, who lived several miles east, near Lake Preston, joined the family to celebrate New Year's.[14]

While traveling around the countryside, Charles discovered a spot just south of Silver Lake that he believed would make an excellent homestead. He waited impatiently for the weather to clear and for the land office in Brookings to open so he could walk the forty miles and file a claim on it before somebody else did. The official land office was located at the territorial capital in Yankton on the Missouri River, and a new one would soon be established at Watertown, fifty miles northeast of Silver Lake. To facilitate the heavy movement of settlers into the area, a temporary office was set up in Brookings. Charles was there on February 19, 1880, to sign an affidavit and file an application for the northeast quarter of Section 3 in Township 110, Range 56. The claim was for 154.29 acres rather than the usual 160, and the filing fee was $13.86.[15]

Quickly that spring a huge rush of settlers entered the region, clamoring for other choice locations near the railroad tracks. Many homesteaders obtained temporary jobs in town to tide them over until their first crop came in. Likewise, many of those who had come to set up stores or to take jobs in town filed homestead claims, either intending to farm a little on the side or, more likely, to obtain title to the land and then dispose of it at a profit. With virtually no housing or boarding facilities available during the first few weeks of the rush, the Ingallses speedily converted the surveyors' house in which they were living into a temporary hotel, serving meals and letting men sleep in whatever space was available. Just turned thirteen, Laura energetically pitched in to help her mother. Especially because of

Mary's blindness, Laura had considerable responsibility thrust on her for a girl just entering adolescence.[16]

Her father, meanwhile, purchased two corner business lots in the new town of De Smet. They were located diagonally across from each other at the intersection of Second Street and Calumet Avenue (or Main Street). Charles quickly constructed a small store building on the lot on the west side of Calumet (and north of Second), and the family moved into it on April 3. The day was a warm and pleasant one, but that evening the weather turned cold, and by the next morning the girls' blankets were covered with snow that had blown in through cracks in the ceiling. Until the tracklayers arrived, teamsters hauled wagons loaded with lumber from Volga so that construction work could continue. "Already you could see Main Street growing up from the muddy ground along the railroad grade," Laura later wrote in *By the Shores of Silver Lake*. "Suddenly, there on the brown prairie where nothing had been before, was the town."[17]

Of the 285 towns that were platted between 1878 and 1889 in southern Dakota Territory, 80 percent were railroad towns. De Smet was typical of them. Like every other town along the Dakota Central branch between the Minnesota border and Pierre on the Missouri River, it was laid out in the shape of the letter T. Calumet Avenue ran north and south, perpendicular to the railroad tracks. Arthur Jacobi, the surveyor who laid out the town in March, simply followed a pattern that had already been used in Aurora, Brookings, Volga, and other places. As was the case with most of the towns east of Huron, the Western Town Lot Company, a railroad subsidiary, was in charge of platting the town and selling lots. All of the commercial lots on Main Street were the standard 25-foot width, and they extended back 165 feet to the alley.[18]

Charles Ingalls was not the first person to erect a building in De Smet; that distinction went to twenty-six-year-old Henry Hinz of Wisconsin, who opened a saloon closer to the railroad tracks. In quick order, other simple wooden structures, most of which were embellished by false fronts, made their appearance on Calumet Avenue or along side streets: a bank, a hotel, a livery stable, a hardware store, a dry-goods store, a tailor shop, a furniture store, a newspaper office, a blacksmith shop, a lumberyard, and a grain elevator. Hope and expectation filled the air as the first arrivers scrambled to get started. Many of them already had tried their luck in other places and had moved with the course of settlement. John H. Carroll, the land dealer

from Fountain, set up business on the east side of Main, north across Second Street from Charles's second store building. Visscher V. Barnes moved from Oakwood and put up his lawyer's shingle. The first arrivals to any new frontier often managed to get a head start, emerging to positions of dominance. Those who failed to do so frequently spent a few months or years in a place and then moved on to give it a try somewhere else. That had been the Ingalls's case up until this time. But if Charles intended to live up to the bargain that he had made with his wife, they would not move again.[19]

Laura later remembered not much liking the new town in the beginning. She did not know anybody, and she felt lonely and afraid. Her father soon sold his first store building to E. H. Couse, who used it for a hardware store. His second one, catercorner across the intersection, became the family's temporary home. With the arrival of warmer weather they moved to their claim south of town, where Charles had built a small claim shanty for them. They would add onto the simple structure later, when more time and money became available. Once settled in, according to her daughter's later description, Caroline took out her little china shepherdess and carefully placed it on a shelf on the wall, a symbol of civilization for her amid the rough prairie-frontier environment.[20]

Plenty of work needed to be done that first year on the claim, and the girls were a great help. Charles dug a well near the edge of the slough and planted some cottonwood saplings around the house. He also broke several acres of ground and planted turnips for themselves and for their cow and also potatoes, beans, tomatoes, corn, and pumpkins. The initial breaking of the sod turned out to be the hardest job, because of the matted roots of the prairie grasses. Later he cut wild prairie grass for hay, and Laura and her mother helped him pitch it onto a wagon and then unload it and build it into stacks for winter feed for the horses and cows. When all of the hay was put up, Charles went back into town to look for carpentry jobs that would bring in some money to help them get through the coming winter.[21]

Cold weather arrived early in 1880. The first snowstorm blew in the first part of October, ushering in what homesteaders would refer to for years as "the hard winter." For the next six months a steady succession of blizzards and Arctic blasts left people in and around De Smet dazed with fatigue and frustration. After the early snowstorm, Laura's parents quickly decided to move back into town, where they would be warmer

and safer. By now there were approximately one hundred people living in the little town.[22] Laura remained uncomfortable around large numbers of people, preferring the open spaces of the countryside, where she felt more in control. At thirteen, she was passing through a formative stage in her personality development, becoming increasingly aware of the opposite sex and trying adult roles for the first time. By serving as Mary's "eyes" after moving from Walnut Grove, she was already working herself into more adult-type responsibilities than many adolescents. When she started school in town that fall, she came increasingly to see herself as someone who stood out from the other children, both in academic ability and in leadership skills.

The new school building in De Smet was located just two blocks west of the Ingalls's house on the north side of Second Street. For a somewhat insecure adolescent, it may have seemed that it actually was "a long, long way to the schoolhouse," which is how she described her first walk to it in *The Long Winter.* Walking with her was little sister Carrie, who gripped her hand tightly as they approached the school. According to Laura's story, a ball came flying through the air toward her, and instinctively she reached up and grabbed it. The boy who threw it was Edmund Garland, called "Cap" by everyone. He lived in his mother's rooming house on the lot directly behind theirs, and Laura seemed to take an immediate liking to this fair-haired boy with the bright blue eyes and effervescent personality. Back in Walnut Grove, she had boys for playmates, as well as girls. If one of them had told her that he wanted to marry her someday, it could be laughed off as a silly notion. Now, however, boy-girl relations began to take on a larger dimension, and the idea of pairing off and even eventually getting married became more real. While Laura sometimes succumbed to her natural instinct to want to play ball or throw snowballs with the boys, she generally conformed to powerful social pressures inclining young girls to behave in "ladylike" fashion and to act out their prescribed roles.[23]

Suppressing a natural tendency toward shyness, Laura emerged as a leader among the girls at school. She was strong willed and possessed an already well-developed sense of right and justice and refused to be taken advantage of, whether by her peers or by adults. Although she would take considerable liberties in constructing her children's novels many years later, Laura seemed to be able easily to resurrect old controversies and conflicts that had occurred when she was a schoolgirl. Although she collapsed three

different people into the fictional character of Nellie Oleson, she seemed still to resent the personal slights and meanness that had been directed at her by Nellie Owens and Genevieve Masters when they were her schoolmates. And though she may have exaggerated somewhat her conflicts with her future sister-in-law Eliza Wilder, her inclusion of those animosities in her story perhaps indicates how important they seemed to her at the time.

The difference between a highly developed value system and sense of right on the one hand and a negative temperament and prickly self-righteousness on the other can be a small one. We can infer that Laura's sense of rectitude and self-assurance derived more from her interactions with her correct and self-controlled mother, who displayed many of the characteristics of the New England Puritan, than from her father. To the extent that she enjoyed interacting with other people and displayed a high degree of artistic creativity, her father was the greater influence. During adolescence a person's character is largely fixed. Certainly, the family environment provided the central crucible for Laura Ingalls's development. But she was also a person of her times. Although more independent and ambitious than most of her peers, she was also much influenced by the cultural environment in which she found herself, constituted in equal parts of frontier small town, Victorian mores, and an increasingly self-aware bourgeois culture. On her way to becoming a mature adult, no other period proved more influential than the six and a half years she spent in De Smet, from the time that her family moved there until she married and started her own home.

Another blizzard blew up without warning not long after the Ingalls family moved into town in the fall of 1880, shutting down the school for the season. For the next several months, it seemed to be one blizzard after another, piling up snow in the streets and between store buildings and people's houses and then sweeping the streets clean again when the wind shifted direction. During one of these blasts it was dangerous for anyone to venture outside even for a few minutes; people could not see their hands in front of their faces and sometimes totally lost their bearings. Like everyone else in town, Charles strung a rope from their store building back to the stable where he kept his cows and horses and stored hay for them.

Trains had difficulty getting through to De Smet in November and December, because snow rapidly accumulated in cuts and blocked the tracks. The last train to make it to Huron came through on January 4. After

that, the townspeople had to rely on available supplies and on their own resourcefulness. The two stores that carried groceries did not have a large stock on hand and ran out. Caroline carefully conserved their small amount of food, but that eventually ran out, too. Flour, sugar, meat, and potatoes— they were all gone. Like the rest of the people in town, the Ingallses resorted to grinding wheat in a coffee mill, making it into porridge or biscuits. It was a wearying task. Mary took her turn, squeezing the coffee mill between her knees. When she got tired, someone else took over, and Carrie climbed back into her lap and cuddled up to her, trying to keep warm.[24]

Laura learned how to twist strands of hay into sticks that could be burned in the stove for warmth. With coal supplies exhausted and nothing else available, the family did what everybody else was doing—burned hay. But to twist the hay tight enough so that it would burn slowly was fatiguing work and left one's hands rough and sore. Whenever the storms abated for a few hours, Charles ventured into the country to haul in more hay from the stacks he had built. It was always dangerous to go out into the cold, especially when another blizzard could burst upon them at any moment. Being cooped up, listening to the wind howl, worrying about the next storm, and wondering if they would survive until another train came through was a depressing experience, leading Charles to lash out at the fates that seemed to be conspiring against them. "Howl! blast you! howl!" Laura had him shouting at one point in *The Long Winter.* But if their circumstances were depressing, the stormy weather also knit the family together more tightly than ever. Everyone had a role to perform; they all could contribute to the family's well-being.[25]

The Ingalls's resourcefulness in facing the menacing situation contrasted starkly with the behavior of the young couple who lived with them during the ordeal. Laura provided no hint of their presence in her novel about the hard winter, but throughout the entire episode George and Maggie Masters and their little baby sat at their table and huddled around the stove with them, trying to absorb the little amount of heat. George, the oldest son of Walnut Grove schoolteacher Sam Masters, had come west to take a construction job on the railroad, and while passing through De Smet he had importuned the Ingallses to let his young bride stay with them temporarily. She had been pregnant when the two got married, and neither set of parents had wanted her to live with them because they were ashamed. What was originally intended as a short stay, however, turned

into a much longer one when wintry weather closed in on De Smet and the young couple had no place to go. In the spirit of charity, the Ingallses invited the couple to stay with them until the weather improved. Maggie Masters, who was Scottish, was a large and good-natured woman. The same could not be said for her husband, George, who appeared sullen, selfish, and self-centered and proved unwilling to help them with twisting hay sticks and grinding wheat. He sat close to the fire and grabbed what little food they were able to put on the table. The young couple's presence in the household made what was already a bad situation even worse, and Laura later left George and Maggie out of *The Long Winter* entirely, believing that their inclusion would ruin her story.[26]

Not everything was gloomy that winter, however. Whenever the storms abated, the girls went to romp in the snow. When they were cooped up inside, Mary braided rugs from woolen strips that were arranged by color in separate boxes so she could keep them straight. Caroline read Bible stories to the girls and also read to them from *Youth's Companion*. Charles, meanwhile, perused old issues of the *St. Paul Pioneer Press* and the *Chicago Inter-Ocean*. Every day he stepped across the street to Fuller's hardware store to hobnob with the other men in town. Sometimes he went to Bradley's drugstore, where checkers were the order of the day. The men took turns swapping stories and telling jokes to maintain their spirits and pass the time. Everyone was getting impatient, and as the days passed, people grew more and more gaunt from their meager diets. Starvation was a real possibility.[27]

One day Cap Garland and a young homesteader named Almanzo Wilder made a risky journey about twelve miles out into the country to pick up a sled full of wheat from a homesteader. They brought the sacks back to the store of Daniel Loftus, who had given them the money to pay for it. When the storekeeper tried to profit from the transaction by selling for an inflated price what the young men had risked their lives to get, Charles and the other men in town were outraged and pressured him into selling it for what he had originally paid for it. Stories about Cap and Almanzo's heroics circulated in De Smet for many years.[28]

The storms eventually abated. Finally on May 9 the first train from the East in four months pulled into De Smet. The town had survived its ordeal. Although activities elsewhere in the territory had continued through the winter (the territorial legislature met in Yankton and established a land-grant college, a penitentiary, a new hospital for the insane, and several

normal schools), the isolation imposed on the town by the hard winter reminded people that they were not far removed from the hand of nature.

If nature still posed major challenges on the frontier, however, the accoutrements of civilization steadily accumulated. Although the first rush into the region had begun to slow, new businesses continued to start up as the countryside filled with homesteaders. By 1882 most of the land within ten miles on either side of the railroad had been entered as homesteads or timber claims or had been preempted for $1.25 an acre. The town's population increased more slowly now; only a few vacant lots remained on Main Street. One of the hustling storekeepers who tried to cash in on the rush of settlers was Chauncy Clayson, who ran a dry-goods store. His mother-in-law, Martha White, who was sewing shirts for him to sell, needed a helper. When Charles learned about it, he figured Laura was old enough to do the job, and at twenty-five cents a day, the money would come in handy.[29]

Laura still felt uncomfortable in the midst of so many adults and was reluctant to take the job. Being a dutiful daughter, however, she suppressed her fears and resolutely walked in from the claim to meet her new employers. Later, in *Little Town on the Prairie,* she explained that her determination not to let the situation get the best of her emanated from her desire to earn money to help send Mary to college. Whatever her motives, the episode casts light on Laura's growing maturity and sense of obligation to the family. Taking on part of the responsibility for her sister's welfare was an extension of the role that she had been playing as Mary's "eyes."[30]

Laura had already displayed traits of feistiness and independence, and later, in her stories about her childhood, she placed special emphasis on them. "Oh, that I had the wings of a bird!" she described herself thinking in *The Long Winter.* If she could have had them, she "would have spread them and flown, fast, fast, and far away." And although she probably exaggerated differences in temperament between herself and Mary, no doubt there was considerable truth in her characterization of Mary as dutiful, obedient, and well behaved and of herself—in contrast—as flighty, impulsive, and naughty. In taking a job in town that she really did not want, Laura subordinated her own wishes to the larger needs of the family and acted out a script that substituted self-control for self-gratification.[31]

Her family and the culture reinforced self-control. Bible lessons and passages that she studied and memorized at home and at Sunday school

had continuing importance in her life. Attending school likewise instilled in her virtues such as modesty, generosity, propriety, and trustworthiness. Each time her mother told her to tighten her corset, it provided a lesson in self-control. When Laura insulted a rival schoolmate, her mother wrote a poetic lesson in her autograph album:

> If wisdom's ways you wisely seek,
> Five things observe with care,
> To whom you speak,
> Of whom you speak,
> And how, and when, and where.

Restraint and self-control were watchwords at home, and Laura learned them well, even if sometimes her emotions got the best of her. She was growing up. In negotiating the rocky road of adolescence, she increasingly discovered that she was playing the role of an adult, and one rule that prominently applied was, "A grown-up person must never let feelings be shown by voice or manner."[32]

Now, as she worked in town with Mrs. White and the Claysons, she bit her tongue when she observed revolting behavior. The adults insulted and quarreled with each other, while the children blithely paid them no attention. The merchant's wife and her mother were all wrought up about some kind of Catholic conspiracy, which grew even more sinister in their minds when a comet appeared in the sky. Laura could not figure out where they got their strange notions. In any case, she kept her mouth shut, and after six weeks of working in town she was able—joyfully—to go back to the claim and stay with her family.[33]

Converting a quarter-section of Dakota prairie into a paying proposition was not an easy assignment, and everyone in the Ingalls family had to pitch in. There was land to break, crops to sow, cattle to care for, a new flock of chickens and a pig to tend to, and a garden to plant and weed. When he had the time, Charles walked into town and did carpentry jobs to earn some much needed cash. It took several years for much of an income to start coming in on a new homestead, so they had to find ways to supplement it. Laura especially enjoyed taking care of the cows. She and her mother worked together to milk them, and then there was butter to churn. Inside, the girls helped Caroline wash dishes, make beds, sweep, scrub, wash and

iron clothes, and—when there was time—mend, sew, and knit. All of these activities taught diligence and responsibility.

Playtime was not something to be taken for granted but had to be earned. Yet, there was always plenty of laughter and fun in the household. At night there were stories and songs and conversation. Just watching the beautiful sunsets was a treat. Colors etched themselves sharply in Laura's consciousness, as is indicated by her vivid descriptions later. She also loved to tramp across the wild prairie landscape, delighting in the beautiful wildflowers and observing meadowlarks, jackrabbits, striped gophers, garter snakes, and other wildlife.

Before the family moved back into town that fall and the girls started school again, Charles and Caroline took Mary by train all the way to Vinton, Iowa, to a school for the blind. Two neighboring farm children came to stay with Laura, Carrie, and Grace while the parents were gone. Laura was sad to see Mary leave home but grateful to know that she would learn many new things at the school that would enable her to lead a more normal life. She took pride in the fact that her own contribution to her sister's education was significant.[34]

Soon the somewhat smaller family was back in town, living again in the store building on Second Street, and Laura and Carrie returned to their studies. They had some new schoolmates, including Ida Brown, the adopted daughter of Rev. Edward Brown, who had come to preach at the Congregational church, and Genevieve Masters, the sister of George and the daughter of "Uncle Sam" Masters, who had brought his whole family to Dakota and lived on a homestead west of town. Genevieve, who later became part of the inspiration for Nellie Oleson in Laura's novels, was mean to Laura, who, however, envied her tall, slim figure, her beautiful complexion, and her pretty clothes. Laura later wrote that she considered herself to be too roly-poly and too plain to be able to compete with girls such as Genevieve. But that did not make her appreciate the other girl's arrogance and meanness any more.[35]

Laura emerged as the leader among the other girls. She possessed a sense of fairness and right and was willing to speak up for them in a way that sometimes got her into trouble. She could display a streak of nastiness, too, when she got her ire up and felt that she was being treated unfairly. The new teacher at the school in the fall of 1881 was Eliza Wilder, a single woman homesteader who had filed on both a homestead and a tree claim near the

town. She was the older sister of Almanzo Wilder and had earlier taught school back in Minnesota. She apparently lacked the knack of controlling young students, however, and, much to Laura's disgust, played favorites, especially, it seems, with Genevieve Masters. Laura got her comeuppance one day when she defied Miss Wilder's efforts to discipline her and got the other students to sing a naughty little ditty she had made up about "Lazy, lousy, Lizy Jane." The last laugh was on the teacher, though, as she was soon replaced. Afterward, the students' behavior greatly improved, and they returned to learning.[36]

Caught between powerful pressures to conform to people's expectations and to indulge her own girlish impulses, Laura was undergoing a major transition; the patterns molded during this period largely guided her the rest of her life. Once again, even though realizing that her mother and her older sister considered it too unladylike, she went to play baseball with the boys, dragging Ida Brown and Mary Power with her. When the weather turned colder, she threw snowballs and rode on sleds pulled by the boys. Quickly now, interactions with the opposite sex became more important, and rather than just playing outdoor games with them, attention turned to parties and pairing up with them.[37]

Shortly before her fifteenth birthday, Laura received an invitation to her first party from her classmate Ben Woodworth, who, along with his family, occupied the second-floor living quarters of the railroad depot, where his father was the agent. She remembered feeling awkward at first at the party, not knowing what to do or say, but she just observed how the others behaved and followed their cues. A special surprise was the orange that had been set at everyone's plate. It was the first one she had ever seen, and she was not sure what to do with it, but when she saw the others eat them in sections, she followed suit.[38]

It did not take the new town long to establish a social whirl—at least a modest one. As elsewhere on the frontier, a literary society quickly was established to enliven things during the colder months. With meetings held in the church or at the schoolhouse, various townspeople volunteered to stage debates, put on skits, sing, give dramatic readings, or participate in spelling matches or anything else that seemed like fun. Laura was not much impressed with a sociable held at Mr. and Mrs. Tinkhams that she and Mary Power each paid a dime to attend, which really was intended for adults. A New England supper hosted by the women of the community provided

a reminder of the social origins of many of the people arriving in the first wave of settlement. And, of course, there were revival meetings to stir up enthusiasm and to make converts.[39]

The Ingalls family felt themselves right at home among the settlers of De Smet, for they, too, were part of the Yankee migration that swept westward from New York and New England during the 1800s, winding up in the Great Lakes states and eventually in Minnesota, Iowa, and the Dakotas. The frontier was a dynamic cauldron of population movement, as individuals and families frequently moved about, looking for ways to make a living. Charles Ingalls was not alone in possessing an "itchy foot." His family was typical of hundreds of thousands who moved forward, backward, and laterally along the frontier, searching for suitable locations. The ones arriving in the eastern part of the territory during the Great Dakota Boom carried with them a distinctive set of political, religious, and cultural traditions. Adding spice to the mixture were the European immigrants who derived primarily from Germany, the British Isles, and Scandinavia.[40]

Shortly after the town got started, John H. Carroll, the land dealer on the north side of Second Street, won designation as census taker for the county. Charles and Caroline Ingalls and their four daughters were among the 116 residents he counted in De Smet. Only fourteen had been born abroad; thirty-four were listed as having foreign-born fathers, and thirty-two had foreign-born mothers. The backgrounds of the residents were mostly Canadian and British, with a sprinkling of Norwegian, Danish, German, and French heritages among them. Later, Scandinavians and Germans would outnumber considerably the English and the Irish. New York was the state that contributed by far the largest number of De Smet's earliest residents, but there were also healthy contingents from New England, Pennsylvania, and the Midwest. Hardly anybody derived from states south of the Ohio River.[41]

As was typical on the frontier, the first arrivals were disproportionately young and male. Children were divided almost equally between the sexes. Among residents in their twenties, however, the ratio was thirty-four men to sixteen women; for those in their thirties, it was twenty to five; in their forties, six to two; in their fifties, three to none; and in their sixties, one to none. The Ingalls's friend Robert Boast was typical of the young men who had come alone and then returned east to bring their brides back with them or to get married. De Smet was typical, too, in that within several years'

time the top-heavy male sex ratio largely evened out as men got married and as other families arrived on the scene.[42]

Typical of the early businessmen who set up shop on Main Street was E. H. Couse, who bought Charles Ingalls's first store building to use for a hardware store. Couse was an active temperance man and a member of the Grand Army of the Republic, the Civil War veterans' organization. Born in New York, he later lived in Illinois and Minnesota before moving to Volga at the end of the railroad in 1879 and then moving to De Smet the following year. Daniel Loftus, the storekeeper who had tried to profit from Almanzo Wilder and Cap Garland's risky dash during the hard winter, was a Pennsylvanian of Irish background who prospered over the years and rose to prominence as president of the South Dakota Retail Merchants Association. Lumber dealer Charles E. Ely, another Civil War veteran, had fought in the Battle of Gettysburg in 1863. An Ohioan by birth, his parents hailed from Connecticut and New York. Charles H. Tinkham, whose wife organized the dime sociable, was a cabinetmaker from Maine who combined a funeral parlor with his furniture store on Main Street.[43]

Not surprisingly, the first religious denomination to take root in town was the Congregationalists—Yankee through and through. Soon after arriving at Silver Lake, the Ingallses were delighted to be visited by Rev. Edwin Alden, with whom they had first become acquainted in Walnut Grove. He was organizing churches under the auspices of the American Home Missionary Society. The first church service in De Smet was held in the surveyors' shanty in February 1880, even before the town was formally established. Later, Charles and Caroline participated in organizing a congregation and became charter members. Rev. Edward Brown served as their pastor until retiring from the active ministry in 1884 at the age of seventy. The Connecticut-born cleric had taught school and practiced law before being ordained and serving parishes in Wisconsin, Minnesota, and Ohio. He claimed to be a cousin of the infamous John Brown of Harpers Ferry fame, which may help explain why Laura later said that his revival sermons sent shudders up and down her spine. Whatever Laura may have felt about Reverend Brown as a teenager, however, during these years she cemented her faith, and it became an indispensable part of her life. Bible-reading and prayer were well-established family habits. Laura apparently never seriously found it necessary to question her basic beliefs. What came so easily to her, however, would not to her own daughter later.[44]

The Congregationalists were soon joined in town by two other Protestant denominations, the Methodists and the Baptists, as well as by a Catholic congregation. For a while, until population grew, ministers found it necessary to divide their time among several parishes, with services in each place being scheduled two or three weeks apart. Nevertheless, religion played a crucial role in the community. The third pillar of society—beyond family and religion—was education. Caroline especially accorded it a high value, having been a schoolteacher herself. The decision to send Mary to the school for the blind in Iowa reflected the family's strong commitment to learning. Of all the girls, Laura stood out as a scholar. She obtained high marks and garnered praise from her teachers. De Smet offered only a rudimentary high school curriculum; a full twelve-year graded course of study would not be implemented until 1908. But considering what was available at the time, the girls received a respectable education. Beyond the content of their studies, the notion that learning was valuable stood out as the most important legacy of their schooling.[45]

Twelve miles south of De Smet lived a little group of settlers who needed a teacher for their one-room rural school. When Louis Bouchie mentioned the matter to the Ingalls's friend Robert Boast toward the end of 1882, he suggested that they approach Laura. They wanted someone for two months, for which they offered to pay twenty dollars a month. That was below the going rate, but if Laura took the job, the money would help the family's finances considerably. The major problem was that Laura would not turn sixteen, as required by law, until February. That detail was easily sidestepped, however, when the county superintendent, in administering her examination, conveniently forgot to ask about her age. So Laura went to the Bouchie school in early December in a wagon driven by her father.

It was not a pleasant experience for Laura, who had not particularly wanted to teach and who was doing this only out of her sense of duty to the family. Living with the Bouchies was particularly troubling, since the wife disliked the rough frontier environment so much that she appeared to be going mad. Laura's pupils were unruly at first, but over the course of eight weeks she started acquiring the knack of controlling their behavior and getting them to learn. Just as important, Almanzo Wilder came every Friday afternoon to pick her up and transport her back to her family for the weekend. Many things might have rendered a fifteen-year-old schoolgirl a target for the affections of a homesteader ten years older. Almanzo, generally

a man of few words, did not likely talk much about it to his friends, but, at the age of fifteen, Laura was pretty, perky, intelligent, strong willed, and independent—reason enough to attract his fancy.

Laura made it plain to Almanzo that her gratitude for his transporting her was only that and not a sign of any special caring for him. Yet, she must have encouraged him to believe that her affections were winnable. Earlier, she had allowed Almanzo to walk her home from revival meetings in De Smet. She would write in "Pioneer Girl" that her attention at the first revival meeting had been directed toward Cap Garland. But whatever feelings she may have had for Cap receded as Almanzo slowly—but successfully—competed for her favor.[46]

Other young men showed an interest in her. There was Alfred Thomas, a young lawyer in town who seemed to lack the courage actually to invite her to go with him to an entertainment one evening, so he lost out. Once a young man named Arthur Johnson escorted Laura home from an evening church meeting. A couple of times Ernest Perry, who lived on a farm just a mile south of the Ingalls's homestead, took her to parties where the young people played kissing games that she did not like. After he tried to slip his arm around her on the second date, she decided to stop going out with him. Fred Gilbert, "a green country boy" who lived on a farm northeast of town, invited Laura to go with him to a Friday night dance, but since she "didn't like his style," she turned him down. With the young homesteader from New York state, Almanzo Wilder, it was not love at first sight, but the two possessed compatible temperaments, and he had the good sense to be persistent without rushing things. Years later, in writing about it, Laura reduced Almanzo's fictional age, partly to create the artificial drama of having him too young under the law to take out a homestead claim but also partly because of her keen awareness of their ten-year age gap. The adult Laura worried that her young readers might think that she had been a "child bride."[47]

In fact, getting married in their teens was not uncommon for young women on the frontier. Most of the wives counted in De Smet's first census had husbands listed as being between four and nine years older.[48] By the time she finished her term at the Bouchie school in early 1883, Laura noticed most of her school chums were beginning to pair off. Strongly influenced by the culture surrounding her, Laura considered it only natural that she should engage in the wooing and courting game herself and not

wait too long to get married. The prescribed role for a young woman, which she in no way resisted, was to find a member of the opposite sex that she could love and be compatible with, get married, and raise a family. No feasible alternative existed. Teaching school to supplement the family's income was only a temporary interlude for her.

Back in town with her family again, Laura returned to school, where she discovered that she had not fallen behind in her regular studies during her two months away. She quickly impressed the new teacher, Ven Owen, as a bright and studious pupil. Meanwhile, on weekends there was much gaiety in the streets, as young people laughed and shouted while darting back and forth in their horse-drawn sleighs. When Almanzo Wilder came by to see if she wanted to go riding with him, she quickly consented. Forgotten was her earlier statement that their rides to and from the Bouchie school did not necessarily mean that she wished to go out with him. She did not much care for the name "Manzo," which is what almost everybody else called him outside of his brother Royal, who preferred "Mannie," so Laura started calling him "Manly." He, in turn, chose "Bessie," the diminutive of her middle name, to refer to her, because he already had a sister named Laura and he had never really liked the name. If Laura was accurate in her book in saying they had waited so long to formally introduce and decide what to call each other, it indicates the level of formality and reserve that characterized their relationship at the beginning. (Laura later wrote that they first told each other their names on the day he picked her up in his buggy at the newspaper office, where she had just picked up some name cards.) With the arrival of spring, sleigh rides gave way to buggy rides. Laura took pride in the fact that Almanzo's team was the best and the prettiest in town.[49]

Meanwhile, Laura took a temporary job sewing for Martha McKee, the town's dressmaker. Mr. McKee, who ran one of the town's lumberyards, had filed a claim on a homestead two miles north of Manchester, the next town down the railroad line, eight miles west of De Smet. Since he was unable to leave his job, his wife was planning to go and stay on the place with their twelve-year-old daughter, Mary, to fulfill the residency requirements under the Homestead Act. She wanted Laura to come and keep them company for several weeks, offering to pay her a dollar a week. Laura decided to do it but was glad to return home afterward. Almost as soon as she returned to her family in June, she was offered another sewing job by Florence Bell,

a milliner in town. Working in the shop with the two of them during June, July, and August was Almanzo's sister Laura. She and Eliza were living together on the latter's homestead just northwest of town.[50]

Charles continued carpentering in town when he was not busy on the homestead. Caroline sometimes came out in the field to help harvest the hay. When the wheat and oats were ready, he used his old hand cradle to cut them, because he did not want to take on the debt burden of buying a harvester, like many of the other farmers were doing. Farm machinery was selling briskly at stores in De Smet, but Charles stuck largely to traditional methods. The agricultural revolution that mechanized (and added to the debt of) farming operations during the late nineteenth century touched the Ingalls family only slightly.[51]

Laura and Carrie resumed school in September, walking in from the farm until cold weather returned and the family moved back into town. Laura saved the first composition she ever wrote. She was anxious at first when Mr. Owen told his students to write on the subject of ambition, not knowing what she might say about it. But having collected her thoughts and relying heavily on a dictionary definition, she wrote a couple of paragraphs that included a quotation from Shakespeare. Later, in *These Happy Golden Years*, she wrote that the teacher had given it a grade of 100 percent. If this early success encouraged her to think of herself as a writer, however, there is no record of it. It would take almost three decades for her to embark on a writing career.[52]

Laura also shone in the subject of history. She and Ida Brown got the assignment of "reciting" the whole of American history from their textbook at a school exhibition in the church. After the "Star Spangled Banner" was sung and the rest of the students performed their songs, recitations, and dialogues, the two star pupils proceeded to the main event of the evening. Laura used a pointer to illustrate the facts as she recited them, referring to pictures of the figures she was talking about and to places on the map. The kind of history they were learning in school—factual, didactic, progressive, and patriotic—would be supplemented later by a notion of lived history when she wrote her books about her own experiences on the frontier. Mr. Owen told Laura's father that with her intellect and memory she should be given every chance to further her education.[53]

That spring, Laura was offered another teaching opportunity, this one a three-month term at the Perry school, located just a mile south of their

homestead. While she was teaching there, the family once again moved from town to the farm. The schoolhouse was new and had nice desks and a big unabridged Webster's dictionary. There were only three students in attendance, and sometimes only one of them showed up. The situation provided considerable free time to study for her own classes, and her pay was twenty-five dollars a month, five dollars more than the Bouchie school had paid her.[54]

The money from teaching school went toward paying for an organ the family bought as a surprise for Mary when she came home to visit. To provide a place for it, Charles constructed a third room on the end of the house for use as a sitting room during the daytime and as a bedroom at night. The presence of an organ was a sign both of the community's cultural high-mindedness and of the family's own improving financial circumstances by 1884.[55]

After their first tentative encounters with each other, Laura and Almanzo sometimes did not see each other for months at a time. He worked hard all spring on his homestead and timber claims, but in May he started coming around again to take her riding in the country in his new buggy. The horses he drove were beautiful Morgans, and Laura looked forward every Sunday afternoon to seeing them swing around Pierson's livery barn on the south end of town and across the big slough to pick her up. Almanzo would drive her to Lake Henry and Lake Thompson or up to Spirit Lake, stopping along the way to pick prairie wildflowers. By the end of the afternoon they had sometimes gone forty miles or more. Several times Almanzo dropped by on the way to Laura's at a farmstead to pick up Stella Gilbert, whose mother was bedridden. He told Laura that Stella worked so hard to take care of her mother and to keep the place going that she deserved to have a little fun. Laura did not object for a while, but after several weeks she told Almanzo that he would have to decide—it was either Stella or Laura; if he wanted to drive Stella around with them, Laura would not be going along anymore. The next Sunday he showed up at the Ingalls's house alone, and that was the end of the threesome driving around the countryside.[56]

July arrived and Almanzo bought a new pair of spirited horses that he planned to train and sell at a profit. Their names were Barnum and Skip. Now when he came by to pick her up for their weekly rides, Laura had to be ready to jump into the buggy as soon as he drove up, because the horses

were hard to control. Soon, however, even she was taking the reins. Now their rides sometimes extended to fifty or even sixty miles.[57]

The two decided to participate in a singing school held on Friday evenings in the Congregational church. These "schools" were organized less for the purpose of learning how to sing than for entertainment and for the financial benefit of the teachers who charged their "students." Most of the participants were young couples, and the classes might just as well have been called "sparking schools." One evening after a Ladies Aid ice-cream social at the church, Almanzo drove Laura into the country and proposed to her. In typical fashion, his approach was indirect, as he asked her if she wanted an engagement ring. That evening (assuming her description in her autobiography is correct) they kissed for the first time.

"Aren't you going to kiss me good night?" she supposedly asked him when he dropped her off at her house.

"I was afraid you wouldn't like it," he replied.[58]

This story reveals something important about their relationship: its formality and decorum and his deference to her wishes. Although she was only seventeen and he was twenty-seven, she clearly already was emerging as the dominant partner.

When school reopened in September, a new two-story schoolhouse was ready for the growing student population. Laura and Carrie and the older students were taught upstairs by Mr. Owen, while the younger ones were downstairs with a new teacher, Gussie Masters, the older sister of Laura's nemesis, Genevieve. Laura's seatmate, Ida Brown, now brandished an engagement ring, too, her beau being Elmer McConnell, a young farmer who had worked for Ida's father that summer. Despite her engagement, Laura was still a schoolgirl. Her girlish inclinations were in evidence one afternoon when she, along with many of her schoolmates, skipped classes to try the new roller-skating rink. When they were all called to account the next morning, Mr. Owen expressed surprise at his prized pupil's action, commenting, "You usually set a good example, Laura."[59]

In November, Almanzo and Royal decided to head south to attend the World's Industrial and Cotton Centennial Exposition in New Orleans and then to visit their parents in Spring Valley before coming back to De Smet. Almanzo was going to enjoy one last fling as a bachelor before settling down to married life. Laura did not expect the brothers' return until spring, but

just before Christmas Almanzo showed up at their doorstep. He and Royal had decided not to go to New Orleans after all, but had traveled through Nebraska and Iowa, taking in the sights on their way to Minnesota. Now, in the evenings, Laura and Almanzo sat up late making plans and talking about their new life together.[60]

Laura's decision to take another teaching job in the spring of 1885 meant that she would not be able to finish her school term and "graduate" with the rest of her classmates (without a twelve-year graded program in De Smet, she would not have been a high school graduate anyway). The Wilkins school was about three and a half miles northwest of De Smet, and for three months' work, beginning in late April, Laura received seventy-five dollars. This time there were seven students to teach and discipline. The youngest was a slow learner and was trying on Laura's patience. Her approach to the problem, based upon her observations of how Mr. Owen had dealt with such situations, was to threaten the boy with a whipping if he did not learn his letters. Her heart was not much in it, however, as she described the episode later in her autobiography: "There was a sinking feeling in the pit of my stomach. I didn't want to whip the poor little rat." Miraculously, little Georgie rattled off the lesson with little prompting. "He could write them as I asked, forwards, backwards or mixed. He could find them anywhere in his primer. I praised him and told him he might go out-doors and play in the shade until noon." A combination of high expectations and sternness, Laura concluded, can accomplish much.[61]

Almanzo, meanwhile, worked hard at putting in his crops and building a little house for them on his tree claim. He had already proved up on his homestead, so there was no need for them to live on it, and he thought that they would enjoy having around them all of the trees that he had planted to comply with the rules for timber-culture plots. Combined, the two properties added up to 320 acres—enough, they hoped, to earn a decent living.[62]

Then one Sunday afternoon Almanzo informed Laura that Eliza and his mother were making plans for a big church wedding for them that fall. Neither of them was enthusiastic about the idea, thinking it would be too expensive. Instead, they decided to short-circuit the scenario and get married in a simple ceremony as soon as Almanzo could get the house ready. Laura's mother helped her make a wedding dress of black cashmere that she would be able to wear again for special occasions.[63]

Laura and Almanzo arranged for Reverend Brown to perform the ceremony, even though Laura would later write that she did not care for him much as a preacher. On the morning of August 25, 1885, at eleven o'clock, they said their vows in the pastor's parlor. As they had agreed upon earlier, Reverend Brown left out of the vows the part about the wife having to obey her husband. Only Mrs. Brown, their daughter, Ida, and her fiancé, Elmer McConnell, were present as witnesses.[64]

The ceremony quickly over, Almanzo and Laura climbed into his buggy and drove back to her parents' place for dinner. Then, for the first time as a married couple, they drove across the big slough, around the corner by Pierson's livery barn, up Main Street, and across the railroad tracks on the way to their new house on the tree claim, two and a half miles north of town. The house had three rooms: the main one, which served as a combination dining and sitting room; to its right, the bedroom; and, off to one side, a many shelved pantry that would be able to store all the food they would harvest from their garden. For the present, the pantry was filled with provisions and with bread, a pie, and a cake that Almanzo had purchased from a neighbor. The kitchen was in the lean-to that came up over the backdoor.

Outside the horses quietly rested in their stalls in the stable that Almanzo had built for them. A cow that Laura's father had given them was chewing its cud in the barnyard, and Almanzo's dog, Old Shep, gazed up at them. Laura was happy to be married and felt at home. Now she had a home of her own. She was Laura Ingalls no more but rather Laura Wilder, a married woman.[65]

# 3

## The Joys and Sorrows of Early Married Life

### 1885–1894

꒛

*A*lthough they could not have known it at the time, Laura and Almanzo had picked a poor time to get married, at least from an economic point of view. Love might carry them a long way, but it could not guarantee financial success. For eighteen years, as a member of a close-knit and loving—but never prosperous—family, Laura had come to understand privation and hardship. Hope and optimism had always won out, but never had the family stayed more than a step or two away from poverty. Because many—if not most—of the people who lived around them on the frontier were in similar straits, it was easier for Laura and Almanzo to accept their own situation. The dream of a better life goaded them on.

Laura later professed not to have wanted to marry a farmer. A farm was a hard place for a woman, she observed in *The First Four Years*, with so many chores to do and having to keep house, assist with the harvest, and cook for threshing crews. A farmer never seemed to have enough money, because the storekeepers and businessmen in town controlled the terms of trade. "I don't always want to be poor and work hard while the people in town take

71

it easy and make money off us," she recalled thinking. But Manly rejected the analogy, countering that farmers alone were truly independent. On a farm a man could be his own boss, and hard work and careful planning would surely bring success. So Laura agreed to go along with him and give farming a fair try.[1]

In marrying Almanzo, Laura had entered into a partnership with someone who seemed to possess all the necessary prerequisites for becoming a successful farmer. Laura later wrote about her husband's childhood on his parents' farm in northern New York, five miles from the town of Malone. The fifth of six children (three boys and three girls), he had grown up in a stern but affectionate atmosphere, where the children were inculcated with the same sorts of values and attitudes that were cultivated in the Ingalls household. Considerably better off economically than the Ingalls family, James and Angeline Wilder and their children lived in a comfortable home, surrounded by substantial barns and outbuildings. The parents considered education an important priority, sending their children to Franklin Academy in Malone, which provided what then was the equivalent of a high school education.[2]

During the early 1870s, however, James Wilder turned his attention westward when hops—one of the farm's main cash crops—failed several years in succession. As often happened in making a decision to move, other family members paved the way. Angeline Wilder's brother, George Day, bought some land near Spring Valley in southeastern Minnesota in December 1870. Shortly thereafter, Laura Ann, the oldest of the six Wilder children, joined her uncle in Spring Valley. Soon afterward, James and Angeline moved west with their younger children, including Almanzo, and bought a farm at the west edge of town.[3]

The mid-1870s were times of hardship in Minnesota, which suffered the effects of the national economic depression, grasshopper plagues, and poor crops. By 1878, when Almanzo turned twenty-one, making him legally eligible to file on a homestead, economic conditions were improving and railroads were poised to move into Dakota Territory from eastern Minnesota. Spirited discussions no doubt ensued around the Wilder family table regarding prospects in the west. The following year Almanzo joined his brother Royal, who was ten years older, and their sister Eliza Jane, seven years older than Almanzo, and headed toward the newly opened prairies of southern Dakota to seek their fortunes where Dakota Indians had so

recently lived. Eliza had taught school in both New York and Minnesota and would continue to do so for a while in Dakota Territory. Meanwhile, like many other women at the time, she decided to file on government land so she could sell it later at a profit.[4]

Royal, Eliza, and Almanzo drove to eastern Dakota in a wagon during the summer of 1879 at the same time that Chicago and North Western construction crews were moving into the region. Rather than seeking a location in Brookings County, which was already rapidly filling up, the Wilders pushed into Kingsbury County, finding land there not too far from the future town of De Smet. Because they were among the first white people to arrive in the area, they found it possible to locate their claims relatively close to each other. They drove down to the federal land office in Yankton on August 21, 1879, to register their claims and pay the required fees. Almanzo filed for a homestead, paying the normal fourteen-dollar application fee, on the northeast quarter of Section 21 in Township 111 west, Range 56 north. The south edge of his claim lay just a mile north of the town site. He also took out a timber-culture entry by agreeing to plant 10 of the 160 acres in trees.[5]

The original Timber Culture Act of 1873 had required claimants to set out 40 acres in trees, but the practical difficulty of successfully nurturing that many seedlings quickly became apparent, and Congress sensibly amended the law in 1878 to require only 10 acres to be planted. Almanzo's timber claim was on the southeast quarter of Section 9, its southern boundary a mile north of the northern line of his homestead. In between lay Section 16, set aside under the provisions of the Land Ordinance of 1785 as a source of revenue for the public schools. The Wilders were well aware that the low filing fees required by the government did not make the land free for the taking. Considerable investments of time and money (for seed, machinery, buildings, fences, wells, windmills, and so forth) were required to succeed on the open prairie. Thus, the phrase "free Homesteads" was quite misleading.[6]

Royal Wilder's homestead, on the southwest quarter of Section 21, adjoined his brother's. Eliza's lay directly south of Royal's, on the northwest quarter of Section 28. Hers was north and west of the De Smet town site. Directly south of her claim was Visscher V. Barnes's homestead, and east of hers was John H. Carroll's, although he later obtained a cancellation and took over the southeast quarter of Section 28, which was also the heart

of the new town. After platting it as Carroll's Addition, he sold lots for a handsome profit. Just as Almanzo had done, Eliza and Royal took out tree claims several miles north of town. Hers was half a mile west of Almanzo's, on the southeast quarter of Section 8, and Royal's was half a mile north of hers, on the southeast corner of Section 5.[7]

Few pioneers around De Smet managed to get to Yankton to file on their claims before the Wilders. Two who did were James McKee, who obtained a tree claim four miles north of the future town on July 28, 1879, and Robert Boast, who took out a homestead entry two miles east of De Smet the same day. Neither Eliza, who continued teaching school before obtaining title to her quarter-sections, nor Royal, who stayed around long enough to obtain title to both of his properties, remained in the area permanently.[8]

Almanzo and Laura, his somewhat reluctant helper, were determined to make farming successful and devoted all of their energy to the task. Much as Laura worried about the "arithmetic of farming" and disliked the drudgery associated with it, she did enjoy their horses, and she reveled in the freedom of the open spaces and the beautiful countryside. Manly had proved up on the homestead a year before they got married and slightly more than five years after filing his claim. Meanwhile, he was trying to get the trees on the tree claim to grow; by living on it they would have an easier time watering and caring for them.[9]

Unlike Laura's father, Almanzo did not hesitate to borrow money to purchase machinery or to take out mortgages on his property. Credit constituted the lifeblood of the agricultural economy. Lacking it, many—if not most—farmers could not have gotten started. Even with it, they often were forced out of business anyway, unable to pay their creditors. It took a while for Laura to discover that Almanzo had placed a five-hundred-dollar mortgage on their house when he had built it. Each time he returned from town with another piece of machinery bought on installments, she could do another exercise in the arithmetic of farming. In *The First Four Years,* she wrote that a sulky breaking plow bought in 1885 had cost them five hundred dollars, half as down payment, the remainder due in a year's time. The following year a new McCormick binder for harvesting wheat cost them two hundred dollars, half to be paid when the grain was threshed and the other half due within a year's time at 8 percent interest. They also obtained a mowing machine and a hay rake on time payments. They also bought a seeder and a new wagon. They needed to pay for coal to heat

their house, seed grain for planting, and medical bills when they got sick. For Laura and Almanzo, success in farming would depend as much on how they managed their debts as on how they managed their crops and livestock. And, of course, much depended on the weather and on the prices they were able to obtain for their output.[10]

Laura's childhood experiences had taught her the vital importance of a woman's labor on the farm. So despite her love for her new house—with its kitchen/dining/living room, its bulging pantry, and its carpeted bedroom— Laura spent much of her time outdoors assisting Almanzo. There was plenty of work to do inside: cooking, baking, washing, ironing, sewing, mending, sweeping, and churning. Outside she could help with plowing and butchering, and she could hold the grain sacks while Almanzo shoveled wheat into them. Laura may have looked small, but she was energetic, and she never shied away from hard physical labor and outdoor work. During the early years of her marriage, she later said in an interview, "I learned to do all kinds of farm work with machinery. I have ridden the binder, driving six horses. And I could ride. I do not wish to appear conceited, but I broke my own ponies to ride. Of course they were not bad but they were broncos."[11]

There was always time for fun as well as work. On Sundays the young couple hitched their horses to the buggy and traveled around the country-side, just as they had done during their courtship. Or they saddled up the ponies, Trixy and Fly, and galloped around. This was a happy, carefree time for them, when they could take their minds off their work and their debts and not worry about the future. Although Laura did not write about it in *The First Four Years,* they sometimes visited friends in De Smet or invited visitors to the farm. Concerts and church socials may have drawn them into town, too, from time to time, and they were able to exchange visits with Laura's parents and sisters.[12]

Migration into the area declined after 1886, and De Smet's population stabilized. Most of the land within a reasonable distance of the railroad had been taken up by then, so prospective homesteaders went farther west to look for government land on which to enter claims. Activity in town, if anything, picked up, however. The two weekly newspapers carried stories and notices about ice-cream socials, church suppers, oyster feeds, dances, picnics, sociables, and various entertainments and performances. After it opened up in August 1884 the roller rink became the site of

many activities, including skating, bicycle races, dances, concerts, and dramatic performances. Until a better place could be found for them, traveling theatrical troupes, choral groups, visiting lecturers, and other entertainers had to be satisfied to perform at the rink, in the school, or at a church.[13]

Amateur baseball also gained a popular following. Large scores were the norm. The De Smet Clippers played a team from nearby Nordland in August 1883. Three years later a group of locals called the White Stockings defeated Lake Preston, while the Clippers took their lumps, losing to teams from other towns. Almanzo displayed little interest in playing baseball or any other games, but he and Laura may have stopped to watch a contest now and then. Nor do we know whether they observed practice drills of the new militia unit—Company E of the Dakota National Guard—or attended Memorial Day exercises, political rallies, temperance meetings, hook-and-ladder team contests, band concerts, or other performances.[14]

The dedication of the Couse Opera House on November 11, 1886, rated as one of the town's most memorable social events. Occupying the entire second floor of Edward H. Couse's new double-wide brick store building, the large hall quickly became the center of all kinds of community activities: dances, suppers, concerts, theatrical performances, lectures, political rallies, school graduations, Memorial Day services, and Christmas parties. In later years, even basketball games were played there and movies shown. Couse's hardware store was on the first floor. The Civil War veteran from New York had steadily built up his business after purchasing Charles Ingalls's store building in 1880. In six years' time he was ready to expand his operation, moving onto the adjoining lot, and, as a public service, filling a need for civic-minded residents: providing the town with a community hall.

Wanting to make the dedication of his new store and opera house memorable, Couse scheduled a supper, various entertainments, speeches, a dance, and—to top it off—a wedding. He offered to give the first couple to volunteer to get married at his grand opening a new cookstove and a set of pots and pans. In short order several couples stepped forward to take advantage of the opportunity, but the storekeeper stuck by his original offer and accepted only the first volunteers. Had Couse decided to build a year earlier, one wonders whether Laura and Almanzo would have considered volunteering.[15]

The Couse Block and Opera House, although it was the most impos-
ing new structure built on Calumet Avenue in 1886, was not the only
impressive building to be erected in town that year. Catercorner across
the intersection of Calumet and Second Street, on a lot he had purchased
from Laura's father, John H. Carroll built a two-story brick edifice for the
First National Bank, successor to the Bank of De Smet. Meanwhile, a block
down the street, Thomas H. Ruth erected a new structure for the Kingsbury
County Bank. Also part of the building boom that year was Gilbert and
Morrison's roller mill. New construction in 1886 added up to fifty thousand
dollars' worth of investment.[16]

Another sign of the town's vitality and go-getting spirit was the growth
of several fraternal organizations, which were proliferating all over the
United States during the late nineteenth century. In addition to Civil War
veterans enrolled in the Grand Army of the Republic, most of the town's
businessmen and professionals joined one or more local chapters of the
Masons, the Odd Fellows, or the Ancient Order of United Workmen. Many
of their wives, in turn, actively participated in the temperance movement.
The liquor question generated much political controversy in De Smet
throughout the 1880s. The Women's Christian Temperance Union got an
early start in Kingsbury County; men and women alike involved themselves
in continual rounds of temperance meetings, lectures, rallies, and picnics.
However, sporadic attempts to establish a literary society on a permanent
basis ultimately failed. A cornet band and a community orchestra were
dependent on the enthusiasm of the participants and the energy of the
leadership. At the end of the decade, De Smet celebrated its first Old
Settlers' Day, making it among the first towns in the region to establish
the tradition. Since the first settlers had arrived on the scene only a decade
earlier, many of the "old" settlers—including Laura Wilder—were still only
in their twenties.[17]

None of the activities mentioned above merited a mention when Laura
later wrote about her and Almanzo's first four years of marriage. Nor did
she refer to any church activities, although religion had been an important
part of family life when she was growing up and would continue to be later.
We can presume that Laura and Almanzo drove into town at least now and
then to attend religious services or other kinds of special events.

For the time being, however, the types of activities and diversions that
earlier had occupied so much of Laura's attention hardly mattered. As a

married women, she bore new responsibilities and assumed new roles. No longer was she merely a helper or a secondary player, albeit an important one. Instead, she acted as a full partner, as responsible as Manly for making important decisions and securing their economic success. Although judgments like this are necessarily inferential, it would seem that, far more than in most marriages at the time, husband and wife talked with each other, agreed upon goals, and negotiated between themselves about how best to accomplish them.

No longer was Laura a schoolgirl or even a schoolteacher. About the time that she finished up with her teaching duties, Genevieve Masters, her old adversary, was just entering upon hers. Had Laura read the local newspaper, she would have discovered that her former schoolmate taught several different country schools, beginning in 1885, including a term or two at the Wilkins school, one of the three at which Laura had taught. In September 1886, Genevieve took a train to Pierre to begin attending Pierre University, a tiny Presbyterian institution that was only a couple of years old. Schoolgirl pranks and jealousies no longer occupied Laura's attention, however, nor would she have to suffer the anxieties and the strains of teaching school anymore. Now she was an adult; the role she had taken on demanded it. Backing her husband, contributing to the support of the household, and raising a family: these were her new tasks, dictated by the culture in which she lived and fully accepted by her.[18]

Laura soon discovered that she was pregnant, with the baby due in December. This was a time of wonder for her—and hope. Their crops were in the ground, the countryside was blooming, and Laura and Almanzo looked expectantly toward the future. She later wrote that the idea for their child's name came from the wild roses that bloomed on the prairie in June. "It will be a girl," she recalled saying to Almanzo, "and we will call her Rose."[19]

Laura had just turned nineteen and Almanzo twenty-nine. They celebrated their birthdays together on the Sunday that came in between with a large birthday cake for the two of them. With adequate moisture present in the spring of 1886, the wheat and the oats that Almanzo had planted looked promising. If they got a decent crop, they would be able to pay a substantial part of their debts. Many farmers around the county were predicting that the wheat crop would be the best one yet. Some of them did, in fact, manage to get theirs harvested. In other places, however, hot

winds blew up dust from the fields. Then, unfortunately for the Wilders, a hailstorm flattened their wheat field in about twenty minutes. Luckily, Almanzo had already harvested the oats, but the loss of the wheat was a major setback for the young couple.[20]

After starting on their tree claim two and a half miles north of town, they decided now to move to the homestead south of the school section, because they would be able to arrange a mortgage on the property if they were living on it. They figured that they were going to need more cash to pay their other debts and to get ready for spring planting the following year. The new place was not as comfortable as the one on the tree claim. The house was a jerry-built structure, with a new room added onto the original claim shanty, which was converted into use for storage. The twelve-by-sixteen-foot addition served as a combination living room, kitchen, and bedroom. As Laura described it in *The First Four Years,* "The house wasn't so bad." At least they were closer to town, and when the baby arrived it would be easier to trade visits with her family.[21]

Laura's mother and Mrs. Power, the mother of Laura's former school chum Mary, arrived on December 6 to assist with the delivery. They also called a doctor from town, and he administered something to deaden the pain. Caroline stayed for several days, and a neighbor girl came over later to help for a few more, but after that Laura and Almanzo were left on their own to cope with the new adventure of raising a child. Just as they had planned, they named their baby "Rose." Arriving just before Christmas, Laura said, she "was a grand present." Now she was more than a bride and a homemaker; she was a mother, and her maternal instincts came to the fore.[22]

Unfortunately, the evidence for these years is scant, and the relationships among the three Wilders are somewhat obscure. But there is every reason to believe that both parents were happy in their new situation and that they were determined to provide for their child as best they possibly could, just as their parents had. Grace Ingalls provided some insights into Rose's disposition and early development in a diary she kept sporadically for several years, beginning on January 12, 1887, just five weeks after Rose's birth. Her first entry noted that Rose was just beginning to smile. Two months later, after a visit from Laura, she described her sister putting her new baby in short dresses. "Rose is a big fat baby now but just as pretty," Grace wrote. A year later, after Rose came into town to live for a while with her grandparents when Laura and Almanzo were sick with diphtheria, she

observed, "She is the best girl I ever saw. She can now say a good many words such as gramma and grampa and bread and butter and cracker."[23]

Rose inherited some of her mother's independence and feistiness. Relentlessly curious, by the time she was two she had become, in Laura's words, "an earnest, busy little girl with her picture books and letter blocks." She could be oblivious to danger and often more than a little mischievous. She liked to stand in a tub under a pump spout and let water run over her face, or roll around in the dust just like one of their horses, or enter a barn stall and kick a horse lying on its side. She could be a worry and a bother, but mostly she was a joy.[24]

Rose's presence helped compensate for the worries that farm life brought. With little to show for their efforts during their first year as a married couple, Laura and Almanzo looked forward to making up for it in 1887. At Christmastime, Almanzo made an extravagant purchase in town of a clock as a present for both of them. The timepiece could stand as a symbol of a more civilized and prosperous way of life. Once again, at year's start their prospects looked promising. In late July the *De Smet Leader* pronounced that there was nothing for farmers to complain about and that on the whole crops were above average. It was good weather for harvesting, the paper reported in August, and a few weeks later it was commenting on thick stacks of grain in the fields.[25]

At haying time, Laura helped Almanzo drive the mowing machine. In their area, dry conditions kept grain yields lower than elsewhere, and wheat prices drifted down to only about fifty cents a bushel. In the end, it was not such a bad year for them. They were able to pay interest on their loans and pay off some of their smaller notes, but they still carried big mortgages on the homestead and on the house on the tree claim. Bad luck showed its face again one Sunday in late July when Laura and Almanzo went for a ride and returned to discover that their barn had burned down, along with the hay and the grain stored in it. A local paragraph in the *Leader* indicated that the fire's origins were unknown.[26]

Then disaster struck again when Laura and Almanzo both contracted diphtheria in early 1888. The disease posed a chronic health hazard in the vicinity during these years. The newspaper cited a number of cases, including the deaths of an eleven year old in November 1885 and of a seven year old in May 1887. At the time of the first-mentioned case, the town put a temporary ban on public gatherings to try to stop the spread of the disease.

Laura came down with it first, and then Almanzo contracted it while taking care of her. In the meantime, Laura's mother came from De Smet and took Rose home with her to keep her safe. Royal Wilder, still a bachelor, came to stay with Laura and Almanzo and nurse them back to health.[27]

The house where Rose stayed during this period of time was not the one on her grandparents' homestead southeast of town but a new one that Charles Ingalls had recently built on Third Street in town. The family moved into it just before Christmas in 1887. It was not a large house—just two rooms on the first floor and one above it—but it was comfortable, and in later years they would add onto it. Charles and Caroline had decided to quit farming and move into town. Thereafter, he earned money by carpentering and doing odd jobs. He was a genial sort and had many friends, serving at various times as justice of the peace, town clerk, deputy sheriff, street commissioner, and school-board member. Grace, who was then ten years old, described Rose in her diary as well behaved during the time that she stayed with them and noted that she quickly picked up new words to add to her vocabulary. In addition, she learned how to walk while living with her aunts and grandparents. Grace noted that the diphtheria epidemic closed her school for a time and that a boy in town died from the disease.[28]

Laura recovered completely from her bout with the disease, but Almanzo was not as lucky. Because he wanted to return to work as quickly as possible, he disregarded the doctor's orders to take it easy for a while and suffered a relapse. "A slight stroke of paralysis," the doctor called it, "from overexertion too soon after the diphtheria." Afterward, Almanzo walked with a limp and operated at less than full strength. It was a severe blow both to him personally, for he had always been such a vigorous outdoorsman, and to the young family, whose financial fortunes depended heavily upon his ability to handle heavy physical labor.[29]

Medical bills depleted the family's meager resources, leaving them with no funds until the next harvest. With drought conditions growing steadily worse, with crop yields so unpredictable, and with the prices they received for them drifting steadily downward, the arithmetic of farming was becoming more and more problematical. Almanzo's feeble condition now precluded their trying to work both of their quarter-sections of land, but then the farmer renting their tree claim decided to leave and someone offered to buy their homestead. He proposed assuming their eight-hundred-dollar mortgage on the property and paying them two hundred dollars in

addition for title to it. Laura and Almanzo accepted the offer and prepared to move back to their tree claim.[30]

They decided at the same time to go into partnership with Laura's cousin Peter Ingalls, who had been working as a hired man for a nearby farmer. With grain prospects as poor as they were, they decided to try raising sheep and bought a hundred Shropshires from the farmer for whom Peter had been working. Peter came to live with the Wilders and helped Almanzo with the chores and other work around the farm. Every day Peter drove the sheep out to graze on the adjacent school section, being careful, Laura later wrote, to herd them "away from the grass that would be mowed for hay." Once again, crop prospects appeared to be favorable at the beginning of the growing season, but hot winds eventually burned up their wheat and left them little to show for the year's effort. Laura and Peter helped Almanzo cut and stack what hay was left. After three years of farming, the Wilders possessed half ownership of a hundred sheep, a few horses and cows, barns to shelter the animals, half as much land as they had started with (with their tree claim yet to be proved up on), some machinery, and a snug little house. Not the stuff of dreams, but Almanzo, even in his debilitated state of health, was willing to keep trying, and so was Laura, at least for another year.[31]

The growing season of 1889 turned out to be the worst one yet. The Wilders' crops, like those of most of their neighbors, burned up again in the hot winds. It should have been a joyous time in Dakota Territory, as the political wheels were spinning and South Dakota finally gained admission as a state. Celebrations in Huron, Pierre, and elsewhere did much to elevate people's spirits, but casting a pall over the festivities that year were abnormally high temperatures, a devastating drought, poor crops, and, in some places, conditions verging on starvation. The last territorial governor and the first to be elected to that position for the new state of South Dakota, Arthur C. Mellette, took it upon himself to travel to Chicago to solicit contributions of food and supplies to provide relief for the destitute citizenry in the most ravaged places. For his efforts he was condemned in various quarters for damaging Dakota's reputation and discouraging people from moving there.[32]

In response to their worsening situation, many farmers organized themselves politically. As early as the 1870s, Midwestern farmers had used local Grange organizations to back political candidates working to regulate

railroad rates and practices. Southern Dakota Territory had been so little developed at the time that the Grangers remained weak and inactive there. But by the 1880s, when the next round of agrarian agitation erupted, Dakota farmers were ready to act. A Farmers Shipping Association was incorporated in De Smet in October 1884 to enable farmers to bypass the commercial elevators by cooperatively receiving and shipping their own grain. When their first elevator burned at the hands of an incendiary two years later, they quickly rebuilt and resumed operations. Started in 1880 by Milton George, editor of the *Western Rural,* a Chicago farm journal, the Farmers' Alliance spread a message of farmer solidarity and developed more advanced proposals for improving farm conditions. The Dakota Territorial Alliance was organized in Huron in December 1884, demanding higher farm prices, fairer taxation, railroad regulation, and the creation of a commission to regulate grain warehouses and investigate grading practices. Local units soon were established to carry on grassroots organization, including a Kingsbury County affiliate. Robert Boast was one of the De Smet residents attending a conference in Huron in June 1890 in which Farmers' Alliance representatives took the lead in establishing an Independent Party whose candidates would speak for the farmers' cause. Two years later this organization evolved into the South Dakota Populist Party. Kingsbury County wasted no time in 1890 in organizing its own Independent group and holding its own county convention to select nominees for office.[33]

If Laura and Almanzo participated in this agitation, it is unrecorded. Almanzo may not even have had any crops during these years to bring to the farmers' elevator. *The First Four Years* remains completely silent about farmers groups and political agitation. The story that Laura told centered on a single family's struggle against the elements and other adversities. Whether Laura simply forgot the circumstances or consciously chose not to talk about politics, or whether she figured that these details would simply clutter her story, cannot be known. The Boasts were close friends of the Ingalls family, and Robert Boast's attendance at the Huron convention suggests that the idea of a farmers' party might have been of interest to the Wilders. In any case, the spare story related in *The First Four Years* needs to be understood for what it is: a bare-bones depiction that emerged against the backdrop of a dramatic economic and political crisis.

Focusing on their own family's situation was only natural for the Wilders. During the summer of 1889 they were expecting their second child. Rose

was two and full of energy. Grace wrote in her diary that the child was "large for her age with golden hair and large blue eyes." She could be a bother sometimes, but she added spice to her parents' lives. Laura apparently had expected her first child to be a girl; perhaps this time she wanted a boy, to balance things out. In the heat of an exceptionally warm day in early August, Laura delivered her second child—a boy. Grace wrote in her diary that "he looked just like Manly."[34]

But something was wrong with the baby; in less than two weeks' time he lay dead, of convulsions, without even a name. The family buried him in the cemetery southwest of town, and afterward they never talked about it. "I know nothing about him," Rose wrote at the age of seventy-nine, "because my mother wanted nothing said about it; I think she never stopped grieving and it was her way to be silent, and want silence about any unhappy subject." Perhaps there were times when Almanzo's and Laura's thoughts turned to their lost boy, but if Rose is correct about Laura's insistence on imposing silence, deep grief and heartache remained repressed, unspoken, and bottled up inside of them. Laura's reaction to this event—the most grievous tragedy of her life—was deeply revealing about her. Her own mother had taught her well the habits of restraint, self-control, and fortitude. There would always be a dark, secret side to Laura that outsiders were unable to penetrate, a side that even those closest to her never fully fathomed.[35]

Two weeks later disaster struck again, this time inadvertently caused by Rose. She was helping her mother fire the cookstove for the evening meal. In an instant, while Laura stepped out of the kitchen, Rose dropped some burning hay on the floor, and in seconds the house went up in flames. Laura was still too weak to effectively fight the fire, and Almanzo and Peter came in too late from the fields to extinguish it. Only some furniture, a few clothes and dishes, and their wedding silver were salvaged.[36]

It was a terrible blow, coming directly after the death of their child. Events seemed to be conspiring against them. But Almanzo and Peter set about building a new two-room shanty near the site of the old one, a place that could get them through the winter at least. Meanwhile, the four of them were able to stay with a nearby farmer, who offered them the use of his house in return for Laura's cooking meals for him. Within a few weeks' time they were resettled in their new shanty, waiting for cold weather to set in and considering what to do next.[37]

By mid-November their decision was made. They would leave South Dakota and return to Spring Valley to stay with Almanzo's parents for a while and decide their next course of action. They drove into town to inform Laura's parents about their plan. At Christmastime, James and Angeline Wilder traveled to De Smet by train to visit them and Royal, and further decisions about the move probably were made then. With the arrival of spring, Laura and Almanzo sold their enlarged flock of sheep for five hundred dollars, which was a neat profit both for them and for Peter. The money allowed Almanzo to convert their tree claim into a preemption purchase; he paid government land officials at Watertown two hundred dollars for the quarter-section and signed the final papers on April 17, 1890.[38]

In filling out the required forms, Almanzo indicated that their one-story frame house had dimensions of fourteen by twenty-four feet with a seven-by-twelve-foot addition. The barn was eighteen by twenty-four feet. There were also a sheep shed and a granary, two wells, ten acres planted in trees, and sixty-five acres under cultivation. The implements he owned included a binder, a mower, a plow, a wagon, and a sulky corn plow. He also listed himself as owning nine horses, five head of cattle, and seventy-five sheep, and he stated that in the two seasons that he had raised crops on the property he had put in wheat, oats, corn, and flax. Almanzo readied a covered wagon for their journey to Minnesota; they would need room for Peter, too. Laura sorted through their things, deciding what they should take along. Once their affairs were in order, they all said their good-byes to friends and loved ones and prepared to leave. By early June, Laura, Almanzo, and Rose, along with Peter Ingalls, were on their way.[39]

If any doubts lingered in Laura's and Almanzo's minds about their decision to leave South Dakota, they likely were quashed by what they saw around them as they traveled: barren fields, destitute families, and radicalized politics. But, as always, hope lingered in the minds of many people for a decent return on their investments the next time around. Crops were looking rather good in places, and farmers would soon be getting ready for the harvest. But Grace wrote in her diary before they left about a sandstorm that blew and blew. "Hard time" socials to brighten people's moods were held often that year in De Smet and surrounding towns, and the county board arranged to issue warrants to purchase seed grain for destitute farmers who were unable to obtain it otherwise.[40]

In Spring Valley a warm welcome greeted them when they arrived at the Wilder farm. Although not immune from the kinds of problems plaguing South Dakota at the time, southeastern Minnesota had fared better. Spring Valley, which was two or three times the size of De Smet, was a visibly prosperous town of around fifteen hundred people, with forty or fifty businesses and a number of brick commercial blocks. There were at least five general merchandise or grocery stores, three hardware stores, two meat markets, two drugstores, six stores carrying men's and women's clothing and footwear, and a variety of other businesses. In addition, the town boasted nine churches, including the Methodist Episcopal church, which the Wilders attended. Enhancing Spring Valley's prospects was a second railroad line that had been extended to it in 1890.[41]

A wide variety of entertainment provided diversion, including traveling theatrical shows, vocal performances, orchestral music, dances, circuses, and other attractions. It is unlikely, however, that Laura and Almanzo became much involved in the community during their year and a half in Spring Valley. Their main concern now was to nurse Almanzo back to health and to figure out a way to make a living. Escape from the harsh Dakota and Minnesota winters might offer a better prospect for his recovery. An idea for a new place to locate emerged from a trip down the Mississippi River taken by Peter Ingalls, Almanzo's younger brother, Perley, and Laura's cousin Joe Carpenter. Perley was twenty-one, just a year younger than Almanzo had been when he had traveled west to Dakota Territory with Royal and Eliza in 1879. But Perley's direction now was southward, as he and the other two were lured by promotional literature extolling Florida's climate and industry. Other adventuresome young men had taken boat trips down the Mississippi, and they decided to try it, too, beginning their odyssey in early October 1890. When they arrived in Cairo, Illinois, they changed course, traveling up the Ohio River and then up the Tennessee in their small sailing craft, which they had dubbed the *Edith*. From Decatur, Alabama, they traveled overland to the small village of Westville, located in the middle of the Florida Panhandle, about seventy-five miles northeast of Pensacola.[42]

Although easy fortunes did not await them when they arrived, Peter Ingalls decided to remain and settled down on a piece of land near Westville, planning to try his luck as a farmer. He later married a woman named Mary McGowin, and they eventually had six children. Letters from Peter

describing Florida's balmy climate, which might speed Almanzo's recovery, were all the stimulus that he and Laura needed to decide to give Florida a try themselves. By early 1891 they were seriously planning to move. In March they auctioned off about eight horses, harnesses, and other items, in preparation for taking their leave. It was not until October 5, however, that Laura, Almanzo, and Rose boarded a train at Spring Valley and headed southeast for Florida. They took some household goods and one team with them to help them get started.[43]

Moving to the piney woods of Florida was an act of faith for Laura and Almanzo, for they had little solid information about the area. Had they realized what they were going to find once they arrived, they probably never would have made the move in the first place. Their primary consideration in going was Almanzo's health, but the hot, moist climate near the Gulf Coast and along the Choctawhatchee River turned out to be more debilitating for Laura than it was energizing for Almanzo. Once, while helping Peter plant some corn, she clutched an umbrella to ward off the hot sun. He finally told her to go back to the house. The entire atmosphere in the South seemed foreign and strange to Laura. "We went to live in the piney woods of Florida," she later recalled, "where the trees always murmur, where the butterflies are enormous, where plants that eat insects grow in moist places, and alligators inhabit the slowly moving waters of the rivers. But at that time and in that place, a Yankee woman was more of a curiosity than any of these."[44]

Even stranger than the climate were the people. From the beginning, Laura felt out of place, considering her new neighbors to be ill-educated and ill-mannered. The local women, for their part, regarded her as a haughty "up-North" person—not one of them. In 1922 Rose captured some of her mother's alienation and fear in a prize-winning short story titled "Innocence": "'Here we are, in the piney woods!' said father. The white road went curving between straight, tall gray trees that had no branches. Far overhead their green-black tops whispered breathlessly, without stopping, telling something terrifying. The gray trunks stood still in a gray light; they knew, but they were silent, and the pale ground looked up at them. A smell of dampness and of wet paintbrushes was in the air."[45] This was a far cry indeed from the vast, treeless spaciousness and the clear, clean sunshine of the South Dakota prairies!

Southern women, in Rose's story, went barefoot and dipped snuff. Snakes slithered through the forest, the piney woods whispered, enveloping

everything in their shadows, and the air was thick and moldy, suffused with strange smells. Unable to relate in any meaningful way to the people living around her, Laura found compensation in her family. To the degree that Rose's story accurately portrayed the relationship between her and her mother, they were extremely close and the relationship was full of love. "For mother was not really grown-up, like father," Rose wrote, "she liked to sing and dress dolls and play games with toes." But if the mother showered love and affection on her daughter, who at the age of five was growing increasingly aware of the world around her, she was also protective of Rose and concerned about the environment into which they had taken her. "Innocence" suggests how closely Laura watched over and supervised her only child and how strictly she disciplined her, aiming to instill in her the habit of self-control. When she spanked Rose once in order to get her message across, the surprised girl yelled in terror and amazement. In Rose's story, her mother paddled her several times, telling her, "Now come in this house, and eat, and don't let me hear another word out of you!" This is how Rose characterized her mother's disciplinary approach:

> Mama was always advanced for her time. She told me once that she made up her mind before I was born that she wouldn't whip me; she did not believe in breaking a child's will. She had to change back to "Spare the rod and spoil the child" before I can remember, because I told a lie. And if she warned me to keep my dress clean or not lose my hair ribbon or something like that, or I'd get a spanking, then she had to keep her word. But she never actually spanked me for not being diligent.[46]

Laura was sufficiently fearful living in Florida that she decided to carry a revolver in her dress.[47] Obviously feeling out of place, she started talking about home almost as soon as they arrived. The family's short stay in Westville indicates that it did not take them long to realize their mistake. Agricultural possibilities in the scrubby pine region were not too promising. So in a few months' time the decision was made to leave, and in August 1892, less than a year after departing Spring Valley, they boarded a northbound train and headed home to De Smet. After staying for a while with Laura's parents in their Third Street house, the Wilders moved into a little house about a block away.

In the meantime Royal Wilder had gone back to Spring Valley to live, setting up in the grocery and notions business. In 1893 he married Electa

Averill Hutchinson, a widow; they had one child, born the following year. Eliza Wilder, after leaving De Smet, had moved to Washington, D.C., where she worked as a clerk in the Department of Interior. She also was married in 1893, to a two-time widower with six children, Thomas Jefferson Thayer, who was eighteen years older. He had relocated earlier from Spring Valley to Crowley, Louisiana, and Eliza made her home there with him; they had a son the following year.[48]

Laura's sisters remained in De Smet. Mary had graduated from the school for the blind in Vinton in 1889 and now spent her days doing handwork and household chores. Knowing exactly where everything was in the house, she swept floors, dusted furniture, made beds, and took care of the houseplants. After dinner she helped with the dishes. She enjoyed teaching Rose how to knit, crochet, and sew and even taught her to read some braille. On Sundays, Mary played the organ, and the family gathered around to sing hymns. Carrie continued to work at the newspaper office as a typesetter while she learned the printing trade. Grace was still going to school. At fifteen, she was the same age that Laura had been when she had taken her first teaching job ten years earlier. So the family was together again, but the happy, generally carefree days of childhood had given way, for Laura, to concerns about her husband's health and the family's economic survival.[49]

Rose later remembered her grandmother being "a real sweet, patient old lady, with brown hair parted in the middle and a shell comb standing up from the knot in back." Caroline Ingalls was not much of a talker, but she was a pleasant woman. Charles continued to do some carpentry work and took on other odd jobs around town. What Rose remembered about him were his bright blue eyes, long beard, and patched shoes.[50]

South Dakota continued to lie under the spell of drought and low farm prices. Things grew worse in 1893 when financial panic struck, plunging the United States into its worst economic depression up until that time. The Florida interlude had done little to improve Almanzo's health. The idea of trying to farm a quarter-section of land now apparently seemed to be out of the question. Instead, he took what jobs he could find, painting and carpentering and the like. Laura, meantime, went to work for a dressmaker for a dollar a day. Money was scarce, but frugal as she was, Laura managed to begin putting money away that could provide them with a stake for a new start.

Rose was a smart child and displayed signs of precociousness. She started school in De Smet a year early, after she was given an exemption

by a sympathetic school board. Writing fascinated her so much that she developed writer's cramp and had to drop out temporarily. In the meantime, she stayed with her grandparents, watched over by her grandmother and Mary. Years later, in trying to recapture what those times had been like, Rose always seemed to think of summer. Responding to one letter writer, she reminisced, "I hope ice cream still tastes as good to De Smet youngsters as it did to me in the hot summers."[51]

Little money was available for ice cream in the Wilder household, so any taste of it must have seemed especially delightful. Rose later wrote about the house that they lived in. In the spring, violets grew all around it on the low, wet land. "We had no furniture because it had been chattel-mortgaged," Rose recalled. "In the whole big house there was only a cookstove and a big box for a table, Papa's and Mama's trunks, and their big bed and my little bed lying on the bare floors. At night there was lamplight only in the kitchen. The blank window seemed to stare at us, and through the empty rooms there were breathings and crawlings and creakings in the dark. And the wind had a different sound around that house, it sounded mean and jeering."[52]

Then someone from De Smet journeyed to southern Missouri to check out rumors about the area's wonderful fruit-growing opportunities. He brought back promotional literature and samples of apples grown there, and Laura and Almanzo were intrigued. Perhaps Missouri was the place they had been searching for.

# 4

## In the Land of the Big Red Apple

### 1894–1911

*

Moving to Missouri proved to be a momentous step for the Wilders. Laura and Almanzo would live the rest of their lives in and around the small community of Mansfield, nestled in the Ozark Mountains in southwestern Missouri. After several decades of moving west and living in various places, Laura would finally settle down in the Ozarks and try to fit into a different culture. It would continue to be a hardscrabble way of life for many years. But if poverty was to be their lot, it did not discourage them, for it was the general situation of most of their neighbors and friends, and sharing a condition makes it easier for people to accept and adapt to.

After their Florida experience, Laura and Almanzo no doubt approached the Missouri move with some skepticism. They hoped not to be disappointed again. Advertising that proclaimed the virtues of the "Land of the Big Red Apple" needed to be discounted and soberly appraised. But what alternative did they have? Continuing to live in De Smet, without land and without capital, offered little prospect for advancement. Almanzo's physical condition precluded the kind of grain and livestock farming required on

91

the Dakota prairies. In Missouri, on a smaller acreage, they might be able to eke out a better income and gradually build up a stake for themselves. The warmer climate, they hoped, would prove more congenial for both of them. "When we came to Missouri in 1894," Laura later wrote, "we were looking for a place where the family health might make a good average, for one of us was not able to stand the severe cold of the North, while another could not live in the low altitude and humid heat of the Southern states."[1]

The idea of moving to Missouri crystallized when Laura and Almanzo listened to reports of those who had visited the state. They also were impressed by promotional literature published by the Kansas City, Fort Scott, and Memphis Railroad, which was designed to attract people to southern Missouri and in the process build up demand for the railroad's services. A forty-page illustrated booklet, "Among the Ozarks: The Land of 'Big Red Apples,'" described several towns along the railroad's right-of-way across the southern part of the state, among them Mountain Grove, Cedar Gap, and Mansfield, all in Wright County. The publication highlighted the fruit-growing potential of the area and featured pictures and reports extolling those opportunities. It also carried recommendations on how to plant and tend orchards. The pamphlet noted that the counties of "Webster and Wright, with Douglas and Christian joining on their south, and Texas on the northeast, abound in cheap timbered lands admirably adapted to fruit growing, which is apparent to every well posted horticulturist who has had a look even from the car window. But further proof is afforded by bearing orchards at many points along the way."[2]

After deciding to move to Missouri, Laura and Almanzo had company with them on the journey. The whole country seemed to be moving in 1894, as the United States slid deeper into the economic doldrums. Twenty percent or more of the workforce lost their jobs. Farmers, whose commodity prices plummeted during the early 1890s, were growing desperate. Transients clogged the roads and byways, searching for a means of survival. Among the migrants were settlers who had moved to the edge of the frontier in the Dakotas and surrounding Plains states and were now retreating to more settled regions back East, hoping to recoup their losses.[3]

The Wilders' move to Missouri was made easier and more pleasant by the presence of another farm family from the De Smet area, Frank and Emma Cooley and their two sons. They also had decided to try their luck in the Missouri Ozarks and were heading toward Mansfield, fifty miles southeast

of Springfield. Their boys were close to Rose in age, and the three would become good friends on the journey. Almanzo removed the backseat from a two-seated hack and applied a fresh coat of black paint. Laura prepared the clothes, bedding, furniture, food, cooking utensils, and other necessary items. They even took along some chickens for eating. In the special writing desk that Almanzo had made for her, Laura tucked away a hundred-dollar bill, which was the fruit of their labors in De Smet and was intended for a down payment on a parcel of land once they arrived in Missouri.[4]

By mid-July everything was ready. The two families headed south on Tuesday, July 17. Laura recorded their daily progress in pencil in a small, five-cent memorandum book. The Cooleys traveled in two covered wagons, one driven by Paul (the older boy), the other by the father. Averaging about twenty miles a day, the two families angled south and slightly east toward Yankton, where they would be able to take the ferry across the Missouri River into Nebraska. The days were extremely hot, and winds roiled the dust from the parched countryside. Temperatures frequently topped 100 degrees, sometimes reaching 110. Crops in many places had completely burned up. In Hutchinson County, home to large numbers of German-Russian Mennonites and Hutterites, they drove past a Russian settlement, and saw more of them as they entered Yankton County.[5]

After resting for a day on Sunday and visiting a friendly colony of German-Russians, the Cooleys and the Wilders arrived in Yankton on the seventh day. Once the territorial capital of Dakota, it was home to the state insane asylum and Yankton College and boasted some of the largest and most ornate store buildings in the state. Laura was not much impressed by the place, calling it "a stick in the mud." She got her revolver fixed while they were there, but they spent so much time driving around looking for feed for their horses that the Cooleys reached the ferry site first. With the wind blowing and darkness setting in, the ferryman hesitated to make another trip across the river with the Wilders' wagon, but they were able to persuade him. Crossing the river, Laura told Rose to turn around and look behind her, saying, "That's your last sight of Dakota."[6]

The days were even hotter in Nebraska, the temperature once hitting 126 degrees, assuming their thermometer was accurate (it later broke). They gawked at the motorized streetcars in Lincoln and were impressed by the handsome courthouse in Beatrice, but the more Laura saw of the state the less she liked it. They drove into Kansas, breathing dust all day; the dust

lay three to five inches thick on the road, according to her daily log. On August 14, the start of the fourth week, they drove through Topeka, the state capital, where Laura was impressed by the streetcars and the smoothness of the asphalt pavement. Crops looked much better here than they had farther north. They also began to notice an unusual sight—large numbers of black people—something that Laura duly recorded in her notebook. Also, somewhat ominously, they began meeting families who had previously moved to Missouri and now were returning and Missourians who had decided that Kansas and Nebraska offered greater opportunities for them than their own state. In Prescott, just north of Fort Scott, they talked to a family who had been traveling through southwest Missouri for two months and did not like it at all. But more wagons seemed to be heading toward Missouri than away from it, and so the Cooleys and the Wilders continued. "The whole country is just full of emigrants, going and coming," Laura recorded.[7]

In the midafternoon of August 22, a little more than five weeks after leaving De Smet, the three wagons crossed the state line into Missouri. That day they met seven emigrant wagons leaving Missouri. The following day they passed through the towns of Pedro, Liberal, and Lamar. In Pedro a man told them that the area around Mansfield was some of the finest country in the world. At Lamar Laura mailed several letters back to De Smet. One described their journey up to that point to editor Carter Sherwood, who reprinted it in his newspaper. "First I ever published," she wrote in the margin of the clipping that her mother sent her. In some of the places that they drove through, weeds in the gardens and the fields betrayed the shiftlessness of the people who were living there, and Laura was surprised to see so few schoolhouses in the countryside. As they approached Springfield, whose twenty-two thousand inhabitants made it the largest city in the southwestern part of the state, their estimates of the area soared. "Well, we are in the Ozarks at last," Laura wrote in her trip diary, "just in the beginning of them, and they are beautiful. We passed along the foot of some hills and could look up their sides. The trees and rocks are lovely. Manly says we could almost live on the looks of them."[8]

From that point on her comments became increasingly enthusiastic. Laura and Almanzo judged the thriving city of Springfield to be the nicest one they had seen yet. Graced by fine houses, it had four business blocks facing the town square that were well stocked with merchandise and full

of customers. To Laura everything was "simply grand." The next day they drove through Seymour, thirty-five miles farther east. Laura observed that in Missouri, unlike South Dakota, the main streets generally straddled an open square, with hitching posts situated all around it where people could tie their horses. They met a farmer who had previously lived near Sioux Falls, South Dakota. He praised the southwestern Missouri climate and predicted they would never want to leave the hills. Getting used to all the stones in the fields, however, might take some time, he cautioned. Laura and Almanzo especially noticed all of the fruit—much of it growing wild—in the fields they passed: blackberries, peaches, plums, cherries, and, of course, apples.[9]

On August 30—some six weeks and 650 miles after leaving home—the Wilders drove into Mansfield, theirs one in a line of about ten emigrant wagons. Laura recorded her first impressions in her diary:

> Mansfield is a good town of 300 or 400 inhabitants in a good central location where it should grow fast. The railroad runs on one side of the square and two stagecoach lines go from the depot, one south to the County seat of Douglas County, the other north to the County seat of Wright County. There is everything here already that one could want though we must do our worshiping without a Congregational church. There is a Methodist church and a Presbyterian. There is a good school. Around the Square, two general stores, two drug stores, the bank, a Boston Racket store, livery stable, blacksmith shop near. There are several nice large houses in big yards with trees. South of the tracks is as good as north of them; two or three big houses, and a flour mill is there by a mill pond.[10]

Almanzo ventured out that afternoon to inspect a farm that was for sale, but he found it unsuitable. They needed to find a place that was affordable but also one that could be made into a paying proposition. It would take some time to find what they were looking for. In the meantime, the Wilders and the Cooleys camped together in a grove of trees west of town, continuing the primitive housekeeping setup they had used on the trail. Between the Cooleys' wagons on one side and the Wilders' on the other, they set up a table and some chairs and hung a hammock in the shade. While the following days were no doubt anxious ones for Laura and Almanzo, as they searched for a place to buy, they also were exciting, since

this was a new beginning for them, a place that could erase the memory of past failures. Day after day Almanzo rode out with land agents to look at farms, only to return empty-handed. But for Rose, who was too young to understand her parents' frustration, it was a joyous time as she and Paul and George picked berries, climbed trees, and roamed the woods.[11]

Finally, Almanzo found a place about a mile east of town that looked liked a real possibility. It had forty acres, and the selling price was ten dollars an acre. Laura, when she saw it, was even more favorably impressed than he. An article published in 1911 in the *Missouri Ruralist* that was signed by him but probably written by her noted that it "looked unpromising enough when we first saw it, not only one but several ridges rolling in every direction and covered with rocks and brush and timber. Perhaps it looked worse to me because I had just left the prairies of South Dakota where the land is easily farmed." Laura was quicker to perceive the potential of the place. It was she who thought of naming it Rocky Ridge. The previous owners had purchased several hundred apple seedlings but had never planted them.[12]

After discussing the situation, Laura and Almanzo decided to purchase the farm. Court records indicate that they paid Thomas M. White and his wife, Charlotte, $400 on Friday, September 21, three weeks after their arrival in town. What the records do not reveal, however, is that in the meantime the family went through a crisis, temporarily losing the $100 bill that Laura had carefully tucked away at the beginning of their journey. Upon discovering its disappearance, she and Almanzo could think only that Rose might have told someone about it or that it had been stolen. Rose recalled afterward how angry and insulted she had felt at the suggestion that she might have betrayed the family's secret. But luckily the bill was found several days later after more fiddling around with the writing desk; it somehow had slipped into a crack.[13]

The significance of the $100 bill in family legend probably multiplied over the years; Laura once told *Missouri Ruralist* editor John Case that they had lacked only $150 to pay for the forty acres, and another time she indicated that they had put a mortgage of $200 on the farm, which was half the price. The former owners had managed to clear only four acres, on which two hundred apple trees had been planted the previous year. Four times that many saplings were set out in nursery rows near the house, ready for replanting as soon as more land was cleared.[14]

The house was a windowless log cabin perched on the edge of a ravine. It had a fireplace that could be used for heating and cooking, and, of course, there was plenty of timber on the property. Rose and Laura quickly started cleaning the house, and then the few pieces of furniture they had brought with them were moved in. Now Laura, who had lived in so many little houses—including a variety of sod dwellings and log cabins—was settled into another one.

Almanzo and Laura began clearing trees and chopping them into fire-wood to sell in town. During their first year or two at Rocky Ridge, the wood they took into town and the income they received from their flock of hens provided what cash they needed for groceries, clothing, and other necessary items. "It was hard work and sometimes short rations at the first, but gradually the difficulties were overcome," Laura later recalled. Almanzo's poor health continued to restrict his activities. "Mr. Wilder was unable to do a full day's work," Laura told a journalist. "The garden, my hens and the wood I helped saw and which we sold in town took us through the first year. It was then I became an expert at the end of a cross-cut saw and I still can 'make a hand' in an emergency. Mr. Wilder says he would rather have me help than any man he ever sawed with. And, believe me, I learned how to take care of hens and to make them lay." Not all of the lumber was sold in town. Some of the logs were used for fencing their land, and others went into building a barn and a henhouse. By the spring of 1895, they had managed to clear about half their land and get it ready to plant their apple trees and crops.[15]

Meanwhile, Rose went to school on the east edge of town. The school was a two-story brick building with four rooms and was only three years old, having replaced the original two-room schoolhouse. Rose already was a good reader, and she was able to beat the other students in her age group in spelling bees. She worked her way through the *McGuffey's Readers* and also read books in geography and American history and a large volume on ancient, medieval, and modern history. Her teachers quickly recognized her exceptional intelligence and allowed her to take books home from the school library, which consisted of a row of volumes on a shelf in one of the upstairs rooms. Winter evenings, with the family gathered around the fireplace in their cabin, Almanzo oiled harnesses and worked on other tasks, Rose did her arithmetic and played at building corncob houses, and Laura knitted or read by the light of a kerosene lamp. All three of them

could thrill to the adventures of *Ivanhoe* and James Fenimore Cooper's *Leatherstocking Tales,* transport themselves back into history with Prescott's *Conquest of Mexico* and Parkman's *Oregon Trail,* or imagine themselves partaking in the exploits of *The Green Mountain Boys, Ben Hur,* or *John Halifax, Gentleman.* They also had their own little library of Tennyson's and Scott's poems.[16]

The Cooleys, who had moved into town to manage a hotel, exchanged visits with the Wilders from time to time, and neighbors and new acquaintances sometimes dropped in for popcorn or just to visit. Laura obtained a reputation for her tasty gingerbread, one of her specialties. Sunday, as always, was a day of rest and for attending church. Picnics in the woods or in shady ravines were always fun. Laura and Almanzo enjoyed riding horseback, and they purchased a donkey and named it Spookendyke, so Rose could learn to ride, too, and take him to school with her. Unfortunately, he seemed to enjoy bucking her off more than carrying her on his back, and she quickly grew to detest him.[17]

The following year a frame room with some windows was added to the cabin, and in the spring of 1896 Laura and Almanzo detached the new room from the cabin, moved it several feet, and added on another new room with a loft above for Rose to sleep in. The old cabin, meanwhile, was converted into a barn. The additions would take a number of years, but eventually the new house would become something of a "showplace" in the area.[18]

The first three years the Wilders were in Missouri the country continued to wallow in economic depression, emerging only during the latter part of 1897. Ruined businesses, massive unemployment, depressed farm prices, industrial armies roaming the countryside in search of bread and jobs all contributed to unprecedented class conflict and a desperate search for political panaceas. Some people discovered their messiahs in various radical organizations and leaders; in the most heavily hit farm areas, the Populist Party and its banner-carrier in 1896, William Jennings Bryan, emerged as popular heroes. Four decades later, during the Great Depression, Rose implied that her family had been among those caught up in the mood of insurgency and had become followers of the "Silver-tongued orator of the Platte." In her introduction to her collection of Mansfield-inspired stories, *Old Home Town,* she recalled the white, yellow, and purple asters (they called them chrysanthemums) that grew up along the fences in people's yards. "To

me," she wrote, "a yellow aster still stands for the hated gold standard; the white aster means William Jennings Bryan, whose free coinage of silver would have taken us back to prosperity. But Bryan was defeated by the soulless corporations and our country was forever ruined."[19]

How much of this political drama from her childhood Rose actually remembered (she was only nine at the time), how much of it derived from information that she picked up later and projected back onto her own past (for example, her estimate of Coxey's Army being sixty thousand strong was wildly inflated), and how much these radical attitudes actually characterized Laura and Almanzo is difficult to say. During the early years of their marriage, they identified themselves with the Democratic Party, which then was not particularly progressive or reform minded. At the time of the Wilders' arrival in 1894, Mansfield and Wright County remained heavily Republican, generally delivering majorities in the range of two to one for party candidates. Before the Civil War, Democratic candidates had usually prevailed by similar margins. The Ozarks, for the most part, were decidedly Republican during the late 1800s, despite having large numbers of families originating below the Mason-Dixon line.[20]

Prosperity was returning by 1898, but Laura and Almanzo decided that moving into town might make it easier for them to make ends meet. Until this time, living at Rocky Ridge could never have provided them with much more than a hand-to-mouth existence, since the farm produced little besides timber that could be marketed for cash. Their apple trees would not start to bear fruit for seven years. They managed to hold onto their property and even expanded it a little in May 1897 by purchasing six acres along the eastern edge for three dollars each. (The farm eventually totaled approximately two hundred acres.) Laura practiced extreme frugality, a habit that sometimes frustrated Rose and may have contributed in a roundabout way to her own spendthrift tendencies.[21]

Almanzo and Laura rented a small one-story house on the east edge of Mansfield, just north of the railroad tracks. Almanzo now was able to have a regular job in town, and they could still easily maintain the farm. After Frank Cooley died, Almanzo approached Emma and bought the draying business from her, including the team and wagon. Laura set up a boarding table in their house and began serving meals to traveling salesmen and other passengers who came through on the trains, as well as to railroad employees. Because of his new dray line, Almanzo spent much time around

the depot, putting him in an ideal position to recommend his wife's good cooking to the men he met.[22]

During the summer of 1898, Almanzo's parents and his widowed sister, Laura, stopped off in Mansfield for an extended stay while on their way to their new home in Crowley, Louisiana. Perley Wilder had already gone to live there, and Eliza Jane had persuaded Laura and her parents to join them there, too. James Wilder had sold their farm in Spring Valley for several thousand dollars and had invested most of the proceeds in Louisiana rice lands. Before he left Mansfield, James, who was eighty-five years old, put up the money for Almanzo and Laura to purchase the house they had been renting. They paid $450 for it on June 22, but it would take them several more years to save enough money to pay off the mortgage on Rocky Ridge.[23]

Living in Mansfield made Rose one of the town girls who had previously looked down their noses at her as a country girl. Now, rather than having to ride—or try to ride—Spookendyke to school, she walked only several blocks. While Mansfield was a typical, quiet country town, some of the things one could see and do there could be exciting to an eleven year old. Several times a day trains rumbled by on the tracks bordering on the family's backyard. Near the depot, drummers and other traveling men came and went, and one could watch the telegraph operator clicking off messages to distant places. Around the square on the north side of the tracks, teams and wagons and buggies were tied up. And there were always people one could observe in the stores and on the sidewalks, going about their business or stopping to chat with friends.

Much later Rose resurrected the town as it had appeared to her when they first drove into it:

> We passed a big Reynolds General Store, with two large windows full of things, the door between them. Men were loafing, whittling, talking and spitting along the high board walk. There were small stores, The Bank of Mansfield, a Boston Racket Store with "Opera House" painted on the windows upstairs, Hoover's Livery Stable and horses in a feed lot, then another big house inside a wire fence. Past a blacksmith shop the dusty road went downhill to cross a little bridge.[24]

In Mansfield, as in other towns, the Fourth of July and Decoration Day were the biggest days of the year. Patriotism was put on enthusiastic display. Missouri was a border state, and many families in and around Mansfield

derived from Southern roots, but the Union veterans in the Grand Army of the Republic maintained a high visibility and worked hard during election time for the Republican cause. The Women's Christian Temperance Union also played an active role in the community. Mansfield was a big lodge town, with active chapters of Masons, Odd Fellows, Rebekahs, and Royal Neighbors. Almanzo was a Mason, like Laura's father, and both Laura and Almanzo were involved in Eastern Star. She normally held an office, as they were passed around among the membership from year to year, serving as warden, secretary, worthy matron, and in other positions.[25]

There was little to distinguish Mansfield from other small towns. Its location along a major railroad route conferred considerable advantage on it, compared with its neighbors to the north and south with no railroad connections. The Kansas City, Fort Scott, and Memphis Railroad, in fact, had been responsible for originally establishing the town when it laid its tracks through southern Missouri in 1881. White settlement in Wright County had begun a half century earlier, during the 1830s. Before then, the area had been home to Osage Indians as well as to Delawares, Shawnees, and other tribal groups. Herds of buffalo roamed through it at one time, and the woods were full of deer, elk, and other animals. The county seat of Hartville, twelve miles to the north, had been founded in the early 1840s. A colony of several hundred black people grew up near it after the Civil War, but Mansfield had few or no blacks living in it. The area around Hartville, in the center of the county, grew up rapidly during the 1840s and 1850s, but the southern part lagged until the coming of the railroad. The largest town in the county—Mountain Grove, twenty miles east of Mansfield—originated in the 1850s, long before the railroad arrived. When the rail link was completed in 1881, Mountain Grove took advantage of its head start. Mansfield also benefited heavily from the trade generated by the railroad. The smaller towns of Norwood to the east and Cedar Gap to the west also got their start with the building of the railroad, but both lagged behind Mansfield and Mountain Grove in population.[26]

By the turn of the century Mansfield had grown to 494 residents, but its population actually declined—to 477—during the following decade. Hartville was overtaken by Mountain Grove between 1900 and 1910, as the former's population declined from 1,762 to 1,660 while the latter's jumped from 1,004 to 1,722. With the advent of automobiles and trucks, the advantages enjoyed by Mountain Grove and Mansfield, located along a

major highway as well as on the main line of railroad between Memphis and Springfield, were reinforced. The railroad tracks followed the path of an old Indian trail sitting astride an east-west ridge of hills across the southern Missouri Ozarks. Cedar Gap, five miles west of Mansfield, at 1,685 feet above sea level, was situated on the highest point in the area and had the second highest elevation in the state.[27]

Many of the earliest white settlers who entered the region during the decades preceding the Civil War originated in areas of similar topography farther east, mainly in the upland zones of eastern Tennessee, western North Carolina, Virginia, and Kentucky. Tennesseans, who predominated among the earliest arrivals, brought their social and cultural traditions with them. Many of the initial settlers were of Scotch-Irish background, an influence of continuing importance over time. Presbyterianism was strong in the Ozarks, supplemented by active cohorts of Methodists and Baptists. Presbyterians and Methodists organized congregations in Mansfield in 1883 and 1884, respectively. Local Baptists had to attend the Mount Pleasant congregation out in the country until they built their own church in Mansfield in 1909. Meanwhile, Catholics were active in Mansfield as early as 1893. Services were conducted by a visiting priest who came from Mountain Grove after 1900, but it was not until around World War II that the first resident priest was established in the community.[28]

With no Congregational church in Mansfield, the Wilders affiliated themselves with the Methodist church. While never formally establishing membership in the congregation, they actively participated in its activities for many years, until age slowed them down. For many years the Methodists had to share their minister with other towns in the area. Southern Missouri's religious traditions, like many other local habits and customs, required some adjustment on Laura and Almanzo's part. While many aspects of the culture were familiar to them—religious revivals, Fourth of July celebrations, pie suppers, band concerts, workings, social visiting, and the like—there was also much that was new. All-day songfests (usually hymn sings on Sundays in the summer) and regularly scheduled court days in the county seat (when people drove in from miles around and made the trials their entertainment) differed considerably from their experiences in South Dakota. The Wilders also struggled with the local speech habits and Ozark twang. While Ozarks dwellers could be just as friendly and outgoing

as anywhere else, they had obtained a somewhat deserved reputation for remaining standoffish among strangers. Traditional rural isolation was beginning to break down by around the turn of the century, however, and during succeeding decades regional characteristics continued to converge with those of the rest of the country. Their locations on major transportation routes running along the "backbone" of the Ozarks, connecting Springfield and points to the east, ensured that Mansfield and other towns like it would be less prone to remain backward and clannish.[29]

As modernizing trends made their influence felt in the region, patterns of resistance drove some local residents to try to maintain their old ways of living. Most people welcomed higher living standards and technological improvements, but they often expressed concern about changes that appeared to challenge traditional habits and values. In *Old Home Town,* Rose described just how provincial, conservative, and suspicious Ozarks dwellers could be; the fictional town obviously was based upon her own experiences growing up in Mansfield during the early 1900s. In her descriptions, the town's residents were, for the most part, narrow-minded, gossipy, overly concerned about other people's opinions, and censorious of their actions. The town was, most of the time, a dull place; the houses displayed no more architectural distinction than boxes, and little beauty prevailed. While a few substantial houses and businesses did exist on the south side of the tracks, the railroad—as was typically the case everywhere—separated the "good" side of town from the "poor" side, otherwise known as "poverty flat." Girls from families living on the north side of the tracks turned up their noses at poor girls from the south side of town.[30]

The tone of Rose's stories was generally ironic and condescending, critical, for the most part, of the narrow expectations, the prudery, the single-minded acquisitiveness, the excessive social control, and the lack of benevolence prevailing among the townspeople. By 1935, however, when she sat down to write an introduction that would tie these stories together and would describe in more detail the look and feel of the town, Rose had moderated her point of view and now professed to discern greater wisdom in the kinds of attitudes and actions that she had witnessed thirty years earlier. Now she focused on the moral softness and political fuzzy-mindedness of Americans that had become apparent to her by the middle of the depression decade.

Rose admitted, with regard to her own childhood in Mansfield:

It was a hard, narrow, relentless life. It was not comfortable. Nothing was made easy for us. We did not like work and we were not supposed to like it; we were supposed to work, and we did. We did not like discipline, so we suffered until we disciplined ourselves. We saw many things and many opportunities that we ardently wanted and could not pay for, so we did not get them, or got them only after stupendous, heartbreaking effort and self-denial, for debt was much harder to bear than deprivations.[31]

Rose had not particularly liked the kind of life that her parents had given her. "We rebelled against it because we did not like it. We wanted a land overflowing with milk and honey," she said, writing during the depression. But there were lessons to be learned from the experience, too, she suggested. The depression with its social and political fallout was teaching people like herself that their parents actually "knew what they were talking about. We suspect that, after all, man's life in this hostile universe is not easy and can not be made so; that facts are seldom pleasant and must be faced; that the only freedom is to be found within the slavery of self-discipline; that everything must be paid for and that putting off the day of reckoning only increases the inexorable bill."[32]

Discounting some of Rose's language here as typical rhetorical bombast, the statement nevertheless revealed a lot about her childhood in Mansfield and about the intellectual journey that she later made as an adult. Obviously she was highly critical of what she perceived as a cultural breakdown and the atrophying of personal responsibility in the 1930s, but she also admitted that her earlier rebellion against her parents' strictures and against society's dictates had been largely misconceived.

Rose clearly felt that as a child she had been reined in too much by her parents, especially by her mother. Even as she moved into middle age during the 1930s, she secretly complained in her journal and sometimes openly let her mother know that she had resented and continued to take offense at Laura's efforts to control her behavior. While the evidence remains heavily inferential, it would seem that her status as an only child had inclined her mother to be overprotective and had strongly influenced Laura to try to mold her daughter's behavior along correct pathways. There seems to have been a rather clear-cut division of labor in the household; raising their only child was primarily Laura's responsibility, although Almanzo certainly doted on Rose and displayed affection toward her. To a large degree, however, he turned out to be absent or the less

significant psychic presence in the family triangle. Based on surviving letters and other documentary evidence, the highly charged—and sometimes stormy—relationship among the three was the one connecting mother and daughter.

Between Laura and Almanzo there was a quiet, sturdy affection and mutual sharing. More than most marriages during the period, theirs was a cooperative one in which husband and wife decided important questions together after discussion and deliberation. If there was a dominant partner, it was Laura. She appears to have been adept at managing her emotions in a manipulative way when she felt it was necessary. "Sometimes my quick mother flew out at him," Rose remembered years later, but most of the time the two probably got along agreeably by largely concentrating their energies within their own specified spheres.[33]

Love bound the three of them together. Rose's status as a highly exceptional child—both intellectually and by dint of personality—also mattered. Laura's own sometimes high-strung personality in some ways resembled her daughter's, although she had learned well her own mother's admonition to keep her emotions under tight control. We can assume that Laura always considered that what she did was best for Rose and that she was doing it for Rose's own best interest, and not for her own. But the mother's ideas about what constituted her daughter's best interest did not always coincide with Rose's. Add to that a large degree of certitude and self-righteousness on Laura's part, heavily reinforced by religious belief, and we arrive at a situation in which the mother's stifling presence could frequently seem overwhelming to the daughter and make her want to get out from under her mother's strict rules and regulations. If Laura harbored high hopes and expectations for Rose, she also had a lot of time to try to shape her behavior so that she would fulfill those goals and desires.

Another major factor in the equation was the family's poverty. Even after moving into Mansfield with her parents, thereby becoming a town girl, Rose felt snubbed and ridiculed by most of the town kids. There were a couple of exceptions—Blanche Coday, in particular—who took a liking to the precocious girl and became friendly with her. But being so smart, so different, and so poor, Rose felt ostracized and isolated from her peers. "No sensitive child who has gone to school from a poverty-besieged home, in patched clothes, with second-hand books, fails to learn that human beings are barbarous. Schoolmates demonstrate that," she wrote in a magazine

article in 1926. "In a few years we were not so poor. My clothes were pretty and my books were new. But the attitude taken toward me by the girls and boys still persisted, and I was too shy, too sensitive, to break it down. I was not invited to parties; I was 'left out.' I was hurt and lonely."[34]

As Rose grew older and could look back on her situation with greater objectivity, she became better able to understand the actual source of her miseries. Even in middle age, however, she was capable of lashing out at her mother and blaming her for her own psychological torments. "It's amazing how my mother can make me suffer," Rose wrote in her journal in April 1933. "She made me so miserable when I was a child that I've never got over it. I'm morbid. I'm all raw nerves. I know I should be more robust. I shouldn't let her torture me this way, and always gain her own ends, thro implications that she hardly knows she's using. But I can't help it." Considering that at the time Rose was suffering from health problems, money worries, concerns about the future, lack of intimate friendships, and being too cooped up close to her mother, her misery was understandable. The two of them seemed to get on each other's nerves when they were living close together, not because they were so unlike each other, but, in part, because they were so similar. An anecdote recorded in Rose's journal in 1933 was highly revealing about one side of Laura's personality: "[My mother] was pleased, self-satisfied, on the street in Mansfield, Saturday, when Mrs. Wilson looked at her palm & told her she could get anything she wanted. 'I always have,' she said complacently, & repeated this when she told Mrs. Craig what Mrs. Wilson had said."[35]

Taking at face value Rose's retrospective commentary—positive or negative—about her childhood and the kind of parenting that she had received can be treacherous. Rose herself admitted that during the early 1930s she suffered a mental breakdown, and she always had a tendency to exaggerate things, to assert things overconfidently, to contradict herself, and to misstate facts in a grand style. She seemed able to convince herself that just because she said something was true at a particular time that it *was* true. Thus, too much should not be made of a journal entry written when she was sick in Albania in 1927, "Influences: 1 to 16: no affection, poverty, inferiority."[36] Her mother's no-nonsense approach to things and frequently judgmental attitudes about people, including her own daughter, certainly grated on Rose. Laura probably assumed that her affection showed itself plainly and that her love shone through so strongly in her actions and

presence that no further statements or gestures were necessary. But letters that mother and daughter exchanged when both were adults and other evidence demonstrated that Laura, in fact, regularly expressed her love and affection openly to her daughter.

At times, Rose admitted that the fault for her misery lay not so much in anything that her mother or father may have done or failed to do, as in the unfortunate and unavoidable financial circumstances that her family found itself in. "My father and mother were courageous, even gaily so," she wrote in a 1926 magazine article. "They did everything possible to make me happy, and I gladly responded with an effort to persuade them that they were succeeding. But all unsuspected, I lived through a childhood that was a nightmare."[37]

These statements—both public and private—about Rose's horrible childhood stand against others that implied just the opposite. "Fifty-odd years ago," she wrote in 1947, "I was a joyously barefoot Ozark girl in a log-cabin; my home is in the Ozarks, and I'm as typical as can be, even to six centuries of Scotch-English ancestry." When she was thirty-one, she wrote the following tribute to her parents:

> My mother loves courage and beauty and books; my father loves nature, birds and trees and curious stones, and both of them love the land, the stubborn, grudging, beautiful earth that wears out human lives year by year. They gave me something of all these loves, and whenever I do something that I really can't help sitting down and admiring, I always come plump up against the fact that I never would have done it if I hadn't been wise enough to pick out these particular parents.

And in 1939, when she was fifty-two, Rose wrote in an article aimed at encouraging women to become more active as citizens: "Luckily I was born poor, and soon knew the long hungry depression that we called The Panic of '93. So I can find something to eat in any field or forest." Here she put the grinding poverty that she otherwise usually deplored into a positive—even gay—light.[38]

Rose's intelligence, her status as an only child, and her failure to make many friends with other children all no doubt intensified the emotional freight of the connection between her and her parents, especially that with her mother. Early on she exhibited an independent streak and a willingness to defy conventional opinion. Many years later she wrote Norma

Lee Browning that she remembered rarely, if ever, completing a school year after leaving De Smet: "In Mansfield I couldn't stand the stupid teachers, and there was no compulsion then; I just quit school." One year, she told another friend, she spent only a half day in school after her teacher disgusted her by unfavorably comparing her own refusal to do a silly exercise with a classmate's dull—but enthusiastic—response. At that point, she recollected, "I stood up, slammed my books on the desk, said in a fury, 'I will not stay here to listen to such stupid, stupid!!' and went home." Such behavior—even if she might have exaggerated it somewhat in the telling sixty years later—was certainly not common in Mansfield nor anywhere else and must have contributed significantly to Rose's being and feeling out of place.[39]

Rose's dissatisfaction with the quality of education offered her is understandable. Ninth-grade classes probably did not begin there until 1900, when she turned fourteen; tenth grade was added the following year. High school enrollment stood at less than thirty at the time. The level of instruction remained low. Thus, when Almanzo's sister Eliza visited Mansfield in 1903 and offered to take Rose with her to Crowley, Louisiana, so that she could finish her schooling there, it provided an enticing opportunity for her to escape the prison of the Mansfield school system and to try her chances somewhere else. She was sixteen by then, and her parents and teachers were incapable of providing her with the kinds of experiences and educational challenges that might arouse her interest. Earlier she had discovered that a family recently arrived in town had a whole wall full of books in their house and she had borrowed them all, including Gibbon's *Decline and Fall of the Roman Empire* as well as a number of English novels and books of literary criticism. Having devoured everything she could find at home, on the shelves at school, and in the community, Rose needed something else to whet her appetite.[40]

The high school that she attended for a year in Crowley was probably not much advanced over the one in Mansfield (having perhaps an extra year of studies), but the move provided Rose with a change of scenery and a chance to make some new friends. Seven students were enrolled in the high school curriculum, and the principal allowed them to study and recite in his office. During the year that she spent in Crowley, Rose whizzed through her course work, including four years of Latin, and she wrote a Latin poem for the graduation exercises. Life in Mansfield, however,

proved no more appealing to her after her return, and the idea of marrying some local farmer or storekeeper and settling down there for the rest of her life held no allure. So Rose learned telegraphy from the local depot agent and hopped on a train for Kansas City, where she took a job as a telegraph operator, earning $2.50 per week. At the age of seventeen she was on her own and headed down a path that eventually would take her halfway around the world and on to literary fame and fortune, astounding and impressing both her parents and her former acquaintances.[41]

During the early 1900s, Laura and Almanzo continued to work Rocky Ridge Farm from a distance while living in town and trying to save enough money to at least pay off the mortgage. Almanzo took a job as a salesman for an oil company, delivering oil, kerosene, and other petroleum products to outlying farms. Laura continued to cook and to save, realizing that cutting expenditures was as important as earning money. As early as August 1899 they purchased a forty-acre plot directly south of the original acreage, and they added more in September 1905. They also did some land dealing in town, purchasing three lots for $100 in February 1904 and selling them again in September of the following year for $225. On June 8, 1910, they sold the house they had been living in to their friend N. J. Craig, who worked as a cashier at the Farmers and Merchants Bank on the square. For it they received $500 and "exchange of property." By that time they already may have been back at Rocky Ridge, tending their orchard, which would have been bearing by then, and taking care of their livestock and crops. A $500 inheritance they received from Almanzo's parents further enhanced their financial situation.[42]

Almanzo devoted special attention to his cows and prided himself in their milk production; Laura, for her part, specialized in poultry. Mansfield, like De Smet, depended primarily upon agriculture for its well-being, supplementing it with some agricultural processing, and—at times—mining operations. During the 1880s, zinc and lead deposits located several miles west of town lured mine operators, who continued to work the diggings on and off in later years. After 1900, a creamery, a flour mill, and a tomato-canning factory started up, and local-business boosters encouraged the growing of tomatoes and other fruits and vegetables to promote faster economic growth. The completion in 1908 of an electric railroad to Ava, twelve miles to the south, contributed to the feeling that Mansfield could become a regional center for processing and shipping agricultural products.[43]

*Becoming Laura Ingalls Wilder*

Statistics reported by state agencies on annual commodity shipments from Wright County around the turn of the century give some indication of the kinds of economic activities that were prevalent around Mansfield at this time:

| | |
|---|---:|
| Cattle, head | 2,875 |
| Hogs, head | 11,200 |
| Horses and mules, head | 300 |
| Sheep, head | 5,590 |
| Wheat, bushels | 20,522 |
| Corn, bushels | 661 |
| Hay, lbs. | 40,000 |
| Flour, lbs. | 225,124 |
| Apples, barrels | 34,043 |
| Hardwood lumber, ft. | 99,000 |
| Railroad ties | 53,550 |
| Cordwood, cords | 3,816 |
| Poultry, live, lbs. | 414,560 |
| Eggs, dozen | 214,380 |
| Butter, lbs. | 572 |
| Strawberries, crates | 1,500 |
| Game, lbs. | 50,240 |
| Pine lumber, ft. | 4,250,000 |
| Canned goods, lbs. | 65,875 |
| Walnut logs, ft. | 9,000[44] |

Annual county averages during the decade after 1905 showed corn to have been the most widely cultivated crop, with 36,851 acres planted and average yields of 23.2 bushels per acre. Wheat trailed with 10,055 acres planted and 10.0 bushels per acre yielded; oats was planted on 2,221 acres with an average yield of 19.8 bushels per acre. (In each case county-wide average yields lagged about 20 percent behind statewide averages.) In addition, about 19,000 tons of hay and forage were produced in the county annually. The number of horses in 1910 stood at 7,908. There were 2,101 mules, 20,374 meat cattle, and 18,006 sheep.[45]

Unfortunately, there is not much information about Laura and Almanzo's activities in town or on the farm during these years. Remaining shreds of evidence portraying their actions and linking them to developments in Mansfield are scanty. Now and then an item appeared in the local newspaper (few issues were published and fewer were saved during the period before

1908). In October 1905 the *Mansfield Mail* noted that A. J. Wilder and family had spent the previous Sunday picnicking with E. J. Knight at Vera Cruz, Missouri. In September of the following year the paper reported that Almanzo had been exhibiting some "mammoth blades" of corn on the street the previous Saturday. On October 9, 1908, a new paper, the *Mansfield Press,* noted that Mrs. A. J. Wilder had gone to Sedalia to visit with a Mrs. Quigley. The following week the paper carried this notice, "Mr. Wilder was anxiously looking for his wife last Sunday but don't want to let on, though, and don't want us to say any thing about it." Several months later it noted that Almanzo had taken a business trip to Ava with Charles Bonnell.[46]

Obviously, the Wilders were familiar figures in the community, but the details of their lives remain obscure. How often they enjoyed chicken-pie suppers sponsored by the various women's organizations, attended concerts of Blind Boone and other performers, participated in songfests at the G.A.R. Hall, watched the *Uncle Tom's Cabin* show, listened to band concerts, joined in Decoration Day exercises, ate ice cream in the park, prayed at evangelistic meetings, or went to school exhibitions is impossible to ascertain. We know that they were active in the Methodist church and in the Eastern Star and we can presume that they were involved with friends and neighbors in many other activities, too.

Through the years Laura stayed in touch with her family in South Dakota. While teaching school west of De Smet near Manchester, Grace met a farmer named Nate Dow, and they were married in October 1901. Carrie continued to work at the *De Smet News and Leader* office. She and Mary lived with their mother in the Third Street house. During the summer of 1903 Carrie was able to travel by train to Mansfield to visit Laura and Almanzo. The previous year Charles Ingalls, suffering from heart disease, had died at the age of sixty-six. Laura visited De Smet for several weeks in May and June, arriving before he died. She was glad for the chance to visit with her mother and sisters for the first time in almost a decade. It was the last time she would see her mother and her sister Mary and the last time that she would visit De Smet until 1931.[47]

Sometime during the early 1900s Laura started giving some thought to writing, perhaps as a way of supplementing the family income. Possibly as early as 1903 she was beginning to consider how she might write some of the stories that she remembered from her childhood. Virtually no evidence

about this remains besides a two-page fragment, written on the back of some oil-company stock requisitions dated February 1903. The incident she wrote about had occurred during the first winter that her family had spent at Silver Lake in 1879.[48] Unfortunately, Laura possessed no models to follow and had no one to ask for advice, either on how to compose them or on how to get them published. For the time being, at least, her energies would remain directed at running her own household, building up Rocky Ridge Farm, and establishing financial security for her and her husband. As she turned forty in 1907, and Almanzo turned fifty, they had to start thinking seriously about how they would support themselves as their physical strength declined.

Rose worked as a telegrapher in Kansas City from 1904 to 1907. It is unclear how often, if at all, she was able to visit. Laura had a chance to stay with her in Kansas City for several weeks in late 1906; when a nationwide strike of telegraph operators erupted the following year, Rose went home to Rocky Ridge, awaiting developments. Afterward, she spent some time as manager of a Western Union office in Mount Vernon, Indiana, and then in April 1908 she boarded a train for San Francisco to take a new position there. The following March she married a real estate salesman named Gillette Lane, and the two of them made a quick trip to Mansfield so that he could meet her parents.[49]

By 1910 Laura and Almanzo were probably planning to expand their little house at Rocky Ridge into more spacious and livable quarters. This would be their dream house, their retirement home and the one they expected to live in the rest of their days. Some of the five hundred dollars from the sale of their house in town went into purchasing building materials for the project, but, as always, practicing frugality, they tried to obtain as much lumber, stone, and other materials as they could on their own property. Using native materials would also add to the uniqueness of their house.

Almanzo had done the initial construction on the house, making several additions over time. He was not capable of doing this larger job himself, so they hired some people from town to help them. Ezra Dennis and his nephew Oral did much of the work on the expansion. Laura had often thought about what an ideal farm home would be like. Almanzo now told her to draw up some plans. Her design included ten rooms, four porches, a native stone fireplace, large windows in the parlor looking out on the countryside, and a library. When Almanzo suggested that they use brick

for the fireplace to avoid having to haul more rock, Laura stamped her foot down. "I objected strenuously," she wrote later. "I argued; I begged; and at last when everything failed I wept." Almanzo yielded, and the rock fireplace was installed.[50]

The task took the Wilders more than a year. Once completed, the house became something of a showplace in the area.[51] It signaled that the Wilders, having arrived in Mansfield two decades earlier with hardly anything to their name, had finally succeeded. If they did not have much money deposited in the bank, they did have a comfortable home that they could grow old in. Little about the couple at this time yet hinted that Mr. and Mrs. A. J. Wilder of Mansfield would ever be anything other than a typical Missouri Ozarks pair who had managed to make a living from the area's rough, rocky soil. But soon that would begin to change.

# 5

## *Building a Writing Career*

### 1911–1923

҉

or the first forty-three years of her life, little about Laura
Wilder seemed to indicate that she differed significantly from
her neighbors. During the almost two decades since she and her
husband, Almanzo, had arrived in Missouri in 1894, almost penniless, they
gradually had built up their farm at Rocky Ridge, converting it into a paying
enterprise that provided them with at least a modicum of security as they
progressed into middle age. Active in church and community affairs, they
were solid, substantial citizens but not particularly outstanding in the eyes
of their neighbors. If anything set them apart, it was their daughter, Rose,
who fit the definition of the "New Woman": a free-spirited career girl of the
type that attracted increasing attention after the turn of the century. Her
spunk and self-reliance suggested that there had been something unusual
in her upbringing, but what it was that might have stimulated her highly
unusual nonconformism remained somewhat mysterious.

Shortly before Laura's forty-fourth birthday an invitation to speak at an
agricultural meeting changed her life. Laura's expert knowledge of chickens
was recognized in the area, and from time to time she was invited to talk
to farm groups about her methods and ideas on the subject. This time,
however, unable to attend the session in person, she wrote her speech and

had someone else read it for her. In the audience was the editor of the *Missouri Ruralist*. The bimonthly farm paper published by Arthur Capper of Kansas combined information about agriculture and practical tips on farming methods with features about rural living aimed at both the man and the woman of the household. Laura's written talk impressed the editor so much that he invited her to submit material to the *Ruralist* for publication. Although later she would tell about the school composition for which she had received a perfect grade in De Smet, until this time she had never paid much attention to writing, beyond exchanging letters with family and friends. The invitation to write for a farm newspaper opened up a new dimension of her personality.[1]

Laura's first article, a fifteen-hundred-word paean to rural living, received featured billing at the front of the issue of February 18, 1911, a week and a half after her forty-fourth birthday. Titled "Favors the Small Farm Home," the essay developed several themes that would recur frequently in her work: the virtues of the rural way of life; the advantages wrought by technological progress in the form of the telephone, delivery of the news, innovations in transportation, and the like; the need for husbands and wives to work together cooperatively in managing their farm operations; and the desirability of small-scale farming. She asserted that a five-acre farm was large enough to adequately support a family. Written in clear, straightforward prose, the article moved from point to point directly and economically. Combining detailed descriptions with broader lessons to be learned constituted a hallmark of her writing from the beginning.[2]

Laura signed her article "Mrs. A. J. Wilder," which is how she would be identified as a farm-newspaper writer. For some reason, Almanzo's name was attached to her second article, "The Story of Rocky Ridge Farm," published in July. Maybe Laura thought that the words would carry more authority coming from "the man of the place," or perhaps it was hard getting used to the idea of being an author and she did not expect to become a frequent contributor. The success story that she recounted in this piece reinforced her earlier contention that an adequate living could be garnered from a small acreage (in this case, it was one hundred acres, not a mere five). Hard work and perseverance had paid off in their own experience, she noted. "Our little Rocky Ridge Farm has supplied everything necessary for a good living and given us good interest on all the money invested every year since the first two. No year has it fallen below ten per cent and one

extra good year it paid 100 per cent. Besides this it has doubled in value, and $3000 more, since it was bought."[3]

Almanzo appeared again as the "author" of the third article, "My Apple Orchard," and his picture graced the cover of the issue. This was Laura's only contribution during the entire year of 1912, however, and she published only one article in the *Ruralist* in 1913, three in 1914, and two in 1915. For several months after the apple-orchard article appeared, Almanzo was listed in the credits of the paper as a contributing editor. Toward the end of the summer in 1912 Laura had taken over as editor of the paper's "Home" column. Her own contributions, however, remained infrequent. Noting a growing tendency to establish neighborhood clubs, she encouraged women to initiate their own local units. "It used to be that only the women in town could have the advantages of women's clubs, but now the woman in the country can be just as cultured a club woman as though she lived in town," she assured her readers. Her other articles in 1914 and 1915 discussed beauty hints ("Washing in buttermilk will whiten the hands and face. Fresh strawberries rubbed on the skin will bleach it, and rhubarb or tomatoes will remove stains from the fingers"); the story of a former city woman who had made a home for her family in the Ozarks ("Women have always been the home makers, but it is not usually expected of them that they should also be the home builders from the ground up"); the "magic" of plain foods; and the Missouri exhibit at the San Francisco International Exposition ("Missouri has met all the states of the Union, all the countries of the world, in fair competition, and has made a proud record").[4]

It is not clear why, when she was given the chance, Laura did not produce more material for the *Ruralist*. Her slowness in producing articles may have derived from her conception of what made a good story; she seemed to be looking for items that were unusual or unique. Later, as she discovered possibilities existing in the common things that could be observed every day, she never lacked for subjects. Her slow start probably also reflected the novelty of the task and its unfamiliarity. She was not used to sitting down and forcing words onto a page for publication. Also, at Rocky Ridge, she lacked editorial guidance and the kind of personal encouragement that might have proved useful. Things would change dramatically, however, after her trip to San Francisco in late 1915. Rose's helpful advice and encouragement at that time would provide the impetus to write regularly for the *Ruralist*. In the meantime, Laura found several other outlets for

her farm journalism, including the *Missouri State Farmer* and the *St. Louis Star.*

Mansfield, its people, and the rapidly changing world also presented potential subject matter, but for the most part Laura avoided writing much about her own community and its residents. Living in town for a time and near it in later years, she certainly would have been able to draw upon the town for material. As regular churchgoers, lodge members, and shoppers in town, she and Almanzo had a wide circle of friends and acquaintances who might have inspired commentary, but they seldom appeared in her columns.

Many things might have attracted her attention. Mansfield's boosters proclaimed their burg to be "the Gem City of the Ozarks," pointing to the abundance of mineral wealth lying buried in the surrounding hills. Although Wright County as a whole, like most of its rural counterparts, lost population during the decade after 1910 (3.1 percent), Mansfield's population jumped from 477 to 757, an increase of 59 percent. Mansfield still trailed the largest town in the county, Mountain Grove (2,212), but the increase did put some distance between it and Hartville (521), which had been founded a decade earlier than Mansfield. Nestled in the orbit of Springfield, fifty miles away by rail or by crude dirt roads, residents of Mansfield still had little to worry about with regard to competition from retailers in that large town (Springfield's population in 1910 was 35,201). Not for another decade would local store owners have to be concerned about their customers driving to other towns to do their shopping.

People in Mansfield were more likely to note the benefits brought by technological progress than the potential pitfalls. An article in the *Mansfield Mirror* in October 1913 boasted of the east-west Frisco rail line (formerly the Kansas City, Fort Scott, and Memphis) crossing through the southern part of the county and the relatively new narrow-gauge short line of the Kansas City, Ozarks and Southern Railway, which from 1908 connected Mansfield and Ava, twelve miles to the south. The laying of gravel on the road between Mansfield and Hartville portended things to come. In short order a bus line connected the two towns. Mansfield was home to three churches, an electric light system, two banks, a bottling works, a canning factory, a creamery station, a telephone exchange, a weekly newspaper, three wholesale produce houses, three hotels, two mills, three

restaurants, a bakery, five real estate firms, and a variety of other businesses and professional offices.[5]

The editor of the *Mirror* also took pride in the town's "beautiful park, with granitoid walk and curbing, macadamized streets around the public square, and granitoid sidewalks." The Mansfield concert band, he boasted, was "one of the best musical organizations in South Missouri, and during the summer months free open air concerts are given in the park."[6] The gap between a local newspaper's account and reality often can be substantial, so readers had to discount some of the *Mirror's* rhetoric. Although much of what we can recapture about the context of the Wilders' lives derives from such newspaper accounts, we need to be wary of broad generalizations asserting what life was *really* like for them. In the absence other resources, though, such articles provide a basis for understanding.

Like their counterparts in other small towns, Mansfield's residents constantly sought to improve their community and trumpeted the progress they had already made. To achieve as much as possible, without spending much money, the townspeople repeatedly promoted the town by reorganizing the commercial club, resuscitating the band, encouraging people to participate in annual spring clean-up drives, and, of course, boosting business. A few property owners complained about the cost of installing new concrete sidewalks in 1913, but the *Mirror* editor reminded them of the improvement's long-term benefits. "We must make the Mansfield Park the beauty spot of Wright County," exhorted another editorial. A public subscription raised funds for sprinkling the streets to reduce the dust that summer, while a better solution for several of the major downtown streets came with their macadamization.[7]

The driving force energizing Mansfield's modernization efforts during the teens was go-getting dentist F. H. Riley, who had quit his practice in Kansas City in 1911 and moved to Mansfield. He quickly plunged into community affairs, generating a continual stream of ideas for fixing up the town and soliciting public support for needed improvements. He presided over the Young Men's Business Club, which was designed to facilitate cooperation among Mansfield's business and professional men and to boost Mansfield's growth and progress. The year after arriving in town Riley spearheaded the creation of what became an annual agricultural and stock show. The following year he organized the townspeople to work on beautifying the town square, which was the center of community life. He concocted the idea

of a six-minute blind auction to raise funds for materials and then organized a "Klondike gold digging contest" in the park, inviting people to search for buried treasure while they spaded the ground to prepare new flower beds. The installation of new iron seats and the electrification of the bandstand completed the transformation of the square. In an article published in the *Mirror,* Riley urged his fellow citizens to join him in boosting Mansfield: "Now let's get down to business. Put your shoulders to the wheel and all push together. We can continue to improve the 'Gem City,' each citizen doing his part."[8]

Every Saturday people flocked into town from miles around, hauling in their cream and eggs and doing their weekly shopping. Many of them stayed to chat with friends or to listen to a band concert on the square. People loved to listen to a band, but enthusiasm among the players periodically waxed and waned, and every few years it was necessary to reorganize and rejuvenate the group. Money was needed to purchase sheet music or to pay the band leader and to take care of other expenses. Concert times varied; Saturday afternoons and Saturday and Wednesday evenings were most common. The music tended heavily toward marches and patriotic pieces, with a heavy larding of popular tunes. When the temperatures cooled, benefit concerts moved into the opera house, and people were charged fifteen or twenty-five cents to help with expenses. Sometimes the women of the community organized chicken-pie suppers to raise money for the band. A band, many people realized, not only provided enjoyable diversion and promoted local pride but also constituted a moral force in the community. An article by H. O. Rounds in the *Mirror* stated the point succinctly, "I know when my son is in a band room practicing under a competent leader six nights a week, that he is far from leaning over a pool table, standing at the bar, or playing cards, for the band is an antidote for these allurements."[9]

Just like band concerts, entertainment and activities at the opera house were reminiscent of the past. Blind Boone, who was famous throughout the Midwest for his piano playing, packed the opera house when he came to town in January 1912. Mostly, however, the troupes and performers who graced Mansfield's stage were less memorable, such as the "marvelous Willard," a magician among whose feats was "the catching of bullets in his teeth fired from a shot gun by a committee selected from the audience," and the Johnston Vaudeville Company, containing eight big acts and "some

of the best acrobats in this section of the country," including one billed as "the human monkey." As with many of the programs that appeared in town, this one was advertised as "a clean moral show."[10]

Before World War I, the opera house remained the social center of the community, drawing people out to enjoy visiting performers of character readings, music, and dramatic recitals. Lyceum series imported a variety of educational speakers and entertainment specialties for the benefit of the locals. Hometown talent performers probably outnumbered these outside acts, however. The opera house provided the setting for high school class plays and graduation ceremonies, locally performed operettas, youth piano recitals, New Year's Eve watch parties, union Thanksgiving church services, political rallies, and election-night poll watching. By 1913 movies had invaded the opera house. As time passed, their frequency increased, while other types of entertainment gradually dwindled. While the contents of the movies, in many cases, reinforced traditional values and beliefs (such as a 1915 two-reeler titled *The Persecution of the Christian Martyrs from the Crucifixion of Christ to the Death of Nero*), their ultimate impact was to introduce alien and often contradictory values and habits of thought that undermined tradition and localism.[11]

We do not know whether Laura and Almanzo chose to attend many of these activities, although we can assume that they did once in a while. They did become active in the Mansfield Agricultural and Stock Show after its debut in 1912. Seeking to promote the community and draw in people from neighboring towns, these fairs provided not only farm and garden exhibits but also a variety of entertainment, including horse races, baseball games, balloon ascensions, trapeze acts, carnival rides, musical performances, lectures, and pie-eating contests. At the second annual fair, held in 1913, Almanzo won first place and a prize of fifty cents for entering the best sheaf of millet in the grain-and-grasses division, and he won a two-dollar premium for having the best fat steer. The following year, he was listed rather than Laura, for some reason, as the prize winner for the best Pen Brown Leghorn chickens, for which he won a dollar. He also received a two-dollar prize for having the best Shorthorn Durham cow. The newspaper reported that "A. J. Wilder's prize-winning Durham cow gives 50 pounds of milk daily." Organizing these exhibits and contests required considerable volunteer labor, and the Wilders frequently offered their services in addition to entering specimens of their own crops and livestock.

In 1917, for example, Almanzo served as one of three superintendents of the horses-and-mules department, and Laura performed in a similar role for the poultry department.[12]

The distance separating Laura and Rose became more and more burdensome for them as time passed. They had not seen each other since 1911, and for both the separation was hard. Rose's marriage to Gillette Lane had begun to deteriorate, and money problems dogged both families. The parents had never been able to eke out much more than a bare living from their farm at Rocky Ridge, and by the middle of the decade the California real estate boom had subsided. Rose obtained a good job with the *San Francisco Bulletin,* but Gillette now had no steady position and was forced to pick up work wherever he could. The two lived from paycheck to paycheck and were unable to repay a loan of $250 that Laura and Almanzo had made to them. In one of her letters at Christmastime, Rose noted that "as usual, we are on the ragged edge of being entirely broke and only the last parting strands of my bank account stand between us and starvation until January first." Her parents, for their part, were hardly better off, still trying to pay off the mortgage on their place and worrying about what they would do for an income as they grew older and less physically able to work on the farm.[13]

Concerned about their welfare and feeling an obligation—as their only child—to look out for them, Rose dreamed up a variety of money-making schemes that she passed on as suggestions to them in letters. In one of them she indicated that with her mother's organizational skills she could launch a "Producers-Consumers League" to bypass local stores in the marketing of eggs and other farm products, to the benefit of both producers and consumers. Once established locally, they could range out as far as Kansas City in looking for outlets for their products. Although her parents would probably make only a few cents a day from the operation in the beginning, by persevering they might be able to turn the concept into "a big thing," Rose predicted. "This is only an idea," she told them, "take it for what it's worth." Another scheme that she came up with involved their working out exclusive agreements with restaurants in Springfield to use products from Rocky Ridge Farm on their tables, not only eggs but also strawberries, milk and cream, ham, and bacon. The hotels then could advertise on their menus, "All our eggs are new-laid from Rocky Ridge Farm" and "All our milk and cream is from Rocky Ridge Farm and is rich and strictly pure."

Rose's expansive vision of what her parents might be able to do with their farm hardly seemed calculated to reduce their workload as they grew older. She suggested, "Increase your herd of cows. Pretty soon buy milk cans, get a separator, and send milk & cream up to the hotel. . . . Next fall buy all the hams from all the country 'round, and all the way to Ava, at butchering time. Have a man make the pickle by your old recipes, treat them like Grandma Wilder used to, smoke 'em over hickory chips—sell them at a fancy price—'Rocky Ridge Farm Hickory-Cured Hams.'" Once Rose had an idea, her imagination would not quit. There were no limits, in her mind, to what could be done if her mother went about it like a businesswoman. "Farming is the business of the future, there isn't a question of it, and there's money in it if it's done on up-to-date principles," she enthusiastically advised.[14]

Meanwhile, Rose was trying to encourage her mother's writing career by suggesting story possibilities. She thought that the *Kansas City Star* could be an outlet for local-color stories. She suggested writing about the prisoners who had supposedly escaped from the Mansfield jail by lifting it off of its foundations ("that really did happen, didn't it? or something as ridiculous"). Rose would later publish a series of short stories in a less than complimentary mode about her memories of life in Mansfield while growing up, but now she encouraged her mother to write something about the town:

> and write it up in a tone rather complimentary than otherwise to Mansfield, picturing it as a peaceful little mountain village where the leading business men on a summer day play marbles in the shade of the depot, or pitch horseshoes in front of the blacksmith shop—the sort of a little story that will appear harmless enough to the editor, and make Mansfield sore as the dickens. It will sell fine. Written in a sort of matter of fact way, you know—YOU know exactly. You could sell anyway three thousand words of that—if you haven't the time, write me roughly the facts and figures and I will work it up for you.

Another time Rose suggested that Laura could take one of her own pieces about certified milk in California and simply "change a name or a sentence here and there and resell it" as a Missouri story.[15]

The great Panama-Pacific International Exposition held in San Francisco in 1915, a year after the opening of the Panama Canal, provided both an

opportunity and an incentive for mother and daughter finally to get together again. Rose encouraged her mother to take a train to California and paid for the ticket. "I simply can't stand being so homesick for you any more," she wrote, offering in addition to give her five dollars for every week she was gone from home as compensation for what she might lose by absenting herself from her chickens. "You can see San Francisco and the Fair, and meet my friends, and we can play together all the time that I'm not working," Rose wrote as a further enticement. The visit would also allow her mother to mingle with Rose's literary and artist friends and would help her think of new subjects to write about when she got home. Rose had recently been invited to submit stories to an eastern magazine, but, not having time to write, she offered Laura the chance to follow up on the opportunity. They would probably pay fifty dollars per story, much more than the five or ten dollars apiece that her mother was receiving from the *Ruralist.* "When you get things to running so that the farm work won't take up so much time you can do things like that," Rose told her. "And with the notes and mortgages paid off and your lovely home all built, you and Papa can take things easier. Next year you can maybe get off and make a little trip together to Louisiana or someplace."[16]

Laura initially resisted the idea of leaving Almanzo alone at Rocky Ridge to do the chores by himself and cook his own meals, but Rose eventually convinced her. Laura was eager to see her only child again and, not incidentally, to try to ascertain the status of her and Gillette's marriage, which Laura suspected was less than perfect. In addition, she would be able to investigate the possibility of their actually moving to the West Coast, which Rose was urging them to do, especially for the sake of Almanzo, who continued to suffer from the cold during the Missouri winters. As retirement loomed, they needed to reduce their pace at Rocky Ridge. Laura also looked forward to obtaining tutoring from her daughter on writing. Laura's writing career appeared to be stalled for the moment, and she was ready to listen to Rose's advice on how to promote it.

Laura boarded a train at the Mansfield depot on August 21, 1915, to begin her adventure, leaving Almanzo and their dog, Inky, behind to take care of the place. She stopped briefly in Springfield to visit an oculist before boarding a train headed north to Kansas City, where she caught a westbound heading toward San Francisco. As they moved onto the Kansas plains, the countryside left her unimpressed. "The land is so *flat,*" she wrote Almanzo.

When a lawyer from Nebraska sitting near her commented on the beauty of the landscape, she and an old Frenchman whom she had been talking to merely smiled at each other. In a letter from Denver, she told Almanzo that everything that she had observed from the train windows since she had left the Ozarks had been ugly. Nor was she favorably impressed by the Utah desert or the surrounding mountains. "They are simply frightful," she wrote. "Huge masses and ramparts of rock, just bare rock in every fantastic shape imaginable." But the Great Salt Lake struck her as beautiful as the train crossed it at night, with the moonlight creating "a path of silver across the water."[17]

Laura found San Francisco to be even lovelier, bathed as it was in light and color and with all its varied scenes, set astride the ocean, the Bay, and the hills. "You know I have never cared for cities," Laura wrote Almanzo upon arrival, "but San Francisco is simply the most beautiful thing." The exposition seemed like a wonderland to her, with its numerous buildings and attractions and rides. Describing it for Almanzo, she enthused, "The coloring is so soft and wonderful. Blues and reds and greens and yellows and browns and grays are all blended into one perfect whole without a jar anywhere. It is fairyland." She returned many times to visit the exhibit grounds with Rose or Gillette; sometimes all three went. "The Zone," with its many arcades and amusements, proved especially interesting to her. One of the places they visited was a mock Navajo village, where they saw Indians making pottery and baskets and weaving rugs. Although Laura did not care for the smell of the place, she discovered the Indians to be friendly and good-natured. She also was impressed by the Samoan dancers and thought that the people she saw in Chinatown were attractive.[18]

More than most people of her age and background, Laura opened herself up to people of other nationalities and races. Not surprisingly, she sometimes reflected some of the baser prejudices common at the time, but, in general, she treated everyone as fellow human beings who had been created in the image of God. One of the articles she wrote for the *Missouri Ruralist* after she returned to Mansfield drove the point home for her readers. In it she described how when she was walking through the Missouri exhibit at the fair she had overheard one woman telling a companion that she thoroughly disliked San Francisco. "Everywhere I go there is a Chinaman on one side, a Jap on the other and a n—— behind," she recalled hearing the woman say. Reflecting on the narrow-mindedness

exhibited by the statement, Laura commented, "These women were missing a great deal, for the foreign life of San Francisco is very interesting and the strange vari-colored people on the streets give a touch of color and picturesqueness that adds much to the charm of the city." Specifically, she noted the beauty of Italian children and the charm of the people in Chinatown. A further lesson that she drew from the story (there were always lessons to be derived from her stories) was that women did not actually need to travel in order to cultivate a sympathetic understanding of varied peoples; they could do it by staying at home and involving themselves in study clubs or in reading books and papers on their own. Then they could truly say, "I have traveled all over the world."[19]

Rose and Gillette (Laura generally referred to him by his first name of "Claire" in her letters) did not have a car, so they needed either to take public transportation or to walk. One day Rose estimated that she and Laura covered ten miles traipsing up Telegraph Hill, over to Fisherman's Wharf, and around the canneries along the shore of the Bay. Laura visited Rose's office at the *San Francisco Bulletin,* and Rose also organized a tea party for her mother with her friends and coworkers. Once they went to Oakland to listen to a Fritz Kreisler violin concert, and while in the area they walked around the grounds of the university at Berkeley. Rose continued to urge Laura to seriously consider reducing her and Almanzo's activities and moving to California. Rose took Laura on a train ride to the Santa Clara valley to look it over as a possible place for them to live. Laura admitted that the valley was indeed beautiful, if one liked intensively managed orchards, but while the roads were splendid and the towns were lovely, she could not imagine paying five hundred dollars an acre for land and trying to make a go of it. She disliked the heat and the dust and considered the "flat, flat land" tiresome. She was prepared to visit other places with Rose but wrote Almanzo, "I truly believe that when I come home and talk it all over with you we will decide to be satisfied where we are and figure out some way to cut down on our work and retire right there." That notion upset Rose, and Gillette joined her in trying to convince Laura that she and Almanzo could make a profit by practicing scientific farming on a small acreage.[20]

An alternative to their moving or trying to extract a larger income from their farm in Missouri was for Laura to increase her income from writing. She arrived in San Francisco as a willing student, ready to learn the proper techniques from her daughter, who by now was becoming well established

at the trade. Rose showed her how to block out a story about the Ozarks that she could complete after returning to Rocky Ridge. The experience was a confidence builder for Laura. "If I can only make it sell, it ought to help a lot and besides, I am learning so that I can write others for the magazines," she told Almanzo in a letter. "If I can only get started at that, it will sell for a good deal more than farm stuff." While Rose worked on her own assignments, Laura took over the housework so that they could have more time together on improving her writing skills. Laura admired Rose's success at her work and hoped that she could emulate it, even in a small way, but she realized that she would never be able to attack the task with the same intensity as Rose. She told Almanzo, "The more I see of how Rose works the better satisfied I am to raise chickens. I intend to try to do some writing that will count, but I would not be driven by the work as she is for anything and I do not see how she can stand it."[21]

Rose recognized the potential that her mother possessed as a writer and otherwise would not have tried to improve her skills. Although Laura lacked Rose's practiced skills with language, grammar, and story structure, she possessed a highly developed ear for description. More important, she had a mature ability to discover significance and meaning in ordinary happenings and convey them to readers in a straightforward—sometimes subtle—style. Laura's broad curiosity and her capacity for empathetic understanding contributed more to her writing success than did her mastery of technique or style. She possessed the potential to be a writer. The question now was whether she could latch onto appropriate subjects and an audience that would develop that potential.

An excerpt from one of her letters home to Almanzo indicated her ability to render full-blooded descriptions:

> We have had the thickest fog ever for several days. All night and all day we can hear the sirens on the different islands and headlands, and the ferries and ships at anchor in the bay keep their foghorns bellowing. We can not see the bay at all nor any part of San Francisco except the few close houses on Russian Hill. The foghorns sound so mournful and distressed, like lost souls calling to each other through the void. (Of course, no one ever lost a soul calling, but that's the way it sounds.) It looks as though Russian Hill were afloat in a gray sea and Rose and I have taken the fancy that it is loosened from the rest of the land and floating across the sea to Japan. That is the feeling it gives one.[22]

At the end of October, almost two months after her arrival on the West Coast, Laura was asked to write several articles about the exposition, including a feature story about the Missouri exhibits for the *Missouri Ruralist*. She wished she had been asked sooner so that she could have been working on them all along. She quickly began the task, realizing that Almanzo, although he was not willing to admit it, was getting impatient for her return. Rose wrote her father to say that Laura was becoming homesick and that she worried about him since she was not there to cook for and take care of him. The feature article that Laura sent to the *Ruralist* received front-page billing. It excitedly recounted how Missouri had "showed them" at the fair, making a proud record by taking more prizes, she reported, than any other state except California. She undoubtedly had Rose in mind, and perhaps was wishfully thinking of herself, when she commented on the successes of Missouri authors. Noting that bookshelves in the exhibit building contained more than fifteen hundred volumes written by authors from the state, she observed, "Hundreds of persons have been surprised to learn here for the first time the fact that our state has produced more successful writers than any other in the union."[23]

An accident shortly before her scheduled departure kept Laura in the hospital for several days, although she could have been hurt much worse. She had been heading downtown with Gillette when he jumped off the streetcar before it came to a complete stop. Startled by his sudden movement, she fell off the car herself, hitting the back of her head on the pavement. Fortunately, she did not suffer a concussion and little damage was done, but the injury did require a short hospital stay until she built back her strength. "She does not want anyone in Mansfield to know about it," Rose wrote Almanzo, "because she says it looks as if she could not take care of herself in a city." By the time she left San Francisco in late October, Laura had largely accomplished the goals of her visit: seeing her daughter again after a long absence, trying to ascertain the condition of the Lanes' marriage, picking up some writing tips, scouting out the possibilities of moving to California, and trying to determine how soon they might expect repayment of the loan that the Wilders had made to the young couple.[24]

Left unresolved in Laura's mind was the future of Rose's marriage and repayment of the loan. Gillette had been a gracious host to his mother-in-law, taking her to the fair several times, and he and Rose had put on a show of togetherness for her benefit. Their marriage, however, did not have

long to last, and Rose soon left him permanently, making the divorce final in 1918. Part of the problem, at least, lay in Gillette's difficulty in finding a job and, with it, the many schemes he had concocted for real estate or other ventures. These seldom bore fruit, and Rose simply tired of them. Laura was told that she and Almanzo would receive their $250 once a real estate deal that Gillette was involved in was finalized, but the people he was doing business with apparently were unable to keep their end of the bargain. At this time, the parents were on both the giving and the receiving ends of the money equation. Later, as Rose achieved greater success as a writer and obtained bigger paychecks, they would increasingly be on the receiving end of her generosity until, in the end, she became heir to the accumulated royalties her mother would earn from her own books.

Home in Mansfield, Laura settled back into her usual routine of cooking, keeping house, tending garden, caring for her flock of chickens, and helping Almanzo when he needed an extra hand. But San Francisco had made a big change in her life. As soon as she returned, she started writing on a regular basis for the *Ruralist*. Almost without fail after this her column appeared twice monthly, and Laura began to earn recognition as a farm-paper writer. Although it was not quite the career step she or Rose might have wished for, it was at least an improvement, and during the next several years her ability to write a column every two weeks that would appeal to a varied readership honed her skill with words, standing her in good stead later when she moved from farm journalism toward fiction writing. Meanwhile, she also became more heavily involved in club activity than she had been earlier, playing a central role in establishing two different study groups: the Athenians and the Justamere Club. In addition, much of her time was spent working with a farm-loan organization, and she continued to be active in church and lodge activities. Middle age became for Laura an occasion not for withdrawal but for increased involvement in the community.

Laura's first *Missouri Ruralist* columns were all individually titled, and they indicated that their author was "Mrs. A. J. Wilder," the paper's "Home" editor. "Life Is an Adventure: Voyages of Discovery Can Be Made in Your Rocking-Chair," "Facts versus Theories," "Haying while the Sun Shines," "Learning to Work Together," "Thanksgiving Time," and "Keep the Saving Habit" were typical of the themes she developed. In May 1919 the column took the regular title of "The Farm Home," and from June 1921 until she stopped writing for the paper three and a half years later, the column was

called "As a Farm Woman Thinks." The paper's twice-monthly schedule required versatility and creativity in conjuring up new subjects. Describing her own experiences at Rocky Ridge Farm could carry her only so far. She looked for interesting items in the newspaper, developments in agricultural methods, and general observations about human nature, based upon her own experience and reading. From time to time she culled something from her memory, perhaps a girlhood experience that might have some lesson to impart to her readers. Earlier, Rose had encouraged her to draw upon her own "life story" for material. The brief vignettes from her past that Laura now sometimes included in her column provided a start in this direction. Later, she would transform some of them into episodes in her novels.[25]

The *Ruralist* columns generally ran between eight hundred and a thousand words. Almost always they described a situation, episode, or development and drew some kind of meaning or lesson from it for her readers. Before San Francisco, the few articles that she had published in the *Ruralist* were mainly geared to concrete descriptions of people (including herself and Almanzo) who had made successes in farming. Now, unencumbered by any particular formula, she turned her attention toward a variety of subjects. Mostly she advised readers about how to enjoy life more fully and how to become better people rather than instruct them about how to become better farmers or homemakers. In focusing her attention upon the values that people should live by, Laura was providing them with moral lessons in nonfictional form that she later would serve up in fictional form in her novels.[26]

Most, but not all, of the values that she espoused served to reinforce tradition and convention. Hard work, honesty, thrift, and self-help were, not surprisingly, central themes. William Holmes McGuffey, Horatio Alger, and the self-help promoters of the 1910s and 1920s defined the essence of American character for many people, including Mrs. A. J. Wilder of Mansfield, Missouri. Her own experiences with her husband on Rocky Ridge Farm proved that hard work pays off. Work imparted meaning to life and made leisure enjoyable. Laura worried that the old incentive to work was breaking down and that more and more people were shirking their responsibilities. People needed to love their work—work with a capital W—for in meaningful labor they would "grow stronger and more beautiful of soul."[27]

Values such as industry, frugality, and independence were in themselves good, but, like anything else, they could be carried too far. Laura emphasized the need for balance in people's lives, because "every good becomes evil when carried to excess by poor, faulty mortals." A frequent theme, based heavily upon her own practice, was the need for thrift, but she realized that economy, too, could be carried to extremes and become miserliness. Even excessive religiousness could turn into fanaticism and intolerance.[28]

This emphasis on balance in Laura's thinking helped her to avoid some of the tendencies that inclined her daughter to shift moods abruptly and to swing wildly from the extreme left to the extreme right in her political views and to adhere fanatically to certain attitudes and principles. Laura, too, believed in self-help and independence. "A bird in a cage is not a pretty sight, to me," she wrote, anticipating an image of free flight that she would later use to describe herself in *The Long Winter.* But self-reliance needed to be supplemented by neighborliness and a sense of community. Laura was especially partial to "workings," where people traded labor with one another in harvesting crops, husking corn, and erecting buildings. One of her columns recounted how once, when a farmer became ill and was unable to plant his crop of oats, his neighbors did the work for him. This "spirit of helpfulness and comradeship" was something that Laura wanted to cultivate in people. Government should remain small and as unobtrusive as possible, she believed, but it did have valid functions to perform. Contrary to those who wanted to abolish federal regulatory agencies after the world war, Laura preferred to treat each department on its own merits. In citing the case of excessive sugar prices, for example, she observed, "If the sugar equalization board is any curb on the sugar trust, it is devoutly to be hoped that the board will be continued, especially when one remembers that five persons are said to control the sugar output of the world."[29]

Laura sometimes betrayed an antiurban bias in her references to the prevalence of noise, dirt, and danger in large cities, but she also appreciated some of the amenities of city life that remained in short supply in rural America. She accepted and approved of the benefits of modern technology, but she also preached the virtues of small-scale agriculture and, like Henry David Thoreau, urged people to simplify their lives. Both now and later when she began to write fiction, she concentrated on the ordinary occurrences of everyday life. In a *Ruralist* column in July 1917 the bouquets of wildflowers that Almanzo brought her put her in mind

of the days of her childhood when she and Mary would walk to Sunday school with their father from their house on Plum Creek. "The little white daisies with their hearts of gold grew thickly along the path," she recalled. "I have forgotten what I was taught on those days also. I was only a little girl, you know. But I can still plainly see the grass and the trees and the path winding ahead, flecked with sunshine and shadow and the beautiful golden-hearted daisies scattered all along the way." These were the kinds of ordinary things that people might be expected to forget as time went by, Laura commented, "but at the long last, I am beginning to learn that it is the sweet, simple things of life which are the real ones after all."[30]

These were some of the lessons that Laura had absorbed after a half century of living: there is beauty in everyday things if people will just look for it; people keep growing all the time; the word *can't* should be eliminated from our vocabularies; there are two sides to everything; don't worry; life is more interesting when we look below surface appearances; we learn by example, so children need to be taught well at home; and people always should be ready to grasp opportunity. Always on the lookout for deeper meanings and for lessons applicable to daily living, Laura understood well that the precepts to be derived from experience can be contradictory. One column, for example, examined the conflicting messages we sometimes receive, such as "a stitch in time saves nine" versus "it is never too late to mend."[31]

Many things drew Laura's ire, among them selfishness, overreliance on experts, the tendency to find fault with others, negative—as opposed to friendly—gossip, swearing, relativistic ideas, and the failure to follow Christian precepts. If a single lesson stood out, it was the necessity of love, a message she derived no doubt both from the warm and loving family environment that she had grown up in and from her own experiences as an adult. The commitment to love was strengthened by her religious beliefs. While seldom mentioned explicitly in her columns, biblical teachings lay at the core of her thinking. Once she observed, "As a child I learned my Bible lessons by heart, in the good old-fashioned way, and once won the prize for repeating correctly more verses from the Bible than any other person in the Sunday school." As an adult she kept close at hand a handwritten list of Scripture verses that she found especially meaningful. Rejecting simple nostalgia as an adequate guide for living, Laura proposed a better approach: "Love and service, with a belief in the future and expectation of better

things in the tomorrow of the world is a good working philosophy." Love naturally grew and matured within the family setting and revealed itself in the willingness of family members to sacrifice for others. Love stood in opposition to anger, which was a destructive force in people's lives. But love had to be given freely; it could not "be demanded or driven or insisted upon. It must be wooed to be won."[32]

Laura's regular columns displayed the workings of her mind. She was engaged in the developments of the time—technological change, social and economic trends, war, and politics—but mostly concerned herself with everyday events. Just as she urged her readers to aim at a sense of balance in their thoughts and behaviors, Laura, in her approach to the world, had two opposing beliefs: a healthy regard for fact and experience on the one hand and a strong sense of idealism and wonder on the other. In warning people not to become overreliant upon experts, she expressed her strong belief that fact superseded theory. Experience, in her view, was the great teacher, and one had to be attentive to it and learn its lessons. But experience and surface appearances did not encompass everything. A developed sense of wonder was also conducive to a fully lived life. People needed to probe beneath the surfaces of things to search for deeper meaning; thus, her admonition to "look for the fairies." Surely there was no harm in idealizing things, and in fact there was much to gain. "There are deeps beyond deeps in the life of this wonderful world of ours," she wrote. Revising the metaphor, she encouraged her readers to emulate the lotus plant and to "strive toward light and purity into the sunshine of the good." The wisdom Laura dispensed in her biweekly columns gave evidence of an active, searching intelligence and later found its way into her novels.[33]

As soon as the United States became involved in World War I, Laura made the conflict a frequent topic in her columns. Rather than condemning American participation as un-Christian or inhumane, she gave her full support to the war effort and to President Wilson and other governmental leaders. In her first column in May 1917, one month after Congress declared war, Laura urged her female readers to do their part in "fighting for Uncle Sam" by taking their place on the battle line just behind the trenches. "Our work is not spectacular, and in doing it faithfully we shall win no war medals or decorations, but it is absolutely indispensable," she asserted.[34]

Soon young men from around the area were enlisting and registering for the draft. As elsewhere around the United States, Mansfield's residents

organized farewell dinners for their "boys" and wished them well as they departed for boot camp from the Frisco train depot. After a farewell dinner at the park on the square in August, the soldiers-to-be lined up for people to shake their hands. Afterward the crowd joined in singing "America," and Reverend John O. Stine pronounced a benediction before the train left the station. Laura observed that with so many local young men leaving, it brought the war closer to home. Evidence of its impact was everywhere. A representative from the State Agricultural College at Columbia came to Mansfield to discuss how farmers could increase their production. A local committee set up to coordinate these activities was chaired by the Wilders' friend J. W. Brentlinger. As the bureaucratic wheels in Washington began to turn, a variety of emergency agencies sprang up to coordinate production and manage the economy.[35]

Much of the initiative for converting to a wartime footing proceeded from local individuals, businesses, and organizations. The Frisco Railroad distributed copies of "The Frisco Man Creed" to all of its employees. It proclaimed, "I hereby affirm my loyalty to the United States and its flag. It is my flag and my country, and I am ready at all times to defend and serve it. I also attest my loyalty to the Frisco railroad, and will do my utmost to protect its property." A number of churches designated the first Sunday in July as "Patriotic Sunday," and their Sunday schools contributed their collections that day to the Red Cross. A local unit of that organization was formally put in place in Mansfield in August 1917. "Mrs. Bessie Wilder" was listed among its seventy-seven charter members. Women also had an opportunity to participate in the war effort by signing up with the Women's Committee of the Council of National Defense. Thirty-six women enrolled in Mansfield at the initial registration, and it is interesting that in reporting the sign-up the newspaper used their first names rather than their husbands' names. In the reports of the activities of women's clubs, church groups, county-fair prize winners, and other women's organizations, the participants were usually identified simply as the wives of their husbands. World War I, therefore, can be seen as part of the transition from "Mrs. A. J. Wilder" to "Laura Ingalls Wilder." But when Mansfield went "over the top" on the third Liberty Loan drive in April 1918, and the *Mirror* listed the names of all the bond purchasers, it was "Mrs. A. J. Wilder" who was named again.[36]

The war became a pervasive presence in people's lives. Following directives from the Food Administration in Washington, Mansfieldians observed

wheatless and meatless days as conservation measures. Daylight saving time went into effect as a means of conserving fuel. The newspaper frequently reprinted letters that had been sent home from men in the service. The Committee on Public Information dispatched "Four Minute Men" to deliver patriotic talks before movie showings and at community gatherings. School concerts included obligatory war tunes on their programs. In newspaper cartoons, in movies at the Nugget Theater, in church-service songs, and in a variety of other ways, the war constantly was brought home to people. "The Kaiser, the Beast of Berlin" packed filmgoers in at the theater for two days in August 1918. The propaganda movie was advertised as "a picture which makes American blood boil and holds the audience with its dramatic intensity." On New Year's Eve, at the end of America's first year of participation, an overflow crowd at the opera house enjoyed a "war entertainment" arranged by Dr. F. H. Riley, president of the Wright County Council of Defense, Mrs. W. M. Divan, chair of the Women's Committee, and Miss Bertha Miller. To open the program, the latter sang "Keep the Home Fires Burning," accompanied by the Mansfield concert band. There followed in succession several other musical numbers, a drill performed by twelve girls trained by Dr. Riley, a humorous skit titled "The Awkward Squad," an address called "The War" by a local politician, appearances by two soldiers who were home on furlough, an "instructive talk" about the Council of Defense, a reading by Miss Miller called "A Voice from a Far Country," and an appeal for contributions of time and money to the Red Cross.[37]

Although Laura was seldom mentioned by the *Mansfield Mirror* as participating in community activities and events outside of her membership in study clubs and the Methodist Ladies Aid, the paper did mention her involvement in the Red Cross Society during the war, which led her to work with people outside her usual circle. For example, meetings at the Masonic Hall in April 1918 for making undershirts, hospital garments, and surgical bandages included study-club standbys such as the wives of N. J. Craig, Dwight W. Hoover, J. A. Riley, W. M. Divan, G. C. Freeman, J. A. Fuson, and P. W. Newton, as well as many other less familiar names. The following month people donated items for a Red Cross sale to raise funds for the organization. Almanzo was listed as contributing a brown Leghorn rooster, two hens, and a bushel of potatoes, while Laura provided fifteen thoroughbred brown Leghorn eggs and a rooster. Six hundred people were

served dinner by the women before the auction, which netted $2,074.35 for the cause. In one of her *Missouri Ruralist* columns, Laura lamented that she had not been able to spend as much time on Red Cross work as some of her friends in town, but later, after thinking about everything that had been accomplished, she felt better.[38]

In President Woodrow Wilson, Laura thought she perceived the perfect embodiment of the kinds of high ideals for which the war was being fought. His high-minded rhetoric coincided perfectly with her own thinking about the need for people to embody elevated purposes and principles in their lives. She praised the "beautiful ideals" that he enunciated in his wartime messages. After the president's speech to the nation announcing the country's war aims in January 1918, Laura lauded its statement of American principles. "As a nation we stand for unselfishness, courage and self-sacrifice," she wrote in a column titled "Victory May Depend on You." Pursuing this theme, she noted, "It is indeed a 'war in each man's heart,' and as the battles go in these hearts of ours so will be the victory or defeat of the armies in the field, for a nation can be no greater than the sum of the greatness of its people. There never before has been a war where the action of each individual had such a direct bearing on the whole world."[39]

After a false report that the Armistice had been signed, followed by a premature victory party, Mansfield's residents participated in a real celebration on November 11, 1918. People were awakened by wild shouting, blaring whistles, and clanging church bells. School was dismissed for the day, and folks bedecked their houses with flags, paraded around town, fired guns into the air, and hung the kaiser in effigy. Several people drove to Hartville to take part in the celebration at the county seat. Laura was on the refreshments committee for the homecoming bash staged the following May for returning soldiers. The war reinforced patriotism and nationalism in the United States, although during the next several years many people would lose their enthusiasm for foreign adventures. But the experience also expanded many people's horizons, making them more aware of and concerned about what was happening beyond their country's borders. A meeting to raise funds for Armenian and Syrian relief was held in the Methodist church, and several of Laura's friends were appointed to the local committee. Laura herself would soon be made more aware of places such as this by letters from Rose, who was traveling abroad.[40]

Laura turned fifty the year the United States entered the war. If aging was supposed to slow a person down, she did not appear to be following form. If anything, she seemed to be getting busier as time went by. In 1917, for example, Laura helped organize and then became secretary-treasurer of the Mansfield branch of the National Farm Loan Association, which received its funds from the federal government. In one of her articles for the *Ruralist* she noted how, from time to time, she would join Almanzo in the field when he needed her help. Just as a farmer needed to be master of many trades, she indicated, a wife, too, must be ready to tackle many challenges. Besides being available to assist her husband at a variety of tasks,

> with brains, and muscle if necessary, the farmer's wife must know her own business, which includes the greatest variety of trades and occupations ever combined in one all-around person. Think of them! Cook, baker, seamstress, laundrywoman, nurse, chambermaid and nurse girl. She is a poultry keeper, an expert in dairy work, a specialist in canning, preserving and pickling and besides all else she must be the mother of the family and a smiling hostess.

In describing the typical farm woman, Laura was describing herself. Still, she wanted more.[41]

Clues to Laura's personality can be found in her *Ruralist* columns. In fact, they are one of the best sources we have, since she did not leave a large cache of letters, diaries, and journals into which she poured out her feelings like Rose did. She possessed a sense of humor, even about herself. In a column about the virtues of tactfulness, she recalled how once, having been less than tactful at a party, she had tried to make amends for it. Waiting for an opportunity to say something nice to the hostess before she left, all she could think of saying was, "Oh, wasn't that water good." The episode left her feeling, she said, "like a little girl who had blundered at her first party."[42]

She insisted so much on the virtues of laughter and cheerfulness that it leads one to suspect that eliciting them in herself was something of a task. In the company of other people, she generally kept her emotions under control and maintained a healthy social distance. Restraint, not exuberance, came naturally to her. Unpleasantness and harsh words repelled her, although she was capable of them herself. She could be highly judgmental of others and was quick to fault those who did not live up to her own high religious and

moral standards. Thus, perhaps she felt it necessary to work at and give the appearance of "friendship and cheerfulness and hospitality" because they were not easily achieved. Every home, she informed her readers, possesses "a sort of composite spirit composed of the thoughts and feelings" of family members that is easily discernible to visitors. "If the members of a home are ill-tempered and quarrelsome, how quickly you feel it when you enter the house," she observed. "If they are kindly, generous, good-tempered people, you will have a feeling of warmth and welcome that will make you wish to stay. Sometimes you feel that you must be very prim and dignified and at another place you feel a rollicking good humor and a readiness to laugh and be merry." She set the second type of person forth as an ideal, but most of the time she probably conformed more to the image of primness and dignity than she did to laughter and merriment.[43]

Laura told people that she was not musically inclined, that the only musical instrument she was able to play was the phonograph, and that she sang only when she knew she would be drowned out by others. Yet, she possessed "a little music in her feet" and later would make her father's fiddle and family's singing a central theme in her fiction. "We do seem at times to have more than one personality," she wrote in one of her columns, a truth that could have been derived from observing herself. If she had a tendency to be bossy with Almanzo at times, she realized her fault and fought against it. A neighbor told editor John Case, who was writing an article about Laura for the *Missouri Ruralist,* that Mrs. Wilder possessed a delightful personality. Always bright and cheery, she knew how to look at the sunny side of things, Case wrote. If Laura and Almanzo sometimes quarreled about how to manage the farm, it was a sign not only of disagreement but also of their mutual willingness to work together and make cooperative decisions. She and Almanzo were partners in every sense.[44]

Above all, Laura grasped hold of ambition and maintained a sense of destiny, not sure exactly wherein her achievement would ultimately lie. It was unusual for a rural-Ozarks resident to hope for such success, least of all a woman at a time when their options and opportunities remained heavily circumscribed. But somewhere inside herself, Laura retained a sense that she was different from other people, that there was something beyond the ordinary that she could accomplish. By the turn of the decade she could already discern in Rose's success a sign that ambition and determination could overcome mighty barriers. Frequently, her mind turned back to the

fairies and the dreams and fantasies that they embodied. In a column in November 1922 she recounted an Irish fable in which the fairy king told a hesitant horseman as he contemplated a high barrier that needed to be crossed, "Throw your heart over the wall, then follow it!" Hesitancy and doubt must be banished, Laura counseled her readers. "If we would win success in anything," she advised, "when we come to a wall that bars our way we must throw our hearts over and then follow confidently."[45]

The wall that barred Laura's way, as she moved into her fifties, was less a barrier denying her access to opportunity than a failure on her part to understand just what it was that she hoped to achieve. During the war, she had been caught up in the frenzy and then had gone through the transition to peace, confronting all the problems others did in trying to return to normal conditions. There were many things to keep her busy: housework, chores on the farm, her women's clubs, church activities, writing for the *Ruralist,* and just being a neighbor. There remained the possibility of taking her writing beyond local farm-journal markets and breaking into new markets, something Rose could help her with if she could come up with some good subjects.

In June 1919, thanks to Rose, Laura's article "Whom Will You Marry?" was published in *McCall's* magazine. Rather than her usual "Mrs. A. J. Wilder," she used the pen name "Laura Ingalls Wilder" to identify herself. The article was part of a series that Rose's editor friend Bessie Beatty was running in the magazine. Beatty had met Laura during her visit to San Francisco in 1915, and it was probably at Rose's suggestion that Beatty now invited Laura to write on the subject of marriage from a farm woman's point of view. The finished product became a tribute to the virtues of farm wives, describing the contributions they made to the success of the farm and the partnership they entered into with their husbands at the time of marriage. There was no reason to pity a farmer's wife, for she, of necessity, combined the desires of the "modern woman" with the traditional activities of housekeeping. "On the farm a woman may have both economic independence and a home life as perfect as she cares to make it," the article asserted. "Farm women have always been wage-earners and partners in their husband's business. Such a creature as the woman parasite has never been known among us. Perhaps this is one reason why 'feminism' has never greatly aroused us." This statement perfectly expressed the thirty-year relationship of Laura and Almanzo.[46]

Laura must have voiced some surprise about or even chided Rose about the amount of rewriting that she had done on the piece from New York City, where she was now living, before sending it to Bessie Beatty. Rose wrote back in reply, "Don't be absurd about my doing the work on your article. I didn't re-write it a bit more than I rewrite Mary Heaton Vorse's articles, or Inez Haynes Irwin's stories. And not so much, for at least your copy was all the meat of the article." She explained why she had deleted some material that her mother had written about large corporate trusts, and she noted that the payment for the article, while modest, was "really a fairly decent price for one article of a series considering that your name has as yet no commercial value." Rose went on to encourage her mother to revise an article that she had already written at Rose's suggestion: the situation of modern girls in comparison with life when she was a girl. Laura expressed reservations about writing on the subject, prompting Rose to comment: "If you really don't want to do it, why let it go. There's no use making oneself miserable for the sake of an article more or less. I thought the subject would be an interesting one to you, that when you really began to think about it lots of new aspects of the question would occur to you, and that it would be fun to turn them around in your mind and work them out."[47]

She returned the draft to her mother with detailed comments on how she thought it ought to be rewritten, with much more attention paid to description and detail. "If you want to do it over, this way," Rose encouraged her, "I don't think there is the least chance that you will fail to sell it. Do it, and send it on again, and then if it has to be reshaped a bit, or cut to fit, I will do that for you and sell it to [Beatty]. You want to follow up your first article with another one very quickly, in order not to lose the advertising value of the first one, but to add to it." Meanwhile, Rose indicated that she had not had time to go over some children's stories that Laura had also sent along to her. "I glanced through them, and think them good," she indicated. "But they are not so important as the articles, for there is no opportunity to make a name with children's stories. I will get to them as soon as possible and see what can be done about marketing them, however."[48]

What the nature of these "children's stories" was is impossible to say. Four years earlier, while working as a newspaperwoman, Rose had used several of her mother's poems, such as "Where Sunshine Fairies Go," "The Faery Dew Drop," and "Naughty Four O'Clocks," in a feature for the *San Francisco Bulletin* titled "The Tuck 'Em In Corner." It would be a long time before

Rose would realize how lucrative writing for children could be. Meanwhile, Laura, for one reason or another, did not succeed in responding to Rose's challenge to write more articles for national magazines, for it was not until 1925 that, once again with Rose's assistance, she managed to place two articles in *Country Gentleman* about living in a farm home.[49]

Meanwhile, life went on at Rocky Ridge, Laura continued to write columns for the *Missouri Ruralist,* dispense loans and do the bookkeeping for the National Farm Loan Association, and stay actively involved in her various church and club activities. It was with great joy and expectation that she and Almanzo heard from Rose that she was planning to return home to stay with them for a while. After living for a time in New York City's Greenwich Village, Rose had traveled to Europe in May 1920, visiting Paris, Vienna, Prague, London, and Berlin, as well as Budapest, Sarajevo, Constantinople, Athens, Cairo, Baghdad, Beirut, and other points. She took an almost mystical liking to Albania, living for an extended period in its capital, Tirana, and befriending a teenage boy named Rexh Meta, who, she believed, in acting as her guide along dangerous mountain trails had been responsible for saving her life. Later she would pay the expenses for his education at Cambridge University in England.[50]

After almost four years of traveling, Rose sailed home to the United States in November 1923. After staying several weeks in New York, where she made connections with old friends and literary people, she boarded a train for St. Louis and then for Springfield, arriving in Mansfield just in time for Christmas. Laura met her at the depot, and, after taking a day to recuperate her energy, Rose had her father drive her into town to pick up her baggage at the depot and to say hello to some people whom she had not seen for years. With their daughter back home to stay with them, Laura and Almanzo were happy and content.[51]

Taken in 1883, this is the earliest known photograph of De Smet's
Calumet Avenue (Main Street). (Aubrey Sherwood)

Laura Wilder as a young woman.
(South Dakota State Historical Society)

Charles and Caroline Ingalls and their four daughters in the early 1890s.
Left to right are Caroline, Carrie, Laura, Charles, Grace, and Mary.
(South Dakota State Historical Society)

Looking somewhat out of place while posing in front of a Florida backdrop,
the Wilders soon returned to their more familiar South Dakota.
(Herbert Hoover Presidential Library)

Laura posed in front of the little house on the east edge of Mansfield that she
and Almanzo called home for several years during the early 1900s.
(Herbert Hoover Presidential Library)

Downtown Mansfield around the turn of the century, looking west on the main
street. The town square is on the left, and the Farmers and Merchants Bank
is on the right. (Herbert Hoover Presidential Library)

Mansfieldians celebrate the completion of the twelve-mile railroad spur to
Ava in August 1908. (Herbert Hoover Presidential Library)

Almanzo putting up hay at Rocky Ridge.
(Herbert Hoover Presidential Library)

Laura's kitchen at Rocky Ridge as it looked in 1924.
(Herbert Hoover Presidential Library)

The living room of the English-style rock house that Rose built for her
parents in 1928 and where Laura wrote her first three novels.
(Herbert Hoover Presidential Library)

Rose in the living room of the Rocky Ridge farmhouse, where she lived from 1928 to 1935. (Laura Ingalls Wilder–Rose Wilder Lane Home and Museum)

Laura and Almanzo at the *De Smet News* office on Old Settlers' Day, 1939. (Herbert Hoover Presidential Library)

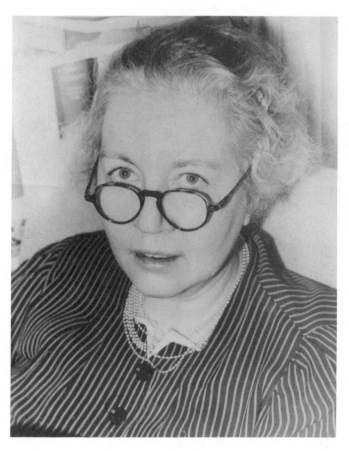

Rose Wilder Lane in 1942.
(Herbert Hoover Presidential Library)

Laura and Almanzo at Rocky Ridge during the 1940s.
(Laura Ingalls Wilder–Rose Wilder Lane
Home and Museum)

The Wilders talking to visitors at their home on
July 4, 1948. (William Anderson)

Laura Ingalls Wilder autographing one of her books,
1952. (American Library Association)

# 6

## *Turning to Autobiography*

### 1923–1932

✍

*R*ose was exhausted when Laura met her at the Mansfield depot after an all-night train ride from St. Louis, with a changeover in Springfield. It had been four years since their daughter had been home, and Laura and Almanzo were delighted to see her again. But she was hardly a girl anymore. Gray was beginning to streak her hair, lines that they had not noticed earlier creased her face, and some of the spring had gone out of her step. At thirty-seven, their only child was approaching middle age, the realization of which left Rose periodically depressed during the next several years.[1]

The reason Rose had come home again, after several years of adventuring in foreign places, is not entirely clear. She had hoped to utilize her experiences in Europe and the Middle East as material for her writing, but little had come from those adventures. Her finances were precarious, she had lost contact with many of her friends, and she was physically exhausted. To her writer friend Guy Moyston she explained, "In Baghdad I got darn tired of picturesqueness, caravanserais [sic] and camels and Arabs—and though, between ourselves, that was not my whole reason for returning, I am now darn glad I left Samarkand without the sunshine of my presence, and beat it back through Paris and New York." She also felt an obligation

to her parents, who at fifty-seven and sixty-seven were unable to work as much around the farm as they previously had. Time was creeping up on them, and now she felt duty-bound to look after them. She searched for some arrangement that would minister to their needs and simultaneously secure her own freedom.[2]

To what extent this sense of responsibility was imposed upon her by her parents and to what degree it flowed from Rose's own dutifulness and personal needs is difficult to sort out. Certainly her parents were delighted to see her and to have her around again; her mother especially could be clingy and stubborn. After only a month at Rocky Ridge, Rose wrote to Guy Moyston, "I don't know whether I shall ever be able to get away from Mansfield again or not. My mother is old and not very well, and wants me to stay here." If not for that, she said, she would have been in New York working to get back to Albania. But while Laura's health was not good in early 1924 and remained precarious for some time (she contracted ptomaine poisoning the following year) and while Almanzo, as always, needed to take things relatively easy, neither of them was exactly feeble. He had another twenty-five years to live, she thirty-three. Feeling obligated to supplement their income, Rose contributed five hundred dollars a year for their support. But her sense of physical entrapment on the farm is difficult to understand aside from her own personal needs and feelings. Perhaps it emerged out of guilt that she had left them at such a young age and stayed out of their lives for so long. Perhaps it was indecision about what to do with her own life. Or it may have resulted from a continuing sense of subordination to her mother, who kindled in her contradictory emotions of affection and resentment.[3]

Being an only child compounded the problem, intensifying the emotional bonds—as well as conflicts—between the generations. "I know, you have the same feeling about your mother that I have about mine," Rose wrote Guy. "Only it isn't so bad for you, because you're one of three, and I'm the only one. And besides, you're a son, and I a daughter. Men aren't expected to stay at home." Both parents were immensely proud of their daughter and reveled in her success. At the same time, they wished she would settle down, lead a conventional life, and raise a happy family. Meanwhile, she was the only one to whom they could look for financial support in their old age. Rose, for her part, was intensely aware that they were growing increasingly dependent upon her. "If we didn't have families,

living would be a simple job," she sighed. "Or perhaps if we had bigger families." She concocted a variety of schemes in an effort to resolve her dilemma: move her parents to a city apartment, send her father to warmer climes for the winter, find a farm for them in California, or—impractically—have them move to England.[4]

Rose's concern for her parents was genuine and well-meaning, but some of her motives for finding them a permanent place to live were selfish. She was as interested in her own freedom as she was in their welfare. One possible avenue of escape that occurred to her was to take her mother on a trip to Paris and then send her home to Mansfield while she proceeded to other places. "It wouldn't be like just packing up and leaving again," she rationalized. Vague feelings of guilt no doubt intertwined with resentment, as Rose fretted about having to behave as her mother's "slavey," dutifully "scrubbing floors and washing windows and hauling water and bringing in wood and washing dishes three times a day and peeling potatoes and waiting on the pigs, and all the rest of it. It's either do it, or see my mother—who's simply broken down under it and should be in a hospital. What the hell can one do? It's ridiculous."[5]

Once the initial glow of being home with her parents wore off, life at Rocky Ridge quickly settled down to dull routine. Almanzo and Laura's days were brightened by Rose's presence. Despite church functions, Justamere and other club activities, occasional visits with neighbors, and trips to town for groceries and other business, living on the farm could be suffocating for someone like Rose. Laura relished having her daughter home with her and let her know it, but she also induced guilt feelings in Rose by reminding her of how lonesome it could be without her. Once, after a friend had departed, Laura commented, "Now can you imagine what it is like when you go, and there is *nobody?*" While her parents hoped that she might stay with them permanently, Rose quickly felt entrapped, considering life in Mansfield intolerable. Letters to distant friends sounded her litany of frustration, hopelessness, and resentment at her imprisonment on the farm. Generally, however, she managed to hide these feelings from her parents and from others with whom she interacted in the ordinary round of activities. Rose acted her part convincingly, leading people to believe that she was enjoying herself. She created a wall between her mundane interactions with people and her personal feelings and thoughts. She made it difficult to penetrate her carefully crafted facade of a gay, witty, happy-go-lucky extrovert who

was interested in everything and everybody. Only in her letters and in sporadically kept diaries and journals did she lay bare her darker moods and more irreverent speculations.[6]

Rose's presence at Rocky Ridge enlivened the household in many ways. A steady stream of her friends from New York and elsewhere passed through the farmhouse to visit her, some settling in to stay for extended periods of time. Catherine Brody, a newspaperwoman from New York whom Rose had met in Paris, stayed with the family for several days while on her way to California. At the end of March, Guy Moyston, who was headed in the other direction after working on a play in California, accepted Rose's invitation to visit and wound up staying for three months. The two mixed fun and work, going on a fishing trip, taking long walks, and bringing in the cows when the sun went down. In the meantime, they started collaborating on a magazine serial and a play. The relationship between them was more than professional. The two had met when she was working for the *San Francisco Bulletin* and he was a reporter for the Associated Press. They corresponded regularly throughout the 1920s, and she eventually turned down his marriage proposal. During the time that he was staying with the Wilders in Mansfield, he went out of his way to make friendly banter with Laura and Almanzo, and they were sorry to see him leave.[7]

On the first Sunday in July, Rose rode with her parents in the Craigs' new Studebaker to attend the annual songfest at Hartville. Every year people drove in from all over to participate in the Wright County Singing Convention at the courthouse. The weather on this particular day was ideal, not as hot as it typically got in the Ozarks in early July, and Rose estimated the attendance at about two thousand people (the newspaper guessed perhaps three thousand). Songfests like this were popular all around the region. The annual event stood out among similar gatherings that were held in churches and other gathering places. The programs typically began with prayers and devotions, proceeding with solos, group performances, and audience sing-alongs. The Hartville songfest lasted for two hours in the morning and another two in the afternoon, with an hour and a half in between for a picnic lunch. Rose probably was thinking of this experience when she wrote a short story published later in *Country Gentleman* about a community songfest held at a church at "Prairie Hollow" in fictional Cedar County. She described the people and the songs and the abundant tables of food, overloaded with chickens, hams, platters of fish, Irish potatoes, sweet

potatoes, yams, peas, beans, corn, succotash, biscuits, jelly, and more. The general tone of the story, though not entirely, was condescending toward the God-fearing churchgoers about whom she was writing.[8]

Laura's social life continued to revolve heavily around the clubs she belonged to. Now she could take Rose along—sometimes willingly, sometimes not—to the meetings. The Justamere Club gathered monthly on Tuesday afternoons in members' homes, and Laura seldom missed a meeting. Once or twice a year husbands were invited to join their wives for an evening get-together. One Thursday evening in early January 1924, a couple of weeks after Rose's return to Rocky Ridge and during Catherine Brody's stay with them, Laura invited her Justamere friends and their husbands over for a homecoming party. More than thirty guests packed the farmhouse and listened to their famous village daughter regale them with tales of her recent travels and inspected souvenirs from the countries she had visited. In June it was her mother's regular turn to host the group at their place, and Rose again provided the program, this time relating "some unique stories on European Battles."[9]

The *Mansfield Mirror* faithfully reported the names of those in attendance at these sessions and often commented that the papers and discussions were "interesting" and that the dainty refreshments served afterward were "delicious." Rose, for her part, complained about how boring they usually were in letters to friends, explaining that she tagged along with her mother only under duress. Nevertheless, she did find the meetings diversionary and sometimes even admitted that her companions at these sessions were worth getting to know better. It was raining on the morning of the scheduled meeting in July, which Rose hoped might serve as an excuse for not going. "But there are so many rows brewing that I will probably miss something if I don't," she noted wryly to Moyston.[10]

Laura also continued to actively participate in the Athenian Club, which she had been a charter member of when it began in 1916. She rode with friends or had Almanzo drive her when the get-togethers were held in Hartville. In February 1925 she hosted a joint gathering for members and their husbands of both the Justamere Club and the Athenians. Guests were instructed to wear costumes from twenty years earlier, and they played old-fashioned games in rooms lighted by candles. Laura also continued her involvement in Eastern Star and usually was elected as an officer in yearly elections. She served as chaplain several times during the late 1920s,

and also acted the role of associate conductor and filled other positions. In April 1925 she went to Mountain Grove with Rose and several other chapter members to attend an Eastern Star instructional school. The following year she and the other officers went to Mountain Grove for a district meeting.[11]

A local chapter of the Women's Christian Temperance Union, which had been active earlier in town, reorganized itself in 1925 with about two dozen members. Although Laura sympathized with the group's purpose, she apparently felt that she was too heavily involved in other activities to join. She sporadically attended meetings and activities staged by the Methodist Ladies Aid. Like similar organizations run by the Baptists, Presbyterians, and Congregationalists, the group mixed Bible readings and devotions with refreshments, gossip, needlework, and planning for bazaars, chicken-pie suppers, and ice-cream socials. Laura brought Rose to a meeting in February 1925 when, following an informal hour of visiting over needlework, dainty refreshments consisting of hot coffee, cake, sandwiches, and pickles were served. To commemorate George Washington's birthday, the rooms of the home where the meeting was held were decorated with flags and hatchets, and each guest received a tiny hatchet as a favor to take home with her.[12]

If Laura had any inkling of Rose's growing dissatisfaction with her situation and her disdain for many of the people around her, she likely kept that knowledge to herself. Rose, after all, was adept at masking her feelings, and she saved expression of her dark moods for letters to out-of-town friends such as Guy Moyston and Fremont Older, her former boss in San Francisco. She hated being saddled with housework—cooking, cleaning, scrubbing, dusting, and hauling water—although no doubt she exaggerated the amount and onerousness. She did have a tendency to make things harder than they had to be. While her dislike for household chores was genuine, her attitude toward the residents of Mansfield remained more ambivalent. She discovered few of them to be witty, knowledgeable, or intelligent enough to be very engaging. But she took a sort of anthropological interest in observing them and wrote some of them into her short stories in disguised form. Her condescending attitude toward Ozarkians in general showed through in the hillbilly stories that she began submitting to magazines. Occasionally, however, she was fully engaged in some of the local activities, such as fox hunting, and she found herself enjoying the company of people such as the Craigs or the Shorts, who took her on fox hunts.[13]

Part of Rose's trouble with "ordinary" people lay in her need to carve out enough time for herself to write. She could not afford too often to wile her days away in gossip and other diversions. When she was in the right mood, her output could be prodigious. During peak periods of production, she could pound away on the typewriter for ten to fourteen hours a day, and block out almost everything else. In 1924, as she labored on a variety of projects, including a novel based on Jack London's life, Rose's incessant typing may have driven her mother to distraction, or, more likely, stimulated her to think more seriously about her own writing career. After more than a decade of writing for farm papers, Laura had become a disciplined writer, able to produce thoughtful, readable prose for a general audience and to meet regular deadlines. What possibilities existed beyond that? Might she aspire to reach a wider audience, as her daughter already had?

Rose thought so, and she helped Laura publish in *Country Gentleman* two short articles describing her kitchen and her dining room as examples of ideal places for living and working in a farm home. Since her first national exposure in *McCall's* five years earlier, Laura had not written any more material for large-circulation magazines. Toward the end of 1924, while visiting friends in Croton-on-Hudson, north of New York City, Rose refashioned her mother's draft of the kitchen article, pulling a new lead for it from the second paragraph, pruning dry details, and organizing the material into several sections that made it easier for readers to follow. When it appeared, with photographs taken at Rocky Ridge, as "My Ozark Kitchen" in the January 17, 1925, issue of the magazine, once again it carried the byline "Laura Ingalls Wilder." For her effort Laura received $150. The publication on June 13 of "The Farm Dining Room" netted her another $150. She told Rose that because Rose's work on it had ensured its sale, it took some of the joy out of the accomplishment, but Rose tried to reassure her that what modifications she had made in the piece were minimal. All she had done to the story, she contended, was "an ordinary re-write job." Although Laura's *Missouri Ruralist* style of writing was not yet capable of gaining her acceptances from high-tone publications such as *Country Gentleman,* Rose sought to convince her that "you have just as much C.G. copy in you as you have Ruralist copy. It's only a question of learning how to handle it." Six months' work and practice, Rose promised, would give her

"the hang of it," but she indicated that Laura would have to listen carefully to her advice and then follow it.[14]

"What I am trying to do is to give you the benefit of these ten years of work and study," Rose told her mother.

> I'm trying to train you as a writer for the big market. You must understand that what sold was *your* article, *edited.* You must study how it was edited, and why, and just what was done. So that next time you can do the editing yourself. Above all, you must *listen* to me. I don't pretend that everything I say is pure wisdom, to be swallowed whole. But every darn word of it is worth good hard thought. If you don't do what I tell you to, you must at least have good reasons for not doing it, and know exactly what they are, and be able to show how and where and why your work is better because you *didn't* do as I said.[15]

It was good advice, hard-won from a decade of learning the writing trade herself. But Rose's sincere desire to transform her mother into a more professional writer, and thereby also enhancing her financial situation, was also inextricably tangled up with her own vague feelings of inadequacy in her mother's presence. Being an only child undoubtedly increased the protectiveness and concern that both parents exhibited toward her, but in the case of her mother the imperative to exercise control appears to have been especially prominent. Rose, in many ways, was just like her mother: ambitious, strong willed, cantankerous, and inclined to act on her beliefs. Both strongly desired freedom of action; both consciously understood the necessity of reining in one's own instincts and inclinations by practicing self-control. Such a personality, however, increases the likelihood that a person will periodically unleash her aggressive impulses on other people. In the case of Rose, whose letters, diaries, journals, and published writings testify eloquently to this pattern of behavior, the evidence is more conclusive than for her mother, because she left more traces behind.

Rose could not appreciate what she considered to be her parents' excessively frugal mode of existence. She had experienced poverty while growing up, and hated it. Deprivation as a child had humiliated her, and the memory of it continued to cast a pall over her. Her parents' penny-pinching habits made no sense to her. She did not understand why they should work so hard to save when it seemed much easier to earn a little extra income. "I never saw any human being so determined to be hideously

and insanely extravagant," she wrote her mother, "you will spend a hundred dollars, any time, for one dollar bill." Able to earn as much as a thousand dollars for a short story that she could turn out in days or weeks, Rose could not understand the mentality of people—even if they were her own parents—who were so close with a dollar. She insisted that her mother, too, could—indeed, should—be earning four or five thousand dollars a year from her writing. But only if she would take Rose's instruction. This relationship between tutor and trainee cast Rose in the dominant position, something that she had not been able to assume with her mother before, despite the widespread acclaim that her writing talents had earned for her. Now, for her mother's own good, she would have to listen to Rose. "Just because I was once three years old, you honestly oughtn't to think that I'm never going to know anything more than a three-year-old," she wrote her. "Sometime you ought to let me grow up." Rose's resentment was palpable, but it was tempered by her genuine love for her mother. She offered Laura strong encouragement and reassured her of her love in closing the letter.[16]

Boosting her mother's writing career was the best way Rose could think of to assist her parents in becoming more financially independent. She did feel obligated for their welfare, but she hoped to escape getting physically tied down to them. She wanted to build up a large enough nest egg so that the interest on it would be sufficient for their needs. It would be helpful if her mother could derive a substantial income from her own writing. Few other alternatives came to mind. One possibility that may have been motivated as much by the income that was attached to it as by anything else was Laura's bid for political office during the spring of 1925. A three-hundred-dollar annual salary came with the post of collector of Pleasant Valley Township. Rose told Guy Moyston, "If she's elected, it will take quite a load off my mind, as the work will go in nicely with her Farm Loan work, and I think if she's once in office she'll stay there as long as she wants the job."[17]

Laura ran on an independent farmers' ticket. Her campaign for the office was largely limited to announcing her candidacy and paying to insert a four-hundred-word statement for several weeks running in the *Mansfield Mirror*. In it she emphasized her character and her experience as an organizer of and as secretary-treasurer for the Mansfield branch of the National Farm Loan Association. "My character is known to neighbors and friends throughout the county," the statement said. "I have been a busy farm woman and have not had time to do as much for the community as I would have liked to

do, but wherever possible I have done my best." In her seven years at the farm association she had carried out her duties competently and honestly, she asserted, which qualified her for the position of township collector. "I am not a politician and have no thought of entering politics," she said, promising, if elected, to fulfill her obligations in the same fair-minded way that she had done for all the other community organizations with which she had been connected.[18]

The election was set for March 31, giving the candidates a little more than a month to conduct their campaigns. Rose reported that things were proceeding "fast and furious," with all kinds of intrigues going on. A week before the election, she commented somewhat mysteriously, "Mama Bess' campaign seems to be progressing favorably. Still, of course, all the whiskey element's against her, likewise the W.C.T.U. and the churches."[19]

When the ballots were tallied, Laura had finished a distant third, garnering only 60 votes, compared with 266 for C. A. Stephens and 122 for Hugh Williams. Rose claimed that the election had been stolen from her mother; they knew for certain, she contended, of more than 100 votes that had been cast for her. "I'm rather much disappointed," she wrote Guy Moyston, "but thank goodness Mama Bess doesn't awfully mind. The steal was so raw that everyone knows it. And of course will go on letting it happen, over and over again. The dear people don't really care a darn about self-government, in spite of all the Upton Sinclairs." Just as likely, Laura's longtime Democratic affiliations and her more recent identification with the independent farmers' movement worked against her, since the Republican Party dominated Mansfield and the area surrounding it. The victor, C. A. Stephens, was a Republican and a Royal Arch Mason to boot, making him a tough candidate to beat.[20]

Laura's election defeat allowed her to concentrate her attention now on her writing. The year 1925 would be a crucial turning point in her career. Now she began to explore how she might use memories and material from her childhood as a basis for articles to submit to some of the better magazines. Laura's mother had died the previous April in De Smet, and Laura had not been able to attend the funeral. She was especially sorry that she had not pushed her sisters earlier to write down stories about the time that the family had lived in Wisconsin. Now Laura wrote her aunt Martha Carpenter to inquire about old recipes that she might be able to use in an article she was planning to submit to the *Ladies' Home Journal* about her

grandmother's cooking. She also wanted to hear other stories about their family. Beyond that, she noted in her letter, Rose might be able to use some of the information in her work. Laura offered to pay her aunt to hire a stenographer to take down the stories verbatim if she were willing to do it.

> As you begin to tell it so many things will come back to you about the little everyday happenings and what you and mother and Aunt Eliza and Uncle Tom and Uncle Henry did as children and young folks, going to parties and sleigh rides and spelling schools and dancing school, if you did, or whatever young folks did do then. About your work and school too. Also about away back when Grandma was left a widow and the Indians used to share their game with her and the children, if I remember right.[21]

Laura told her aunt how wonderful it would be to have those stories preserved. She would make copies of them and pass them to the other cousins. "I am very busy these days with my writing," she noted, "though I do not pretend to write anything like Rose. Still I have no trouble in having the little things I do write published." Aunt Martha responded with many details about life on the Wisconsin frontier during the time that she was growing up, about Indians, maple-sugar parties, corn husking, quilting, and school experiences. She also sent a recipe for cottage-cheese pie.[22]

The correspondence with Aunt Martha might have inspired Laura to start thinking seriously about her own childhood as a subject, but apparently it did not occur to her yet that it would be of much interest to anybody. Laura's writing career was getting nowhere fast. Her articles for the *Missouri Ruralist* stopped after 1924, perhaps because she now hoped to branch out in new directions. Soon Rose would be gone again, too, temporarily. Throughout 1925 Rose grew increasingly frustrated with the dullness of Mansfield, the drudgery of her household duties at Rocky Ridge, and the growing feeling that her life was slipping through her hands, leaving her older each day with little to show for it. Living in the United States itself seemed to constitute more and more of a burden for her. In long letters to Guy Moyston—sometimes two or three a week—she described her feeling of entrapment, her desire to return to Albania, and her wish to see him again. She thought of being cooped up with her parents as a sort of self-imposed sentence, which by the spring of 1926 she would have fulfilled, allowing her once again the freedom she so strongly craved. She had been

away from her parents for so long that she felt bound somehow to "square things up" with them before departing once again.[23]

Yet, in the meantime Rose felt like a martyr. "I am so miserable, doing all the cooking and cleaning and everything," she wrote Moyston. "You never have understood how wretched I am here, and I suppose no one can." The work itself was not a problem. "I don't mind housekeeping. I love it," she explained. "I would have the happiest time keeping a little Breton cottage. But I certainly do hate farm-housework, sour milk, splashy cream, bringing in wood, walking knee-deep in cats and dogs and trying to do things with no tools."[24]

Adding to her frustration was her declining output, despite the fact that she was converting a series of Ozark stories that she had produced into a novel called *Hill Billy*. Having grown accustomed to writing two to three thousand words a day, she now was generally lucky if she could produce just one thousand on a regular basis. She realized that much of her problem derived from moodiness; one day she was up, the next day down. The weather, her progress with her work, checks in the mail, relationships with other people, and thoughts of distant friends and places all fueled her volatile moods. Living in the same house with both parents could be especially wearing. Rose loved her parents and wanted to be a good daughter to them, but her sense of responsibility to them was constantly contrasted with their many differences.[25]

Laura and Almanzo's world was, from Rose's perspective, narrowly limited. While she shared many of their values, she also felt herself emancipated from what she considered to be their more rigid attitudes and expectations. "You see, I don't fit any rule whatever," she wrote Guy Moyston:

> Where is perseverance, thrift, caution, industry—where are any of the necessary virtues? Simply not in me. It is, really a sad thing for my parents. I mean this. I mean it quite gravely and sincerely. They would have had comfort and joy and pride from me, if I had married fairly well, had a good home, been steadily lifted a little in the world by my husband's efforts, become, let us say, a socially successful woman in Springfield, with a car and accounts in the good stores, and friends visiting from Kansas City and St. Louis. This unaccountable daughter who roams around the world, borrowing money here and being shot at there, learning strange languages and reading incomprehensible books even in her own language, is a pride,

in a way, but a ceaseless apprehension, too. We are all of us, after all, largely products of our environments, and thirty years on this Ozark farm. . . . It's a marvelous thing, and a triumph of character and intelligence over environment, that they go as far with me as they do, that they know as much of the world and its affairs as can be gained from St. Louis newspapers.[26]

When she was absent from Rocky Ridge, Rose usually was able to consider her relationship with her parents—and especially with her mother—in more rational terms. But living elbow to elbow with them day after day inevitably stimulated friction, and every other frustration reinforced and magnified their differences. Although she was approaching forty, Rose remained, in the eyes of her parents, their little girl, and often they still seemed unwilling to acknowledge that she was an adult. "My mother can not learn to have any reliance upon my financial judgment or promises," Rose complained. "It's partly, I suppose, because she still thinks of me as a child. She even hesitates to let me have the responsibility of bringing up the butter from the spring, for fear I won't do it quite right!"[27]

The same Rose who could fulminate so bitterly about her mother's overprotectiveness and condescension also wanted to take Laura on a special trip, one that she would always remember. The idea of driving to California to visit Rose's former boss and admired friend Fremont Older took shape in July, and she thought that afterward she could seriously start planning to leave home again. Finally, in the second week of September, after she had finished the Ozark novel that she had been working on and Laura had gotten her things in order at the National Farm Loan Association, they left Mansfield and headed toward California, with Rose's friend Helen Boylston riding along for company.[28]

Helen had been living with the Wilders at Rocky Ridge since coming back with Rose from the East the first of the year. Known as "Troub" (short for "Troubles") by her friends, Boylston was a nurse from New Hampshire who had met Rose while doing Red Cross work in Europe in 1920. Now she was interested in becoming a writer, and Rose encouraged her and was helping her get started. Soon after Troub's appearance on the scene, a two-year-old Buick that Rose had paid six hundred dollars for back East arrived in Mansfield by railcar. Beyond the reaction Rose anticipated from the townsfolk ("Nothing that has recently occurred in Mansfield is going to

make the sensation that the car will, when unloaded"), she thought of the vehicle as a freedom-giver—both for herself and for her parents. Though she complained that her bank account could not justify the expense, Rose believed that it would be well worth the cost "to so delight my father and Mama Bess. They will really be speechless. And I think the car will work a complete revolution in their lives. There is so much liberation in a car; it extends horizons so." Simultaneously, she viewed it as a ticket to her own liberation, constituting "part of the price of my liberty to go back to Albania. I am sure it will make a great change in their lives, give them many more interests, and if I can now fix them up financially, in this next year, I will go away again with a clean conscience and a light heart."[29]

Laura took easily to driving at first, but before long she decided that she would rather leave the driving to others. Almanzo, on the other hand, was a more difficult learner. At sixty-eight, it was harder for him to learn something so completely foreign to his experience. One time his tendency to treat the new vehicle like the horses that he had known and loved since childhood almost led to disaster. He was practicing with Rose when he attempted to slow the car down by pulling back on the steering wheel and yelling "Whoa!" while simultaneously bracing his foot on the accelerator. They veered off the road and hurtled through the ditch and over an embankment, jolting to a stop against a tree. Rose lunged headfirst into the windshield, and Troub had to pick broken bits of glass out of her face with tweezers. Almanzo, however, eventually became a fairly competent driver, and having a car greatly enhanced his and Laura's mobility.[30]

That summer the road past the Wilders' house was upgraded and slightly rerouted as part of a general highway-improvement program that gathered steam in Missouri during the 1920s. In 1926, the east-west route through Mansfield and in front of their house was designated as federal Highway 60 under the new numbered-highways program. On the one hand, such improvements were welcomed. The old washboard trails people had grown accustomed to driving over could be brutal, breaking springs on cars and forcing Rose sometimes to put chains on her tires in rainy weather to better negotiate the mud. On the other hand, the family resented the road builders' plan to move the highway over and cut through the hillside in front of their house, exposing bare earth and reducing the size of their lawn.[31]

People in Mansfield and other small towns welcomed the enhanced mobility that came with better roads and naturally hoped to be able to

benefit economically from them, too. Over time, however, the realization dawned on them that improved transportation could work both ways. Better roads did enhance efficiency and stimulate economic opportunity. Conversely, while benefiting primarily the larger towns and cities such as Springfield and Joplin, they often hurt smaller towns that people now increasingly drove past, such as Mansfield and Mountain Grove. Beginning in 1925, however, great expectations were aroused by the grading and graveling of Highway 60 and of Highway 5, the north-south road through Mansfield. N. J. Craig, one of Mansfield's most exuberant road boosters, was actively involved as a prosecuting attorney in securing the land necessary for the right-of-way of the new highways. In 1929 a Highway 60 Association was formed to promote the route and the towns along it. Later in the year a Capital to Capital Association came into being to promote a north-south highway along the route of Highway 5, which its backers hoped would eventually connect Des Moines, Jefferson City, and Little Rock. By the early 1930s already, parts of these long-distance routes were getting hard-surfaced.[32]

Automobile ownership in Missouri exploded during the decade after World War I, just as it did across the country. The number of registered motor vehicles in Missouri grew from 16,387 in 1911 to 297,008 in 1920 and then jumped again to 763,375 in 1930. By that time there was 1 for every 4.7 people in the state. Vehicle registrations in Wright County tripled from 881 to 2,692 during the 1920s. Mansfield's residents increasingly relied on their automobiles to make shopping trips and to attend sporting events in nearby towns. Laura's excursions to Hartville for Athenian meetings became easier as cars and roads improved. A story in the *Mirror* in July 1927 about a family gathering in Mansfield made this observation: "Modern conveniences, good roads, cars, etc., help to annihilate distance so now instead of being 'distant' relatives, they are only near neighbors to their Wright county relatives." Rose made a similar point in a short story she wrote titled "Thirty-Mile Neighbors," appearing in the May 16, 1925, issue of *Country Gentleman*. "Times change," she noted. "Neighborliness goes now on rubber tires and takes in, more swiftly, a wider radius." The dismantling of hitching posts in nearby towns during the late 1920s registered the demise of the horse as a mode of transportation. Another indicator of the automobile's growing importance was the introduction of angled parking for automobiles in Mansfield in 1931.[33]

It took six weeks for Laura, Rose, and Troub to drive to California and back. Summer roadwork on the highways forced them to take many detours while motoring through Kansas, but "Isabel"—the name they gave to the car—responded well throughout the trip. They encountered their only serious trouble when the muffler blew out along the way, costing five dollars to repair. Every evening the threesome rested in a hotel for the next day's journey. As they moved from the wooded, broken terrain of the Ozarks onto the open spaces of Kansas, Laura was reminded of how sunsets and starlight looked on the prairie. In a note to Almanzo, she stated her gratitude for being able to live in a place like Missouri, for she did not think she could stand to live where the wind blew continuously, as it did in Kansas.[34]

The trio proceeded through Colorado, Utah, and Nevada, Troub taking over all of the driving chores after Rose's nerves got the best of her. When they entered California, they drove through Yosemite National Park and then went to San Francisco, where Rose visited some old haunts and tracked down old friends. They spent a long weekend at Fremont Older's ranch, where many of the people who had worked with Rose at the *Bulletin* came to greet her. The threesome then proceeded down the coast through Monterey, Carmel, Santa Barbara, and Hollywood and drove to Los Angeles, where they stayed for a day. While they were there, Grant Carpenter, an old friend of Rose's, took them to lunch and gave them a tour of Universal Studios. They returned home by the southern route, driving through Arizona, where they saw the Grand Canyon at night, the Painted Desert and New Mexico, the Texas Panhandle, and Oklahoma. Although Laura frequently fretted about leaving Almanzo home alone and kept pushing to get home quickly, she did enjoy the experience immensely. Commenting about it afterward, Rose noted that "the trip did her no end of good, and now that it's over she begins really to enjoy it, and will for years."[35]

The California adventure, however, failed to jump-start Laura's writing in the same way that her 1915 excursion to the West Coast had. A decade before she had returned and begun writing regularly for the *Missouri Rural-ist.* This time nothing so dramatic resulted. Worse, Rose announced that she was ready to return to Albania. She figured that she had completed her two-year "sentence" at Rocky Ridge. More to the point, she had accumulated almost six thousand dollars, mostly on returns from her investments with the Palmer and Company brokerage firm. With additional anticipated income from sales of *Hill Billy,* she made plans to spend several months

in Paris studying languages with Troub and then to proceed to Albania. Rose would turn forty before the end of 1926, and she was becoming increasingly conscious of her need, in the words of biographer William Holtz, to discover "a kind of integrity in her life, one that would let her meet the world confidently on its own terms and then to write about it as a free agent rather than a market-bound hack."[36]

During the next two years, while Rose sought personal and professional fulfillment in Paris and Tirana, Laura and Almanzo were left alone again at Rocky Ridge, lonesome for their only child but quite capable of taking care of themselves, despite her concerns about them. Now with Isabel in the garage and Almanzo able to drive it, they were more mobile than they had been before and could go to church and into town to shop and do their other chores more easily than before. Local news items in the *Mansfield Mirror* reported them taking trips, either alone or with friends such as the Craigs or newspaper editor O. B. Davis and his wife, to Hartville, Mountain Grove, Ava, Seymour, and Springfield. They went on a camping trip during the summer of 1926 but decided against driving to the Grand Canyon when they were unable to find anyone to take care of the farm and the animals while they were gone.[37]

Farming went badly in 1926. Almanzo experienced difficulty in finding a hired man to help. His Jersey cow was "just as mean as ever," but now their dog, Nero, drove him up to the barn every evening. O. B. Davis reported in the paper that one of Almanzo's cows had produced twenty-four pounds of milk at one milking. Their small operation constituted a tiny segment of an infant dairy industry in the Ozarks that accelerated during the 1920s. Wright County led the state in the number of milk-collecting stations. Meanwhile, efforts were being made to promote grape and strawberry production in the area, including the formation of a Fruit Growers Association to represent producers' interests. The *Mansfield Mirror* enthusiastically reported that thirty-nine hundred railroad cars of strawberries were shipped out of the region during the 1927 season. When a Bermuda Onion Growers Association started up, Almanzo became a charter member. In addition, the growth of tomato production around Mansfield supported a canning factory in town.[38]

Although things were not going so well for them on the farm, Rose informed her parents that they no longer needed to worry about money, since her Palmer account was performing spectacularly well. They followed

her recommendation to entrust some of their own money to her broker, because the way the stock market was behaving it seemed that there was no way anybody could lose. She urged them now to spend on things and not to worry at all about money. "If I were to drop dead this minute," she assured them, "I have enough to double your present income if you never touched a cent of the principal."[39]

Almanzo continued to be largely a private person. According to Rose, he never used the telephone. He did serve as an officer for the Wright County Fair and Stock Show in September 1926 as one of three superintendents in change of the horses, mules, sheep, and goats. Laura, meanwhile, kept busy with club activities while Rose was gone. A new study group called the Interesting Hour Club was formed toward the middle of 1926, and from the beginning Laura was an active participant. Its membership overlapped somewhat with that of her other clubs; for the most part these were the wives of lawyers, doctors, Main Street store owners, and other town notables. Topics for their monthly discussions were intended to be interesting and instructive and, occasionally, useful to the community. A session on the Panama Canal might be followed by one on Russia; one on "Prominent People" might precede one with papers about the geography, social customs, Methodist missions, and birds of South America. When the topic "Interesting Places" came up in July 1927, Laura read a paper on "Western Views," while three of her fellow club members talked about places they had visited. Several months later Laura presented a talk on "the possibilities of the Ozark country." In March 1927 she was on the program again with a discussion of "Mexico and Her Relations with the United States."[40]

Popular culture proliferated rapidly during the 1920s in the form of radio, movies, sports, music, and other entertainment, but it largely passed by the Wilders. A year and a half after F. H. Riley closed the Nugget and moved to Mountain Grove, the theater was resurrected under the name of the Bonny in November 1925. If Laura and Almanzo went to see Clara Bow in *It* or to any other movies during these years, the fact is not recorded. Laura, who according to Rose hated anything having to do with sex, would certainly have disapproved of the ad that ran on the first page of the *Mirror* in July 1927 for the hit movie: "Some girls have 'IT,' millions wish they had 'IT.' What is 'IT'? Soon you'll know!" Further signs of the times could be discerned in advertising for *Ankles Preferred,* which showed at the Bonny

five weeks later: "She thought it was her brains that was making her success in business—BUT—It was her pretty ankles." By 1928 Mansfieldians could drive to Springfield to take in one of the new "talkies." Meanwhile, the local theater manager purchased a new projection machine, enabling continuous showings rather than making moviegoers wait between reels, and a new Wurlitzer pipe organ was installed for their listening pleasure.[41]

The Mansfield band went through one of its cyclical periods of inactivity in 1926, but it reorganized at the end of the year and again performed in the bandstand on the town square the following year and then performed concerts in surrounding towns in 1928. The Mansfield Grays reorganized their baseball team, too, in 1927, but it seems unlikely that Laura and Almanzo took any interest in it. And it is impossible to imagine their getting involved in the rapidly proliferating sport of golf, which was so appealing to their good friend N. J. Craig. Golf courses sprang up outside of towns all over during the decade. One was built in Mountain Grove in 1927. Mansfield obtained its golf links, located two miles north of town on Highway 5, the following year. In addition to entering local competitions, Craig drove to Springfield to play in tournaments with like-minded enthusiasts.[42]

Automobiles, sound movies, and golf courses represented modernizing forces during the 1920s. People in places such as Mansfield grew increasingly aware of the need to make improvements in their towns if they were to remain competitive with their rivals and avoid economic decline. After a decade of rapid increase during the 1910s, Mansfield's population growth rate leveled off during the 1920s, increasing by a relatively modest 13.7 percent to 861. Perhaps because the general economic prosperity fostered complacency during the years before the stock market crash of October 1929, town-boosting efforts lagged during the latter part of the decade. The chamber of commerce lapsed into inactivity, only to be resuscitated after the economy entered its downward slide. Promotional efforts sputtered, as some residents volunteered their time and money for organizations such as the Highway 60 Association, the Ozark Playground Association, and the Missouri Development Association, which was headquartered in Springfield. Campaigns to promote construction and stimulate new industry in the community obtained limited results. After a bond issue had earlier been rejected by the voters, Mansfield proceeded to build new water mains and a new waterworks in 1927. The city also purchased a new

fire truck. Concrete curbs were installed along Commercial Street, and the possibilities of putting in a swimming pool, a new city park, and other improvements were discussed. A new railroad depot, built in 1927 after the original one—dating back to the 1880s—burned to the ground, further dressed up the town. The *Mirror* proudly reported that the structure "is one of the best depots between Springfield and Memphis, and is a credit to the progressiveness of our thrifty little city." Another significant development during the decade was school consolidation, which proceeded after voters approved it in a special election in 1926.[43]

But nothing could hide the fact that, a half century after its founding, Mansfield was essentially stagnant, struggling to hold on to its position in competition with surrounding towns and was in danger of losing ground if it did not promote itself more effectively. By the end of the 1920s, the "problem of the country town" was growing increasingly urgent as economic and social changes that had been unleashed during the nineteenth century by the Industrial Revolution continued to erode old habits and attitudes. Counteracting modernizing tendencies that were transforming almost every aspect of life, a wave of nostalgia gained momentum during the decade, stirring memories of bygone days and fostering resistance to trends that were steering people away from their old moorings. Old-time fiddlers contests, a chicken-calling contest on the square in February 1927, and historical columns in newspapers reflected this tendency. Another manifestation was the *Mansfield Mirror*'s front-page reproductions of the syndicated poems of O. Lawrence Hawthorne, whose verses re-created a romantic vision of an earlier homespun, small-town America. One of his offerings, "There's No Place Like Home," typified Hawthorne's rosy, nostalgic, determinedly positive tone:

> Home is a garden of beautiful flowers.
> Home is a playground with love keeping score.
> Home is a haven of rest and contentment.
> Home is a harbor on joy's golden shore.

> Language could never portray its endearment;
> Only the heart knows what Home truly means.
> Memory treasures the pleasures of childhood,
> Taking us back to its radiant scenes.

Home is the secret of manhood's achievement.
Home is our comfort when shadows draw near.
Home is a temple of endless devotion,
Growing more sacred with each passing year.

In their syrupy evocation of everyday things, Hawthorne's poems presaged the kind of treatment Laura would later give to her own experiences when she started writing her autobiographical novels.[44]

Two years in Paris and Tirana failed to advance Rose any closer to her goal of publishing significant material and achieving personal fulfillment. In a letter to Clarence Day she complained, "More and more, I am oppressed by the sense of emptiness, of not-worth-whileness. Of all my days going." She was gripped by a sense of wanting to accomplish something more. "What *is* there to accomplish?" she wailed. "It's like being cursed with a mad desire to print an impression on running water." By early 1928, she was ready to return to Rocky Ridge to live with her parents and to churn out more salable stuff so that she would be able to escape once again to someplace else.[45]

In New York in mid-February on her way home to Mansfield, she lingered for several weeks visiting friends and having some work done on her abscessed teeth. Seven years after striking up her relationship with Guy Moyston, she decided to break it off. She had loved him, she insisted, but she valued her freedom too much to marry him. In a farewell letter she quoted from Robert Frost's poem "Diverging Roads," saying that she had chosen to take the road "least traveled by." That statement could have served as her epitaph.[46]

Back at Rocky Ridge by late April, she wrote Fremont Older that she found it hard to understand why she had come home. A lot of little reasons could be adduced, but they did not add up to a logical explanation. Already she was homesick for Albania, but she could see many things that needed repair and refurbishing in the farmhouse. She tried to explain to Older the compulsion that drove her to want to build things, "I dream of lavish water-systems and oil-burning central heating plants with vapor and vacuum heat, and stone walls—miles of 'em—and other insanities. I suppose I'll probably carry 'em out. You know, I would be an entirely different woman if it weren't for the pernicious influence of houses. My intelligence sees

their perniciousness clearly enough, but I have no character. I can't take 'em, and I can't leave 'em alone."[47]

For someone who spent so much time in the realm of words and abstractions, the chance to do something concrete—to build something permanent—constituted an irresistible urge. Much of her time in Albania had been spent planning and working on her house in Tirana. Rose recognized the "uncontrollable passion" she possessed for houses. "I should have been an architect and decorator, instead of a writer," she laughed. Houses, she admitted, were her vice; she loved to remake them. Two other factors came together in 1928 to launch her on another house-building venture— one positive, the other negative. The positive development was the ten thousand dollars she received for another Ozarks novel she had written, which she considered to be mere trash. Acknowledging that *Cindy* was competent so far as it went, Rose told a friend that it was "utter rot." The money from it, however, was now available to build a house for her parents.[48]

On the negative side, 1928 turned out to be a difficult year in many ways for Rose, most important in that she continued to be unable to latch onto a subject that she felt was truly worthy of her talents and one that would elevate her beyond the hackwork level at which she considered herself to have been working. Telling her agent, Carl Brandt, that she was really not a good writer, she categorized herself as only a fair writer who managed to sell things by writing better than average prose and being vividly pictorial about it. She also recognized in herself a tendency to overwrite. She consoled herself by noting that at least her stories would do nobody any harm. Her real trouble, she told Clarence Day, was that she had not yet figured out where she stood in the "literary business" or where she wanted to go. Instead, she had let circumstances jostle her in every direction. All of her book ideas had come from other people; she possessed too little experience of her own to draw upon for subject matter. With this in mind, she briefly considered writing stories about pioneer America, like the ones her mother and father had told her when she was a child, but the subject held little appeal. "Don't dislike it, and I readily admit all the admirable qualities," she told Day. "I'm simply not interested. I was brought up on pioneer stories, and never a spark from me."[49]

She continued to grasp for significance but, not being able to find it, turned her attention to building a house. Perhaps the idea to build an English-style cottage for her parents related somehow to her earlier

fantasy of moving them permanently to England. It is unlikely that Laura and Almanzo encouraged her in the undertaking or even went along with it willingly. The best evidence for this is that as soon as they had a chance to move back into their old farmhouse, after Rose left Rocky Ridge permanently in 1935, they quickly did so. That the daughter was ministering more to her own needs than to those of her parents in building the house seems apparent. Perhaps her motive—either consciously or unconsciously—was to exercise an amount of control over them. No doubt she felt that she was doing it for their own good, but since her mother, at least, was reluctant to accept the favor, the construction venture was emblematic of the power struggle that went on continuously between mother and daughter, at least in the latter's mind.

By the time Helen Boylston returned to Rocky Ridge in June to resume residence once again with the family, Rose had already progressed considerably with her plans not only for the new house but also for a tenant house that could be used by a hired man. Once Laura and Almanzo were installed in their new house on the other side of the hill, Rose and Troub could take over the old farmhouse and modernize it for themselves. A cook/housekeeper could be hired, allowing them more time for writing. All of Rose's plans seemed to make perfect sense to her. While the work was proceeding, she was so busy with arranging and supervising the details that little time was left to worry about her own writing.

Originally estimating that the house would cost four thousand dollars, Rose eventually paid about eleven thousand. Between the start of construction in August and final completion just before Christmas, Rose had dozens of details to attend to. Based on a design described as a "sort of modified English cottage" in style, the five-room house sported a field-stone exterior and brick windowsills. It was well built, with steel door casings, steel-casement windows, and French doors. Most of the suppliers were located in Springfield, and Rose spent a considerable amount of time corresponding with them and the contractors and driving back and forth to talk to them. Everything else was set aside for the duration. Explaining to Fremont Older why he had not received a letter from her in two months, Rose reminded him of how engrossing such a task could be. "I've thought, ate, dreamed, nothing but House," she noted.[50]

Meanwhile, Laura refused to visit the construction site until the work was completed. "She wanted a new house, but didn't want to bother with it in

the building stages," Rose told Older. But how much Laura really wanted a new house is hard to say. She had always taken great pride in the farmhouse that she and Almanzo had built and expanded over the years. She had written lovingly about it in the *Missouri Ruralist* and the *Country Gentleman.* Through its picture windows she could look across the countryside and toward town. Perhaps when Rose offered to build her and Almanzo a new house, she felt that they could not refuse it, but that did not necessarily mean that she had to like the idea either. Rose remained curious about what her parents' reaction would be to the finished product. "I do hope the family will like it," she wrote Older. When Laura and her friend Mrs. Craig went over the hill to inspect the new house on December 22, Rose recorded in her diary, "Mama Bess delighted." Afterward, however, she described the scene somewhat differently in a letter to Older: "Certainly I should have thrilled all over when my mother walked into the new house. I expected to, and would have done, but for a strange but unexpected turn of events, which I might tell you about, but won't write. The longer I live, the more I am amazed and fascinated by the endless variety of living." We might infer that Laura's first reaction to her new home was less than enthusiastic.[51]

This was a time of transition for both mother and daughter. Rose experienced mental upheaval in 1928; her mind was going through "a series of geological adjustments," as she put it. "Earthquakes and volcanoes and tidal waves accompanying." She was in a state of confusion, struggling with conflicting attitudes and points of view. In a few years' time, her opinions would find a firm resting place: on the far right of the political spectrum. At this time, however, she continued to play with ideas and test them against her own experience and knowledge and against the opinions of people such as Older. Crime and punishment, cultural decadence, eroding values, religious belief, the ultimate nature of reality—these were among the topics Rose was struggling with. While reacting favorably to Herbert Hoover's victory over Al Smith in the presidential race that year, Rose was unengaged in politics at this time, at least not interested enough to write much about the subject.[52]

Laura, whose interests and concerns spanned a much narrower range, was likewise moving in a new direction. After serving for a decade as secretary-treasurer of the Farm Loan Association, she resigned the position in April, shortly after Rose returned to Rocky Ridge. Having her daughter back home again filled up more of her days. She also spent considerable

time in several kinds of club activity, taking Rose with her. Around August 1927 Laura became involved in the Embroidery Club, which had been going strong for several years. Rose also joined the group, attending their Thursday afternoon get-togethers with her mother and Troub. Laura did not simply drag them with her against their wills, because sometimes when she was unable to attend the sessions, they went to them on their own. Beginning in 1929 the two also accompanied Laura to Wednesday and Thursday evening Bridge Club parties held in various homes. The *Mirror* reported Laura entertaining "her bridge club" one Wednesday evening in September 1930 while Genevieve Parkhurst, a friend of Rose's, was passing through town on one of several visits she made to Rocky Ridge. Rose herself invited the members to the place to play on another occasion.[53]

Laura gave little sign at this time that she was working on or seriously contemplating any major new writing effort. Her household chores, club involvements, and church and other activities consumed most of her energies. Around Christmastime and during the first several weeks of the new year, the whole household became caught up in a chess craze after receiving a set as a present. For days on end, everyone's schedule revolved around the game. Mostly, though, life continued along well-charted paths; there was no need to worry much about money, even if Rose was not selling many articles, so long as the stock market remained buoyant. At times, three—or even four—typewriters could be heard pounding away in the old farmhouse as Rose and Troub were sometimes joined by their friends from the East, Catherine Brody and Genevieve Parkhurst.[54]

With the completion of the new cottage and her parents' move into it, Rose had more time to concentrate on writing; still, no great ideas emerged as subjects to write about, so she resumed producing pieces for *Country Gentleman, Ladies' Home Journal,* and other publications. Living in the Ozarks did provide her with material that she could transform into fiction, but there were few people she felt able to identify with and engage in meaningful relationships. One person she grew increasingly close to was Corinne Murray, who ran a laundry in Mansfield with her husband and who shared her liking for bridge. More frequently she considered the people whom she encountered every day to be provincial and ignorant. Ambivalence characterized her attitude, because while in the abstract she tended to romanticize people, individual specimens of humanity frequently inspired her pity or contempt. She expressed her mixed feeling in her

journal entry for May 28, 1929: "I believe that most lives are exciting, intensely emotional daily, about little things; that most Americans are vaguely decent persons, vulgar, self-centered, insensitive, stupid, but well-meaning." Two months later she wrote Fremont Older, "People mostly lead such *dull* lives. It's horrible to contemplate, really, the dullness, the stupidity, of living, for most people. In this little town I see it every time I'm with a group for any length of time, for an afternoon." She admitted that things were little different anywhere else. San Francisco was just as dull—even New York—but she noticed it more in Mansfield because she knew the dull people there better.[55]

Some people who crossed her path were worse than dull; in Rose's estimate, they were essentially subliterate and incapable of functioning like normal human beings. Quoting from a letter that a loan applicant had written to her mother, she noted the ignorance of the writer; schooling could do nothing for someone like this. "How long will it take us to recognize the necessary existence of classes?" Rose wondered. "There's such a cruelty, in forcing ambition upon this poor creature, who, without ambition, as a servant born and bred, accepting the inevitability of being a servant, would be a busy, contented, and doubtless most excellent servant all her days."[56]

Rose often experienced violent mood swings. In early October 1929 she was suffering from a severe case of the blues. Tired and bewildered, she wished she could discover "something—anything, even the very least little thing—*graspable* in living." All she could see was an "endless stream of time pouring through the fingers and leaving nothing, nothing at all." A month later, after the stock market crash, with everything in her life seemingly going to hell, she observed that she was feeling almost gay. She refused to sympathize with people who wanted to end it all; she said she could not believe that suicidal people really did not want to live. "Our whole resentment of the terms on which we live comes from such an ardent love of life that we can't bear it to be less valuable, beautiful, perfect than our love impels us to imagine it," she wrote Fremont Older. In an attempt to analyze her own mood swings, Rose guessed that she was the manic-depressive type.[57]

The stock market debacle at the end of the year and the onset of the Great Depression left a deep impression on both Rose and Laura. The money they had invested in the Palmer Company evaporated. Money worries, which for

a short time had receded, now began to obsess Rose. She quickly abandoned any intention of moving back East, feeling herself tied more than ever to Rocky Ridge, both because of her obligation to support her parents and because it was cheaper to live there. It was at just this time that Laura began writing a memoir of her childhood and adolescence. Later, after the memoir's transformation into a series of children's novels, her writing would start bringing in the kind of steady income that would finally allow Rose to make good her escape. Laura's pioneer stories, like the two that Rose would write about her parents' and grandparents' adventures on the late-nineteenth-century frontier, were partly shaped by their thinking about the depression and the experience that the country was going through at the time.

The year 1930 began badly for both households at Rocky Ridge. Laura's teeth were bothering her, leaving her so sick that Rose finally took her to St. Louis to have some dental work done. Bills piled up. Rose found it harder and harder to sell articles to the magazines, and the book market seemed to have disappeared entirely. She felt like she was working harder than ever—sometimes ten hours a day—but managed to place only one short story during the first half of the year. Compounding their problems was a heat wave that withered crops and left the thermometer hovering around one hundred degrees every day.[58]

Rose grew more and more despondent as troubles accumulated. "This life is really nauseating," she wrote in her diary in January. But in the middle of everything Laura finished writing her autobiographical account about her childhood, beginning with her earliest childhood memories and ending with her marriage to Almanzo. In writing her *Missouri Ruralist* columns, she had sometimes included brief vignettes based on childhood memories. Rose had been encouraging her to expand upon them with stories for possible publication. What Laura had written this time was a straightforward first-person account of her recollections of growing up on the frontier. A few of the episodes included in the narrative had been used earlier in the *Ruralist*. She apparently wrote the memoir during the first part of 1930. On May 7 she delivered her handwritten copy to Rose, who took about ten days to type the manuscript and make her own emendations. The final result was approximately two hundred pages long. Rose mailed it to her agent in New York, Carl Brandt, on May 17, hoping that he might be able to find a magazine that would publish it as a serial. Meanwhile, she extracted

some of the early material her mother had written about her childhood in Wisconsin and fashioned it into a separate twenty-page story titled "When Grandma Was a Little Girl." She and her mother apparently thought that this might work as the basis for a picture book for young children.[59]

In writing her story in pencil on cheap, lined tablets, Laura inserted marginal notes, directed at Rose, indicating why she was doing things a certain way, asking questions, or pointing up potential difficulties. These were all intended to assist Rose in the process of typing and revising the manuscript. No doubt mother and daughter also talked to each other face-to-face from time to time about how to rectify various difficulties in the text or clarify things that readers might question. It was only a short walk over the ridge from one house to the other, and they must have made the trek frequently. Her motive in writing her life story, Laura told her daughter, was not money, but prestige.[60]

Carl Brandt attempted to interest a number of magazines in Laura's autobiography. *Good Housekeeping, Ladies' Home Journal, Atlantic Monthly,* and *Country Home* all turned down the idea of serializing the story. Yet, there was some encouraging feedback, too. While Rose was visiting in New York City in October, Graeme Lorimer of the *Saturday Evening Post* characterized "Pioneer Girl" as "a grand piece of work, fascinating material and 'most intelligent writing'" and informed her that the *Post* would undoubtedly have taken it had they not previously purchased some other submissions along the same line. Moreover, Lorimer indicated, the magazine likely would still buy it if it could be reworked into fictional form. "But I know you don't want to work it over into fiction," Rose commented when she passed the information along to her mother. "I haven't any doubt at all that it will go in book, but what I want to do is to exhaust serial possibilities before offering it for book publication."[61]

While she was staying in New York, Rose switched literary agents, dropping Carl Brandt for George T. Bye, whose list of clients included such stellar personages as Lowell Thomas, Franklin P. Adams, Heywood Broun, Will Durant, Damon Runyon, and Rebecca West. In correspondence with her new agent, Rose sounded almost apologetic in suggesting that he might want to get involved in trying to place some of her mother's material, explaining that she realized that probably not much—if any— money would be in it for him. Bye, for his part, was not very impressed when he saw Laura's manuscript. "*Pioneer Girl* didn't warm me enough the

first reading," he wrote Rose. He did not think it dramatic enough to draw in many readers. Rather, it appeared to be the work of a "fine old lady" who was "sitting in a rocking chair and telling a story chronologically but with no benefit of perspective or theatre." Ironically, had the *Saturday Evening Post* or some other publisher been willing to take the autobiography at this time, Laura probably would have become a one-shot nonfiction wonder, and Laura Ingalls Wilder—the beloved children's author—probably never would have been discovered.[62]

Laura's transformation from memoirist to novelist began when Berta Hader, a literary friend of Rose's to whom Rose had sent a copy of "When Grandma Was a Little Girl," interested Marion Fiery of Alfred A. Knopf's juvenile department in it. Fiery quickly wrote to Laura, indicating her interest. "I like the material you have used: it covers a period in American history about which very little has been written, and almost nothing for boys and girls." Instead of a picture book for very young children, however, she thought Laura's stories would be more interesting for beginning readers between eight and twelve years old. She suggested that the manuscript be expanded from its original six or seven thousand words to about twenty-five thousand and that more details about the everyday life of pioneers be added, including information about food, clothing, games, bullet molding, and so forth. She also thought that the use of the terms *Ma* and *Pa* for Laura's parents sounded a little too colloquial and that a stronger title was needed.[63]

Meanwhile, Rose visited with Fiery, who told her basically the same thing. Rose wrote home to say that the children's book editor "is crazy about your writing; indeed, everyone is who has seen it. She says you make such perfect pictures of everything, and that the characters are all absolutely *real.*" Laura would be able to start working on the revisions before Rose returned to Rocky Ridge, so Rose told her where to look in her files for the manuscript of "When Grandma Was a Little Girl." Explaining what it was all about, Rose told her mother, "It is your father's stories, taken out of the long *Pioneer Girl* manuscript, and strung together, as you will see."[64]

Rose suggested that Laura buy another tablet and write another fifteen thousand words or so. If it seemed easier for her to write in the first person, she should go ahead and do it that way. After she returned home, Rose could go through the manuscript again and change everything into the third person. They could modify the lead and expand the time span covered to an entire year rather than just a single winter. "Of course I have said

nothing about having run the manuscript through my own typewriter," she reassured Laura, "because the changes I made, as you will see, are so slight that they could not even properly be called editing. It is really your own work, practically word for word."[65]

It took Laura two months to come up with the additional pages requested by Knopf. Meanwhile, Rose had passed on to Fiery Laura's larger autobiographical manuscript, but the editor apparently was no more interested in it than the other editors who had already seen it. On further reflection, she said that she had changed her mind about the names, concluding that using "Ma" and "Pa" would work just fine, because they reflected the atmosphere of the time. On May 8, according to Rose's diary, Laura came to Rose's place for tea, bringing her manuscript with her. Rose was busy at the time working on a story called "Vengeance," which she had begun three days earlier, so she set her mother's manuscript aside for the time being. It took two weeks for Rose to finish writing, editing, and retyping the story, the name of which in the meantime had been changed to "A Spool of Thread." She mailed it to her agent on May 20.[66]

The following day, a Thursday, Laura went to Rose's house at breakfast, and they roughed out fifteen thousand words of the Knopf juvenile. After finishing her own work, Rose immediately started getting her mother's book into shape for submission to the publisher. She finished fifty-six hundred words on Friday, leaving time to gather some wildflowers and ferns with her friend Corinne Murray. On Saturday she recorded in her diary that she had almost finished her work on the manuscript. Laura walked over in the afternoon and read it, and she and Almanzo stayed to eat dinner with Rose. On Sunday, Rose completed her editing and copied the first chapter. The next two days were long ones of typing; Rose finished copying the manuscript by half past four on Tuesday afternoon, when Laura came to read the final chapter. On Wednesday, she prepared the manuscript for mailing, having completed the entire task of blocking out the story, editing, and retyping it in a week's time. Considering the short amount of time that she spent on the task, whatever changes Rose made in her mother's manuscript had to have been done quickly and relatively lightly. Significantly, this, the first of eight books that mother and daughter would collaborate on, received the lightest editing.[67]

Rose composed a note to Marion Fiery to send with the manuscript expressing her hope that Fiery would like the finished result since the

stories included in it meant so much to her mother. Concealing her own role in helping produce the manuscript, Rose commented disingenuously, "I don't know just where or how I come into this, do you? But somehow I do, because my mother naturally consults me about everything concerning her writing." She suggested that contractual details be worked out with the Bye agency. Unfortunately, Fiery had gone on a trip to Europe by the time the revised manuscript arrived at her office, and she did not get a chance to look at it until mid-August. Meanwhile, Laura and Almanzo finally felt able to leave on an automobile trip to De Smet in order to attend the annual Old Settlers' Day celebration there on June 10. Within a month's time, the gears were turning at Knopf, and they decided to publish Laura's book under the title *Little House in the Woods*, after considering and rejecting other possibilities, such as "Trundle-Bed Tales," "Little Pioneer Girl," "Long Ago Yesterday," and "Little Girl in the Big Woods." Marion Fiery wrote to say that she had found the manuscript "delightful" and that she was "quite keen" on it.[68]

Rose asked George Bye to handle the contract negotiations, indicating that for him it would merely be a matter of collecting the royalties and remitting them directly to her mother, minus his agency's customary 10 percent commission. She sent her mother's address (Mrs. A. J. Wilder, Mansfield, Missouri) so that he could communicate directly with her. Laura was not widely known yet as "Laura Ingalls Wilder," but in short order she would be. She already was planning two more children's books and had started one of them, Rose indicated to Bye. "It's really awfully decent of you to bother with this small fry; I do appreciate it," she told him. "And I don't expect you really to bother. I want it to be nothing more than a bit of semi-annual office routine which will adequately pay for itself." Whether Rose had any notion at the time that a "juvenile" book could earn substantial prestige and wealth for an author or whether she was deliberately trying to obscure her own role in the book's production is hard to say, but doubtless she considered her efforts in this instance to have been merely formal and perfunctory. After spending two weeks on a fifteen-page story for magazine publication, she had devoted exactly one week to working on her mother's book.[69]

Then word arrived from Marion Fiery that the Knopf firm had decided to close its children's department. It was a simple cost-cutting exercise, prompted by the effects of the depression. Fiery said that she was

heartbroken and suggested that they reject the contract with Knopf, which under the circumstances would be able to do little to promote the book, and rather try to place it with Harper and Brothers or Macmillan. It was probably because of Fiery that the manuscript came into the hands of Virginia Kirkus at the Harper and Brothers children's department. Kirkus's off-the-cuff response to the idea of a fictionalized true story about a pioneer girlhood was less than enthusiastic at first; she had seen and been unimpressed with too many similar stories already. However, a quick reading of the manuscript engendered a completely different response in her. "But the real magic was in the telling," she later recalled. "One felt that one was listening, not reading." She would later consider her "discovery" of Laura Ingalls Wilder to be one of the milestones of her book-publishing career. News that Harper's would take Laura's manuscript arrived at Rocky Ridge by telegram from Marion Fiery on Thanksgiving Day. The displaced children's book editor requested that Laura send her an autographed copy of the book after it was published. "I do feel such a personal interest in it and I'd love to own it," she wrote.[70]

Laura's new editor, Virginia Kirkus, wrote expressing her great pleasure that Harper and Brothers now was being given the opportunity to publish her book. "May I take for granted your permission to make certain editorial changes in the transitions between the main story and the anecdotes told within the story?" she inquired. "There may be some other minor changes, but these seemed to me the most striking. I assure you that the pattern of the whole will not be touched." Harper's enthusiastically promoted the book in hopes of boosting lagging sales. "Big" was added as a modifier to "Woods" to balance "Little House" in the title. Now the book would be called *Little House in the Big Woods*. Helen Sewall, a well-known illustrator, was contracted to do the illustrations for the volume, which now was in the form of a narrative storybook rather than the picture book that had originally been envisioned.[71]

After so many months of delay and worry, the process moved ahead swiftly now. On December 18, Virginia Kirkus relayed the good news that the Junior Literary Guild had chosen the book as an April selection. Page proofs arrived at Rocky Ridge on January 20, 1932, and Laura sat down to tea with Rose before going about correcting them. By the end of March, Laura had received her author's copies, and she went to Rose's for tea to

let her inspect them. "Very well done," Rose jotted in her diary. Official publication occurred on April 6. Laura could have been only extremely happy to see her work in book form and the glowing reviews that quickly accompanied it. After telling Rose that her motive in writing was not money, but prestige, she now began to reap it.[72]

# 7

## Becoming a Celebrated Author

### 1932–1937

*✍*

The publication of Laura's first book in 1932 at the age of sixty-five transformed her life. Henceforth she would be known primarily not as "Laura Wilder" or "Bessie Wilder" or "Mrs. A. J. Wilder." To her thousands—and eventually millions—of admiring fans, she would be "Laura Ingalls Wilder." Her identity now rotated less around her roles as farm wife, club member, or small-town citizen and more around her status as a widely acclaimed and increasingly popular author of children's novels. During the next eleven years, as seven more books were published, young people wrote to her begging for more stories of her childhood on the frontier, and librarians and schoolteachers installed her in their literary pantheon.

Popular success came immediately with the publication of her first book. Following the praise showered on the manuscript by Marion Fiery at Knopf and Virginia Kirkus at Harper and Brothers and designation of the book by the Junior Literary Guild as its April 1932 selection, *Little House in the Big Woods* received strong recommendations from reviewers. Praising the story's "refreshingly genuine and lifelike quality," the *New York Times* observed that its characters were "very much alive" and that the portrait of Pa, especially, was drawn "with loving care and reality." *Atlantic Bookshelf*

called the story "delightful and absorbing." *Books* urged that it be read by all Middle Border children and by many others. "Too few, nowadays, can tell as real and treasurable a story," the publication noted. "Moreover, this story is delightfully told."[1]

Laura must have been pleased with all of the favorable attention. Not only was she now a published author, but the response was overwhelmingly positive. Although no notice of the book's appearance ran in the *Mansfield Mirror*, news of it must have spread rapidly around town. Laura now began to reap the prestige she wanted, and financial returns began to trickle in also, slowly at first, but accumulating to considerable proportions over time.

Rose, too, was pleased with her mother's success. When Marion Fiery had informed her in September about Knopf's decision to publish the book, she had written in her diary, "Am feeling grand." Two months later, when Harper and Brothers took over the manuscript, the following entry appeared: "I am thankful." Positive comments declined in frequency during the months preceding publication of *Little House in the Big Woods;* mostly the diary's pages recorded cries of pain and despair. In June, Rose raged, "I must leave here." Two months later: "The whole situation is getting too much on my nerves and I don't sleep well." In September: "Feeling dull & sunk" and "Feel stupid." Then in November: "Accomplished nothing. Am bothered & worried by teeth." Her final assessment of 1931 consisted simply of "Last year was catastrophic."[2]

Rose's despondency flowed partly from health problems. Her teeth, especially, were plaguing her. Several times she went to St. Louis to have them worked on. At other times pains in her shoulders and legs left her feeling sick and tired. The final cutoff in late November of income from the Palmer account devastated her and dashed all hope that she would be able to depend on it without having to continue to grind out the kinds of stories she increasingly disliked. Within days, Helen Boylston packed up and headed back East, where it would be easier for her to support herself financially. Rose owed Troub about twenty-eight hundred dollars. Laura, upon hearing the news of the Palmer Company's failure, "took it very well, considering," Rose noted in her diary. But money worries left Rose "sick with fear." She did not know how she would pay her bills. Then a "begging letter" arrived from Laura's sister Grace in Manchester, South Dakota. She and her husband, Nate Dow, were growing desperate and did not know

where to turn. Rose discussed the situation with her parents over dinner at her place. "Couldn't sleep til after midnight," she recorded in her diary." Six days later: "Had another panic all night." And a couple of weeks after that: "Sick panic and was unable to do anything at all."[3]

Even during this period of intense financial difficulty, however, considerable cash flowed through Rose's bank account. She had a great deal more to work with than did most Americans. In October a $1,200 check (minus 10 percent for her agent) arrived for the sale of "Immoral Woman" to *Ladies' Home Journal,* and radio announcer Lowell Thomas sent her $500 in partial payment for ghostwriting a book for him. Next month, another $1,200 followed upon acceptance of "The Dog Wolf," by *Good Housekeeping.* It all went toward reducing debts that she had accumulated. She continued to subsidize the Cambridge education of Rexh Meta, the young Albanian she had met in Albania, and to support her parents with annual income supplements. It seemed that no matter how much money Rose earned, there was never enough, and in 1932 her financial situation deteriorated even further as her magazine markets evaporated. Even when her stories sold, they brought in less money: between $500 and $750, rather than the $900 to $1,200 she had become accustomed to.[4]

Departing from her usual Ozark themes, Rose began working in October 1931 on a serial set on the Dakota prairies during the 1880s. Calling it "Courage," she wanted to write it to exalt the resourcefulness and bravery of the frontier homesteaders, as typified by her grandparents, Charles and Caroline Ingalls. Stories that she had heard over and over again from her parents formed the basis for her short novel. Progress came slowly, however; she set the project aside several times before finally finishing it. Even before the appearance of *Little House in the Big Woods* in April, Laura brought Rose the draft of a new novel that she had written about Almanzo's childhood. Rose spent a week working on it in March, then continued to revise it during May and June, completing her work and typing it sometime between August 12 and 16. Her and her mother's writing careers were becoming increasingly intertwined. The editing job Rose did on the first novel had been desultory, but she either felt it necessary or simply decided that she wanted to spend more time working on the second one, *Farmer Boy.* After this, Rose would play a much larger role in editing and restructuring her mother's manuscripts. Meanwhile, her own writing began to depend much more heavily upon material given to her by her parents.[5]

For some time Rose had been growing increasingly frustrated at her inability to come up with new and compelling subjects for her writing. She possessed style and technique in abundance; subject matter was something else again. She never claimed that writing was particularly enjoyable; it was simply a job for her, she told people. But she could turn out an amazing number of pages when she was on track. The problem was that increasingly everything that she did left her feeling unfulfilled and empty. She judged her work to be merely clever—focused upon surfaces and inauthentic. Despite her many exciting adventures and travels that took her halfway around the world, Rose lacked the kinds of experiences that she believed would have served her well for fictionalizing. Her frustrating search for a compelling subject to write about derived from, and in turn contributed to, her deep-seated lack of personal identity. Although she remained unwilling to commit herself romantically to any single person after her divorce from Gillette, Rose retained a wide array of friends and corresponded regularly with many others. But she lacked the capacity to give unlimited love to anyone. After traveling to many exotic places and living on both coasts and in foreign countries, Rose did not have anyplace to call home. No place had earned her full commitment, nor any person. She seemed destined always to be dreaming of someplace else.

What drove Rose to write now about the Dakota frontier, after indicating earlier that the homesteading experience had never excited any interest in her, is hard to say. Possibly her parents' trip back to De Smet for the annual Old Settlers' Day celebration there on June 10, 1931, made her think about it. They had talked about going the previous year, when the town had its big fiftieth-anniversary celebration, but things had not worked out. Laura had found time, however, to write a poem for the occasion and had mailed it to editor Aubrey Sherwood, who published it in the *De Smet News*. It was titled "Dakota Prairies," and, while somewhat more pretentious in language than that of many similar home-town versifiers, it did little to bring distinction upon its author:

> Ever I see them in my mental vision
> As first my eyes beheld them years agone,
> Clad all in brown with russet shades and golden
> Stretching away into the far unknown;
> Never a break to mar their sweep of grandeur

From North to South, from East to West the same,
Save that the East was full of purple shadows,
The West with setting sun was all aflame;
Never a sign of human habitation
To show that man's domain was begun;
The only marks the footpaths of the bison
Made by the herds before their day was done.
The sky down-turned a brazen bowl to me,
And clanging with the calls of wild gray geese
Winging their way unto the distant Southland
To 'scape the coming storms and rest in peace.
Ever the winds went whispering o'er the prairies,
Ever the grasses whispered back again,
And then the sun dipped down below the skyline
And stars at just the outline of the plain.[6]

She signed the poem "Laura Ingalls Wilder," no doubt to assist local folks who had known her and her family in identifying her. Seven years later, when she started writing about her Dakota-prairie experiences, she sounded many of the same themes and called up similar images: prairie vistas, flamboyant sunrises and sunsets, open spaces, wild geese, waving grass, and whispering winds. Unlike her poem, which asserted that "man's domain" on the prairie commenced with the arrival of white settlers, Laura's books did pay some attention to the original settlers of the prairies and plains, the Native Americans. Nevertheless, both early and late, she thought of the westward movement not as a conquering army, displacing an already well-established Indian presence on the land, but as a benign and progressive transformation that introduced the blessings of civilization to the region.

When Laura and Almanzo finally departed for South Dakota on June 6, 1931, Rose noted in her diary that she was "astounded to see them actually start on the trip." Laura's manuscript had just been sent to the publisher a week and a half earlier, and all they could do at that point was wait for a response. Laura and Almanzo would be able to reacquaint themselves with old places and talk to old friends whom they had lost contact with for almost four decades. They traveled a route similar to the one that they had taken down to Missouri in 1894. What had required a month and a half to negotiate now took only several days, as Nero, their Airedale dog, rode with them on the car's running board.[7]

De Smet had, of course, undergone considerable change. Though many of the places they visited remained familiar to them, much was different. No buildings remained standing on their old tree claim north of town, and just a few of the trees they had planted had managed to survive. Grain was growing on the hill on the homestead where Rose had been born. They drove around to look at Spirit Lake and at the old family homestead. Grace helped Laura go through Caroline's and Mary's belongings, which were being stored in a room of the house on Third Street while it was being rented. (Mary had died in 1928.) Later Laura and Almanzo drove west to Keystone in the Black Hills, where they visited Carrie and went sightseeing.[8]

Back in Mansfield three weeks after starting their journey, both were happy to be home, telling Rose, "East, west, home's best." She could respond only by thinking of how utterly complacent and dated her parents' viewpoint seemed to her. Laura had kept a diary during at least part of the trip, but if returning to some of her old haunts had made her think more about her childhood, it did not lead her immediately to concentrate her writing energies on her adolescent years in De Smet. After *Farmer Boy*, Laura would write about her childhood chronologically, elaborating upon the episodes that she had written about in "Pioneer Girl." Her third book would be set in Indian Territory in Kansas; not for another six years would she start writing about her Dakota experiences.[9]

Interestingly enough, Rose turned her attention to life in Dakota before her mother did, even interrupting her work on editing "Farmer Boy." Toward the end of June 1932, she rode a bus to St. Louis to have some dental work performed. Upon returning to Mansfield, she set her mother's manuscript aside temporarily and put in five weeks of intense work on "Courage," which she now was calling "Let the Hurricane Roar." The new title derived from an old song that her mother remembered singing. Laura wrote Carrie to find out if she knew the words of the song. Day after day, while they suffered from the intense heat of July and early August in the Ozarks, Rose cranked out a story about a blizzard on the Dakota prairie. Some days, as she recorded it in her diary, the heat was merely "terrific"; at other times it was "devastating." Mostly, there was no rain. Worse, Rose worried that there was no further income in sight for her. As her bank balance dwindled, she noted in her diary, "I am truly frightened." A day later she escalated the adjective to "terrified."[10]

No doubt much of the power in Rose's story about fortitude and courage on the frontier derived from her own fears and timidity in the face of financial disaster and other calamities. The years 1930 and 1931 had been difficult for her; 1932 and 1933 turned out to be even worse. She slid into despondency, worried about her finances, her writing career, her personal relationships, her teeth, her general health, her deteriorating looks, her advancing age, and the seeming shackles that tied her down to her parents. Living in the midst of many people, she was desperately lonely. She began to realize that there probably would be no more great loves in her life, and she was prepared to write off the opposite sex. Few of her acquaintances appeared very interesting to her; most of them seemed dull and "stupid" (the latter a term she applied frequently to herself). Having recently turned forty-five and depressed by her lack of accomplishment, she grew increasingly aware of her own mortality. Morbid thoughts about death and even suicide frequently overwhelmed her.

Rose was especially exasperated by the large amount of time she had to (or chose to) spend on her mother's second manuscript. She always resented things that seemed to reduce her personal freedom; this seemed to be just one more example of her mother's literally "tying her down." Midway through revising "Farmer Boy," Rose became acutely depressed. On May 29 she wrote in her journal, "I am old. I am alone, a failure, forgotten, here in this dull alien place, I am losing my teeth." More to the point: "I am not leading my own life, because any life must coalesce around a central purpose, and I have none." Two days later she wailed, "I am really a stupid person. . . . I am too childlike and simple. Other people doubtless understand each other's meaning & purposes well enough, but I continually keep pulling at mama's sleeve and yammering, 'Mama, mama! answer me, please!'" Her resentment toward others "tying her down" was genuine, but she also realized that, having failed to locate any central purpose in her life, she often flailed about. On June 8 she arrived at an important realization: "My whole trouble was that I am not master of my material in writing my mother's second juvenile. It was a little job that seemed inconsequential— and is—and therefore it was able to do all this to me without my knowing it—The truth is that for better or worse, no matter how hopelessly a failure, I am a writer. I am a writer. Nothing else in the world is so important to me—to my own inner self—as writing is." Because she had to spend so much time on her mother's material, she was unable to work on her own,

a situation made all the worse by her assumption that her mother's work was essentially trivial. Laura, for her part, may not have been interested enough in what Rose was writing to actually sit down and read it. At least, Rose did not think so. In one of her cynical moods, she had written Guy Moyston, "Oh, it isn't hard to keep Mama Bess from reading my books. She never reads 'em. She just likes to have 'em around."[11]

Very likely it was while working on her mother's manuscripts and talking to her parents about their traveling to De Smet that Rose began to think about writing a story located in Dakota. Now stories that they had related to her over the years could serve as background material, especially the incredible tales about the hard winter of 1880–1881, when De Smet and the other towns along the Chicago and North Western Railroad tracks were snowed in for months. The events of that winter had become almost legendary among those who had lived through it. These stories, passed on by her parents and filtered through Rose's lively imagination, inspired *Let the Hurricane Roar.* It, along with *Free Land,* published in 1938 and also based upon stories her parents had told her, became Rose's two most outstanding pieces of fiction. Thus, the collaboration that occurred between mother and daughter worked in mutually beneficial fashion: Laura lent Rose factual material to draw upon for her writing, while Rose lent her professional expertise to polish and edit Laura's writing.

Laura sometimes may have resented Rose's appropriation of stories that she and Almanzo had told her for use in her own fiction. After getting started on writing novels, Laura at least hoped that Rose would avoid using stories that she might want to make use of later. Once, upon glimpsing a newspaper advertisement for the book edition of *Let the Hurricane Roar* that identified the names of the leading characters as Charles and Caroline, Laura immediately assumed that Rose had used her parents as models in writing the book, and she appeared to be resentful of it. Generally, however, Laura was quite willing to help her daughter in any way that she could. A few years later, Almanzo helped Rose with her research in preparation for writing *Free Land* by filling out a long questionnaire that she had prepared for him, asking about specific details of farming and frontier life as he had known it back in the 1880s.[12]

A month after Rose sent the manuscript of "Hurricane" to George Bye, the *Saturday Evening Post* bought it for three thousand dollars, publishing it as a two-part serial in October 1932. Rose indicated that her purpose in

writing the frontier romance transcended its ostensible subject matter; her real subject was the depression that the country was experiencing at the time. The story, Rose said in *Better Homes and Gardens* in December 1933, was intended as a reply to pessimists in the United States. "It was written," she said, "from my feeling that living is never easy, that all human history is a record of achievement in disaster (so that disaster is no cause for despair), and that our great asset is the valor of the American spirit—the undefeated spirit of millions of obscure men and women who are as valiant today as the pioneers were in the past."[13]

Despite the self-doubts that she spilled into her journals and diaries, Rose remained a fiercely individualistic person, proud of having made it "on her own." In this way she reflected her parents' own sternly independent spirits. Because Rose's and Laura's royalty checks arrived at opportune times, the family never had need of government relief. Somehow they managed to get by with little money. What they refused to acknowledge was that most families did not have the luxury of periodic checks arriving in the mail paying them hundreds or thousands of dollars, and many did need government handouts merely to survive. Laura and her parents, however, held fast to the belief that anyone with gumption and wit and a little persistence could make it without having to take government charity.

On August 12, immediately after depositing her serial in the mail, Rose resumed working on her mother's manuscript of "Farmer Boy." Only four more days were needed to finish the task, and it was ready to be mailed on August 15. Despite the success of Laura's first book, however, Harper's initially turned the manuscript down. Book sales were plummeting, and they wanted more work done on the story to ensure healthy sales. Meanwhile, the country was sliding deeper and deeper into the economic doldrums, leaving millions of people destitute and desperate. Missouri suffered along with every other state. One advantage that many Ozarkians had, however, is that they were used to poverty and more self-sufficient than others.[14]

Manufacturing collapsed in Missouri after the stock crash; value added by the sector dropped 51 percent between 1929 and 1933. Unemployment statewide exceeded the national average, jumping to 16 percent of the labor force in 1930, 27 percent the following year, and 38 percent in both 1932 and 1933. The relief load was especially burdensome in the Ozarks. Among the hundreds of miles of railroad track that were abandoned in the state during the decade, the twelve-mile-long short line of the Ozark Southern

Railroad between Mansfield and Ava was torn up and removed in 1935. Happily, Mansfield's two banks, the Farmers and Merchants Bank and the Bank of Mansfield, managed to weather the maelstrom and stay in business at a time when three hundred of their counterparts around the state were forced to close their doors.[15]

Farm receipts plummeted even faster than those of other products. The index of prices paid to farmers declined from 146 in 1929 to 65 in 1932. Farmland values nose-dived, along with agricultural prices, from an average of $53.23 per acre in 1930 to $31.36 per acre five years later. Drought compounded the agricultural problem, as devastating heat and lack of rain turned 1930, 1934, and 1936 into especially difficult years for farmers. Temperatures topping one hundred degrees wilted plants, livestock, and people for days on end. Springs and streams around Mansfield went dry. Crops burned up, and animals shriveled up and died. Almanzo had to haul water to the farm. In July 1934, Rose—her nerves on edge—was suffering from nausea and agonizing headaches. She wrote Adelaide Neall that everyone was on the verge of insanity. Further adding to people's miseries was an infestation of army worms and other pests that damaged crops, and worse.[16]

The depression drove Republicans for cover in Missouri, as elsewhere, and 1932 was a big year for the Democrats. Mansfield, traditionally safely in the Republican fold, granted New York governor Franklin D. Roosevelt a slight margin over President Herbert Hoover in that year's election contest, 362 votes to 303 (54 percent to 46 percent). Democratic candidates for other offices obtained similar margins over their Republican opponents. Countywide, Roosevelt and his Democratic running mates did slightly better, garnering 56 percent of the vote, 8 percent less than he obtained in the state as a whole. It did not take long for historical patterns to reassert themselves, however. In the off-year elections in 1934, Mansfield reverted to form, casting only 33 percent of its ballots for Democratic newcomer Harry Truman, who obtained 59 percent statewide in a successful bid for the U.S. Senate. Straight-ticket voting continued to be the norm, as candidates for the various offices obtained almost identical vote totals. District Seven, which included Wright County, sent conservative Republican Dewey Short back to Congress in 1934, after a four-year hiatus, and for the next twenty-two years he vociferously spoke out against liberal, New Deal–type programs in Washington in terms virtually identical to the conservative,

antigovernment rhetoric spouted by Rose Wilder Lane and her parents. In 1936, Roosevelt's big year nationwide (with 61 percent of the major party vote), he garnered only 37 percent in Mansfield and 41 percent in Wright County. Although compiling a victory margin of almost two to one statewide, the president trailed his opponent, Gov. Alf Landon, throughout most of the Ozarks region.[17]

Government programs initiated by President Roosevelt and Congress to try to cope with the problems brought on by the depression may have failed to convert most Ozarkians into Democratic voters, but the New Deal did exert a major impact on people's lives. A considerable number of farmers and unemployed workers obtained jobs under the auspices of the Public Works Administration, building roads and working on other construction projects. The Civil Works Administration pumped $17,500 into Wright County in November 1933, with $3,500 of the total set aside for Mansfield. Work-relief jobs continued to be provided under the massive Works Progress Administration (WPA) appropriation of 1935, while direct relief payments came to a halt early the following year. The most dramatic visual evidence of WPA activity in Mansfield was the new grade-school building that was erected at the end of 1936. Several dozen women obtained employment in WPA-sponsored sewing rooms and workshops in Mansfield, as well as in Hartville and Mountain Grove. Meanwhile, other programs, including the National Youth Administration, supplemented welfare families' incomes in return for work done in the schools. Through early 1936, federal dispersals of relief funds totaled $265,000 in Wright County.[18]

Of the two major programs that were designed to foster economic recovery, the Agricultural Adjustment Administration (AAA) made by far the bigger impact on the county. Its counterpart, the National Recovery Administration (NRA), had little impact because it exempted stores having five or fewer employees in towns of less than twenty-five hundred people. J. E. Craig became the chairman of the local NRA committee and went to a meeting in Springfield to be briefed on the organization's operations, but apparently the agency had little or no effect on Mansfield. The AAA and other agricultural programs, on the other hand, proved to be much more important in this mainly agricultural region. The program paid farmers to induce them to reduce their production in an effort to raise prices. County wheat committees were inaugurated in September 1933 to help administer

allotment contracts. A corn-hog program was also set up. Missouri farm prices rose 80 percent between 1932 and 1937. During the summer of 1934, as drought and heat ravaged the area, a cattle-buying program went into effect, and emergency crop and feed loans also were extended.[19]

Like their good friend N. J. Craig, the Wilders remained loyal Democrats as late as the 1920s, but the philosophy behind Roosevelt's New Deal rubbed them the wrong way. The idea of granting government "handouts" to the needy and of extending the regulatory reach of federal agencies into local communities and businesses went against notions of individualism and self-reliance that they had grown up with. Although Laura had worked for almost a decade with the federally sponsored Farm Loan Association, now she, Almanzo, and Rose all perceived the intrusive hand of government as having become far too powerful and meddlesome.

Almanzo's knee-jerk reaction against government interference in people's lives was told humorously in a story that Rose related to Mark Sullivan, a literary friend. Because of the thin clay subsoil and hilly terrain on Rocky Ridge it was impossible to plow most of the acreage. Nevertheless, her father did like to turn up an acre or so of relatively level land for oats or millet for bird feed, and he also liked to grow a little popcorn for the family. One day while he was plowing with old Buck, his thirty-year-old Morgan, a young agent from the Department of Agriculture parked alongside the road and walked into the field to ask some questions about his farm operation. When he informed Almanzo that federal regulations prohibited him from planting more than two acres of oats, the farmer retorted that if the fellow did not immediately leave his property, he was going to go get his shotgun. The agent, who was writing this down, offered Almanzo an opportunity to change his words for the record. At that point the old man made his meaning perfectly clear, in Rose's telling of the story. He said, "God damn you, you get to hell off my land and you do it now. I'll plant whatever I damn please on my own farm, and if you're on it when I get to my gun, by God I'll fill you with buckshot."[20]

As the 1930s wore on and government activities continued to expand, the family grew ever more resolute in their opposition to Roosevelt and his claque of New Dealers. Within weeks of the president's inauguration, Rose began referring to him as a dictator, and her parents agreed. All three of them mutually reinforced each other's suspicions about FDR and his minions. Rose eventually would devote her energies to attacking the direction in

which the government was being taken by the liberals in Washington. In the meantime, she and Laura continued their literary pursuits, with their subject matter increasingly converging. But just as Laura was beginning to win some recognition for her children's novels, Rose was sinking into the depths of depression, burdened by a sense of personal powerlessness and inadequacy.[21]

Rose's journal entries during 1933 reveal her at her lowest point. Growing older, suffering from various health problems, lacking friends to whom she could fully relate, searching for some significant project that would elevate her above literary hackwork, and sensing that she would never discover love again, Rose turned morose and suicidal. At least some of her depressed state of mind revolved around frustrations emanating from her close proximity to her mother. They seemed to grate on each other's nerves when they lived too close to each other. Having to take precious time from her own writing to devote to her mother's books nagged at her, but her sense of duty compelled her to do it. Their main points of conflict revolved around money and power. Rose considered her mother to be manipulative in trying to extract money from her, even though she often showered her parents with expensive and not-always-wanted gifts, like the house that she built for them. Ultimately, power and control lay at the heart of their disagreements. Rose never had been quite able to cut the knot that bound her to her mother, and now, as she was approaching fifty, her mother still sometimes seemed to view her as a little girl, while Rose, for her part, seemed to want to establish her own control over her parents' lives.

What Rose successfully hid from other people, she set down at length and in explicit detail on paper at night. Starting a journal in January 1933, she admitted, "So far, I am almost superlatively a failure. There has been no success in personal relationships, in adjustment to the world, in work, or in money." Attempting to understand her own sense of failure, Rose pondered, "I have never really felt that I am I; I feel no identification with myself. My life is not *my* life, but a succession of short stories and one-act plays, all begun by chance and left unfinished."[22]

Rose's years of living at Rocky Ridge had all been wasted. "Since 1927 I have spent most of my time and about $15,000 on it, without pleasure or any satisfaction. I do not like the place, I do not like to live here, and I see no prospect of ever leaving." What may have prompted Rose to start writing this journal was her sense of being tied down to working on her

mother's second novel, "Farmer Boy." When Harper's asked for a revised version of the manuscript, Rose spent two and a half weeks in January 1933 working on it and then most of February retyping it. By March 2 she was finally finished. In the middle of all of this, her dog, who was named Mr. Bunting, was killed by a car. This, combined with all of her other worries and concerns, prompted long crying jags over the next several months. In addition, she was pessimistic about the likely sales of *Let the Hurricane Roar,* which had been published in book form. It should not have been too surprising, therefore, that she directed, either consciously or unconsciously, many of her accumulated frustrations against her mother.[23]

Rose did not count what she was doing for her mother as being important. "I am getting nothing whatever done," she wrote in her journal on January 27. "Preparing to rewrite my mother's second juvenile, Farmer Boy. Work on it every day till teatime, going over first typed mss. with pen. Would like to finish it this month, but can't possibly. Meantime my own work stagnates: I do not even think about it." Rose recognized "a curious half-angry reluctance" on her part to help other people with their writing: "I say to myself that whatever earnings there may be are all in the family. Also I seize upon this task as an excuse to postpone my own work. But there can be no genuine pleasure in generosity to my mother who resents it and does not trouble to conceal resentment."[24]

Rose's journal became a record of her mental illness during her depressed period in 1933. Displaying great insight into her own personal pathology, Rose nevertheless found it difficult to translate self-knowledge into transformed behavior. A day after being traumatized by Mr. Bunting's death, she recorded, "I can not love. That's what's wrong with me. I give everything except real warmth, myself. Living is hell and all life is to be pitied." One week later: "Why am I such a monster? I *am* a monster. I always have been. There is no true warmth in my nature. I have no heart." In late March: "My mind is paralyzed, not any longer by fear and worry, but by exhaustion. Day after day, I am simply motionless. Not even waiting, any more." At the end of the month: "I am mentally sick. Can't stop crying." And one month later: "All these days I have been sick in my mind. I haven't yet stopped crying. I read all day and am ashamed because it is only a way of trying to escape."[25]

During the midst of all this, Rose acknowledged the pent-up resentment that had been accumulating in her against her mother. Describing a scene

that took place at her parents' home on April 9, when Laura suggested that they turn off their electricity in order to cut down on expenses, Rose let all of her animus out. "It's amazing how my mother can make me suffer," she wrote. "Implicit in every syllable and tone, the fact that I've failed, fallen down on the job, been the broken reed. But never mind, (brightly) she's able to manage nicely, thank you!" Once again, money—or Rose's impression that her mother was dunning her for money—triggered her outburst. She recognized that Laura was reaching out for some kind of companionship and wished she could be friends with her. Yet, in her view she had "not the faintest notion what she's doing to me. . . . She made me so miserable when I was a child that I've never got over it. I'm morbid. I'm all raw nerves. I know I should be more robust. I shouldn't let her torture me this way, and always gain her own ends, thro implications that she hardly knows she's using. But I can't help it."[26]

Such words need to be considered in context and against Rose's own contradictions of them. She recognized herself that she was not thinking straight during this period of time. On May 20, she wrote in her journal, "I have been mentally sick ever since Bunting died. But quite suddenly one day I was whole again, though shaky. I am now almost sane once more."[27]

Laura signed a contract for "Farmer Boy" that month. Harper's had agreed to take the new revised manuscript in March, two weeks after Rose mailed it, but at only a 5-percent royalty for the first three thousand copies and thereafter the standard 10 percent, which is what Laura had received for *Little House in the Big Woods*. Rose was upset at being forced to take the reduced rate, but she followed the recommendation of her agent, George Bye, who told her, "If you can get a first class publisher to take a routine seller like a juvenile, with little chance for a flash sale, these days, at only slightly offish terms, I'd accept." By June 1 proofs were in hand, and Laura went to Rose's place to check them.[28]

Reviews again were favorable, although there were fewer this time. Calling the story of Almanzo "a delightful tale," the *Boston Transcript,* like other publications, located its appeal in its faithful description of farm life before mechanization, radio, movies, and other modern trends transformed the rural way of life. The *New York Times* praised it as "a genuine bit of American life, vividly and charmingly described and centering about a very real and natural small boy." *Books* noted, "Altogether there is reason to be grateful to Mrs. Wilder for another light thrown on our domestic past."[29]

Even before *Farmer Boy* was published, Laura was working on another volume to carry her own story forward. She intended to focus on her family's brief stay on the Osage Indian Reserve in southeastern Kansas when she was only two or three years old. To try to pin down some of the facts and hazy details that had been lost to time, Laura and Rose began to research them, writing to libraries and historical societies and even making a trip to Kansas to see if they could find the location of the rude cabin where her family had lived. *Let the Hurricane Roar,* meantime, went into its third printing, and *Publishers Weekly* reported that it was a best-seller in Chicago. Rose worried that she should be taking advantage of momentum generated by the book's sales to get more short stories published, but she had a hard time getting started. "I should be giving editors pioneer stories," she told herself. Working on her mother's first two novels and on her own *Saturday Evening Post* serial set in Dakota Territory had turned her attention toward the frontier. Both before and after publishing *Hurricane,* she recorded efforts to write a story she was calling "The Hard Winter," and in 1937 she would rely on her parents' accounts to write another Dakota pioneer story, *Free Land.* Now, however, she began to concoct a grandiose and highly unrealistic scheme for a multivolume novel that would chronicle the entire westward movement of the United States, with a great cast of characters representing all phases of American economic and social life. This would be a grand, sweeping panorama of national history, echoing American themes with which she now identified. The leftist critique of American values and mores that she had formulated during the early 1920s now gave way to celebration of them. It took her only a few days to realize that her fantastic plan was only a mirage. To some degree, however, her historical impulse found realization in the frontier novels that she helped her mother write, and several years later Rose would make another attempt at writing a historical book, this time about the state of Missouri.[30]

Apparently their writing activities led Laura and Rose to withdraw from most of their outside activities during the early 1930s. Whereas earlier the *Mansfield Mirror* had frequently recorded their presence at meetings of the Justamere Club, bridge parties, and various other social gatherings, now there was scarcely a reference. Laura's age as well as her need to work on her books would have figured prominently in her withdrawal from community activities. Not that the family became social recluses. They continued to entertain at home from time to time. The newspaper reported the visit of

the family of Julian Bucher, who had spent summers with them when he was a boy, at "the beautiful country home" of the Wilders in September 1934. The J. W. Brentlingers spent a Sunday afternoon visiting the Wilders a month later. A former Mansfield boy, Ogden Riley of Peoria, Illinois, stayed with them while visiting old friends in and around town. And there certainly would have been other unreported visiting back and forth between the Wilders and their friends and neighbors. The Craigs continued to be valued friends, and Rose grew more and more attached to Corinne Murray, who shared many of her interests.[31]

Mostly, though, Laura, Almanzo, and Rose kept each other company, often walking back and forth across the ridge to each other's houses to talk, share meals, or take tea. The diary that Rose kept regularly from 1931 to 1935 chronicles the frequency of these visits, which waxed and waned depending on the weather, work schedules, and other factors. Mostly it was Laura and Rose getting together; less often Almanzo was involved. Waffles or pancakes and sausage might make breakfast. Laura invited Rose over to make doughnuts. Fried spring chicken was sometimes on the menu, or fresh greens out of the garden, or tapioca cream and sponge cake. Sometimes they saw each other every day; at other times maybe only once a week or less (assuming that Rose was fairly thorough in noting these encounters in her diary). Most commonly they got together two or three times a week. In addition, there was always the phone, and sometimes even Almanzo used it to call Rose.[32]

Laura and Almanzo owned a radio, and Rose came to listen to several of President Roosevelt's fireside chats, although the family was more interested in local gossip or things around the farm than politics. Sometimes they played chess or dominoes. They celebrated each other's birthdays, and at Christmastime they got together to trim a tree. Almanzo was known to shoot a game of pool, and now and then they drove or walked into town to take in a movie—maybe a Charlie Chan feature or Wallace Beery in *Treasure Island* or Pauline Lord in *Mrs. Wiggs*. They may have gone in to listen to Saturday-night band concerts on the square and probably attended some of the ceremonies and festivities around Memorial Day and Fourth of July.[33]

Often they drove to nearby towns to visit friends, shop, eat, or take in entertainment. Sometimes Corinne Murray or a friend from out of town went with them, or a group got together to visit some place such as the Shrine Mosque in Springfield. Cedar Gap, Mountain Grove, Seymour, Ava,

and Hartville were short distances away. Sometimes they ventured farther out, traveling to Branson, or Crystal Lake, or down into northern Arkansas.

Rose's life changed dramatically when a fourteen-year-old orphan named John Turner showed up on her kitchen porch one cold, rainy afternoon in September 1933, offering to do some work in return for food. Rose responded to her mothering instinct and not only gave the boy a job weeding the flower bed but also took him into her home and nursed him and put him into the Mansfield high school. Later, upon discovering that John had an older brother named Al, who was still living on their uncle's farm near Ava, she took him in, too. Although the relationship between her and the boys was not always a smooth one, she discovered in them a new purpose for living. They helped restore in her a sense of fulfillment and nurturing, brightening her outlook on life. No longer expecting to find a loving relationship with a man, she invested her affectionate instincts in the boys, who partially reciprocated her feelings but who also could be a great frustration to her. At the end of the year she recorded in her journal, "John is a deep joy to me. There is endless interest, amusement, fascination, charm, in such a relationship with a child."[34]

Even so, the year ended dismally for Rose. Much of her malaise flowed from her ambivalent attitudes toward her mother. "I want to keep on going but do not quite see how," she wrote, "and there is no alternative—rather than justify my mother's 25-year dread of my 'coming back on her, sick' I must kill myself. If she has to pay funeral costs, at least she will cut them to the bone and I will not have to endure her martyrdom and prolong it by living."[35]

It would be a wonderful thing if Laura had written and saved letters, diaries, and journals the way her daughter did. Had she done so, we could understand more about her thoughts and feelings as she wrote her novels. As it is, we can know in excruciating detail the innermost dreams and expectations, frustrations and suicidal wishes of Rose; about Laura's inner life we know relatively little. The most revealing evidence about her is to be found in her published writings—including her newspaper journalism—and in a few letters that have been preserved.

Laura finished her "Indian juvenile" on February 1, 1934. Afterward, the family drove to Mountain Grove, where they ate some "awful food in [an] awful restaurant," in Rose's words, and went to see a movie, *The Invisible Man,* which Rose described as "rotten." But they all had "a gay, noisy time"

driving home. Laura had worked on the manuscript during the second half of 1933. In this, her second autobiographical volume, she directly confronted the presence of Indians on the frontier. The story revolves around the family's moving to "Indian Territory" in Kansas and then being forced to leave when the federal government enforced the terms of a treaty with the Osage Indians by requiring white intruders who were squatting on the reserve to vacate. Although she had neglected to mention Indians in her first book about the allegedly "vast, empty forest" of northwestern Wisconsin, and while Indians were treated only marginally in her later narratives, Laura was not unaware of their presence on the frontier, and her thoughts about them were well-meaning, if often ambivalent.[36]

What is notable about Laura's attitudes toward Indians is not so much that they contained a considerable degree of narrow-mindedness and prejudice but that they, to some degree at least, transcended generally accepted notions that were held about racial inferiority and the Indians' alleged backwardness. Wright County had few blacks residing in it. Most of them were concentrated near Hartville, where their annual picnic was a big event in the area. Missouri had been a slave state and was the site of a number of Civil War battles, including the Battle of Hartville in 1863. Not surprisingly, Missouri's white population, deriving from a largely southern background, by and large accepted common racial stereotypes imputing black inferiority. Some towns enforced traditions that blacks would not be allowed to settle in them. Bigoted language was commonplace, and the idea that the races were equal would have been considered radical in the extreme by most people. Within this context, Laura could have been forgiven for harboring some of the prevalent prejudices directed against blacks, Indians, and other minorities. Her religious training and the precepts of fairness and benevolence that her parents imparted to her inclined her toward a more enlightened viewpoint.[37]

Rose waited three and a half months before tackling her mother's "Indian story." She was trying, with middling success, to churn out more of her own material, often running dry but managing to complete two short stories, "Hope Chest" and "Perfect House," during the first part of 1934. It was only when she could not get started on another story that on May 20 she reluctantly turned to the task of working on her mother's novel. Laura stopped by after the first week to see how things were going, and Rose gave her a copy of what she had completed up to that time. The days were

excruciatingly hot. Once Rose recorded the temperature at 125 degrees; the next day it was 135, breaking the thermometer. Laura was sick for a while, and once Rose walked the mile back and forth between the houses four times. Her eyes were giving her trouble, and she went to Springfield to have minor surgery on her eyelids. Most days, however, she managed to stick to the task, and by June 10 she had finished her revisions on her mother's manuscript. After an early dinner, they all walked into town to watch Clark Gable, William Powell, and Myrna Loy in *Manhattan Melodrama*. After enjoying a day off from her labors, Rose took a little less than two weeks' time to copy what they were calling "High Prairie" and to get it ready to mail to the publisher. The whole job took her five weeks; afterward there was nothing to do but wait for word from New York.[38]

Despite the heat, which continued to hover around 100 degrees, Rose made another short stab at writing "The Hard Winter" before finishing a story called "Object Matrimony," which quickly was bought by the *Saturday Evening Post* for nine hundred dollars. She also worked on a story called "Old Fashioned Christmas" before deciding to escape the July heat by going with John Turner on a five-week rail vacation to Florida, arriving back home on August 27. She wrote more short stories by the end of the year, but Rose again grew restless, more than ever eager to escape Rocky Ridge. Her mother was getting on with her writing now, and Rose had the additional responsibility of taking care of Al and John, who soon would be ready to head off to college. On February 26, 1935, she wrote in her diary, "I can not stand this house, this sunk-in-the-muck way of living, any more. I must get out."[39]

By the time that day finally arrived, Rose's departure from Mansfield had taken on a sense of inevitability, and the parting turned out to be not nearly so traumatic as she had imagined. In April she received an offer from the McBride Publishing Company to write a volume about Missouri for a series of state books that the company was in the process of publishing. At the time, Rose was just finishing a preface for a collection of short stories set in a fictionalized Mansfield that she had previously published. Longmans, Green, and Company was publishing the collection under the title *Old Home Town*. The McBride offer seemed especially enticing to Rose, since she had increasingly been turning her attention toward history. A state-oriented book would allow her to develop some of her ideas about how history should be written with regard to a single state about which she possessed

some personal feeling and knowledge. The fifteen-hundred-dollar advance offered by the company also attracted her. Rose started researching the book in mid-May by reading books and taking notes about Missouri history at home, but she quickly concluded that to do a decent job she would need to use a good research library, like the one at the State Historical Society in Columbia. Thus, the decision was made to go live in the college town for an extended period of time while she did the necessary research. It was easier for her to move out under the circumstances, since neither she nor her parents realized that she would never return to live with them.[40]

Laura decided to ride with Rose and Corinne Murray on July 20 for the 170-mile drive to Columbia, where Rose installed herself in a room downtown in the Tiger Hotel. From there, it was only a few minutes' walk to the State Historical Society Library on the University of Missouri campus. Laura and Corinne drove home the next day. Life would be different for Laura and Almanzo without Rose, who had been living at Rocky Ridge for the previous seven and a half years. Only later would they all come to understand that she had left the place for good. Rose bought a secondhand Ford to travel around the state to gather material for her book, and Corinne Murray drove back to Columbia to accompany her on the trip. Unfortunately, the anecdotal, historical manuscript that Rose produced for the McBride Company did not meet their expectations. They had more of a contemporary travel book in mind, and her manuscript never was published. The better part of a year that she had spent working on it was wasted.[41]

Laura's third book, whose title had gone from "High Prairie" to *Little House on the Prairie,* appeared toward the end of September 1935. Ida Louise Raymond at Harper and Brothers had sent it to a Midwestern librarian for evaluation before deciding whether to publish it. The librarian who read the manuscript liked it very much. As soon as copies were available, Laura gave one to the *Mansfield Mirror,* and they printed a story about it on the front page. Once again reviewers were quick with praise for the book and for the illustrations of Helen Sewell, which were described as "childlike and inviting" by one reviewer and "just right" by another. "Furiously interesting," M. L. Becker called the book. Families should sit down and read it aloud, *Books* suggested. "Mrs. Wilder has caught the very essence of pioneer life, the satisfaction of hard work, the thrill of accomplishment, safety and comfort made possible through resourcefulness and exertion,"

the *New York Times* reviewer wrote. "She draws, too, with humor and with understanding, the picture of a fine and courageous family, who are loyal and imaginative in their relationships to one another."[42]

During late 1935 and early 1936 Laura worked on a fourth volume, this one about the family's stays in Minnesota. She skipped over the interlude in Burr Oak, Iowa, perhaps because the memory of that period when her little brother, Freddie, died was too painful, perhaps because describing the move away from Walnut Grove and back again would complicate the story too much. Instead, she wrote it as if they had simply lived in Minnesota once. Writing in the middle of the Great Depression and during some of the worst drought and heat the country had ever experienced, Laura must have felt a sense of déjà vu in describing the difficulties of pioneer life in Minnesota during the 1870s. The challenges facing the family had included drought, grasshoppers, prairie fires, and crop failure, similar in many ways to the devastation wrought by the hard times of the 1930s, with its dust storms, insect invasions, and market collapse.

Rose, in Columbia, had the manuscript in hand by the end of March 1936, but she put it aside for the time being. "Have to finish my mother's goddam juvenile, which has me stopped flat," she noted in her diary on May 10. In June and July she finally tackled it. This was the first volume that Laura had written without Rose being nearby for consultation. Now the revision process would have to take place at a distance, with letters passing back and forth between them. Not surprisingly, Rose resented the demands on her time occasioned by her mother's book. Once again her own material was selling well, which was encouraging. She earned $9,717 (minus commissions of $946) for her efforts that year, her best performance since 1926.[43]

The kinds of things that mother and daughter previously would have discussed over tea or breakfast now had to be taken care of in letters. Laura depended on Rose's judgment almost entirely to make the necessary modifications. To aid in the process of revision, Rose constructed a series of detailed questions about food, clothing, furniture, buildings, and a dozen other things that they both wanted to get right and to be understandable to their readers. The collaborative process that continued to develop between the two was not simply a one-way street, with Rose in the driver's seat; both were intimately involved in the process. Working together at such a distance was hard, but they managed. After several weeks at the task, Laura

sent a list of suggested cuts and modifications, telling her daughter that it would be better if Rose made the changes on the version that she had in her possession. "I have no copy of the thing here that I can go over," Laura explained. "If I should try to use the first scraps of scribbling, I would get us all confused for I changed it so much from them. That makes it hard for me to tell you where to cut."[44]

Laura made a map depicting Plum Creek and its relation to other landmarks, including their original dugout, the new house that her father had built for them, the stable, the swimming hole, the fish trap, the firebreak, the path to the Nelsons, and the road to town. "This was and is prairie country," she reminded Rose, warning her not to confuse it with the hills and the gorge that they were so familiar with at Rocky Ridge. Aware that her memory was less than perfect on many details, she nevertheless was able to remember many particulars, even though she had been only six years old when the family moved to Minnesota. Following the precedent set in the first book of elevating the girls' ages, in this one Laura made them all a year older than they actually had been at the time.[45]

Laura's original manuscript had failed to mention the railroad tracks on the edge of town that she and her sisters had to cross on their way to school, and Rose asked about the omission. Her query jogged Laura's memory. She drew another map to show where the railroad had been and how it was situated in relation to the half dozen or so buildings that she remembered being in the town at the time. Rose was full of questions. She asked about how potatoes, carrots, and other vegetables could have survived in the ground after rabbits had eaten their tops, and Laura explained that Minnesota's soil differed from Missouri's, making it better able to preserve things that remained in the ground. She asked about the big "crab" that her mother had seen in the creek, not believing that a fresh-water crab was likely to be found there, but they decided to leave it in the book anyway. She asked about vanity cakes, about the rooms at the back of a store where a party was held, about the recipe for vinegar pie, about when school terms were held, about the desks and books and blackboards, about sidewalks and song lyrics, and about many other things.[46]

Laura dutifully answered all of Rose's questions as best she could, thanking her for making suggestions and for correcting her mistakes. "I know they are many," she admitted. "I have written you the whys of the story as I wrote it. But you know your judgment is better than mine,

so what you decide is the one that stands." Many of the scenes were so vivid in her mind that she did not always consider that her readers might have a hard time visualizing what she was talking about without more elaborate description. Regarding the map of the town that she had drawn, she noted, "I see the pictures so plainly that I guess I failed to paint them as I should." Not always, however, did Laura follow her daughter's advice. When Rose suggested that it would make more sense for Laura and Mary to have visited the town before walking there on their first day of school, her mother responded that she did not think they actually had seen the town before their first walk to school, so that was the way it stayed in the final draft.[47]

Laura was careful not only to get the details as accurate as possible but also to try to capture the right tone in describing relationships within the family. The pains she took to get the language—as well as the facts—right increases our confidence today that her descriptions of personality and personal interactions were essentially correct. While Laura's father never used language any stronger than "Gosh all hemlock" or "I'll be darned," her mother would never have stooped to even such expressions. "Her language was rather precise and a great deal better language than I have ever used," Laura admitted. She said that she and Grace had been more like their father in that respect; Mary and Carrie had been more like their mother. Referring to something that Rose had written about Ma saying that "she vowed she didn't believe those young ones were *ever* going to sleep," Laura commented that her mother would never have called them "young ones." She always referred to them as "children." Nor, being a lady, would she ever have used the expression "I vow."[48]

One technical problem had Laura stumped. During a blizzard when Pa was in town, Ma had to go out to the barn to take care of the animals, raising the question of how the scene should be written, since Rose always emphasized that everything should be described as Laura herself had observed it. But if Laura could not have gone out to the barn, she would have been in no position to describe the action inside. There was a problem, however, in that Laura would not have been tall enough to reach the clothesline that they had stretched from the house to the barn to prevent their wandering off in the storm, and Ma could not have held her hand because one of her hands would have been on the clothesline and the other would have been carrying the milk pail. "I don't know how to handle it,"

Laura wrote Rose. "Seeing the inside of that stable and how Ma did the chores seems rather necessary to the interest of the whole thing. But How? I am beat!" In the end they decided to let Laura stay inside the house and imagine what Ma was doing, moment by moment, as she went out into the storm.[49]

While attempting to get all of the details straight, Laura and Rose were not above manipulating facts or even making things up in order to convey the proper impression to the reader or to keep the story moving. For example, in describing how the creek flowed past their dugout—foaming and roaring as it pushed around the bend—Laura told Rose, "I have an awful suspicion that we drank plain creek water, in the raw, without boiling it or whatever. But that would make the reader think we were dirty, which we were not. So I said a spring. There could have been a spring near where Pa watered the oxen or there could be one near the plank footbridge. As it is located in my imagination, you may put it where it is most convenient."[50]

Rose spent about two months working on the manuscript. While mother and daughter were in correspondence about it, Laura added tidbits about happenings at Rocky Ridge. An electrical mishap had sparked a fire in the woods behind their garage by the barn. Luckily, they had been able to rouse the neighbors to help put it out. Almanzo had been in such a hurry to douse the flames that he ran out in just his shirt and shoes, without his pants or socks. More serious was some trouble that Al Turner had gotten into, which Laura advised Rose not just to forgive and forget. "If he gets off too easy," she cautioned, "he might think he got away with that all right and you would help him out again and try something again." Rose probably recognized in her mother's advice the same sort of strictness that she herself had been subject to while she was growing up. Laura seemed to be uncertain about the best way to treat the problem. After considering all of the ramifications, she concluded, "Oh Dam! I don't know what to do."[51]

Even more difficult to deal with was the situation of Corinne Murray and her husband, who were living in the farmhouse while Rose was in Columbia. Jack Murray had been observed hauling water away in big cans in his truck to use in their laundry operation downtown. His apparent motive was to save on water bills. The situation was bothering Laura, who earlier had urged Rose to let the Murrays stay at the place. Now she advised

getting rid of them and closing the house. Finally, as Rose recorded it in her journal four years later, Laura presented her with a simple choice: "come back at once to stay (and throw Corinne out) or get out myself. She added that she had ordered Bruce [the hired man] to kill my dog. (Which he did.)" In evicting Corinne, Rose softened the blow by giving her all of her possessions except for her books, and meanwhile gave the house back to her parents. They wasted little time in moving back into the house they had always preferred living in, and the rock house that Rose had built for them was left standing empty for the time being. Once separated from Rocky Ridge, Rose evinced no desire to return to it and did not come back to Mansfield to visit until Almanzo died in 1949.[52]

Rose finished revising and retyping the Plum Creek manuscript just before midnight on September 21 and sent the original to Laura the next day with detailed instructions about how to send it to George Bye. He would forward it to Ida Louise Raymond, who was waiting for it at Harper and Brothers. Rose informed her mother that she would hold on to the carbon copy until hearing that the original had arrived safely in New York, because to lose the manuscript would be ghastly. Previously, they had simply mailed packages from the Mansfield post office, keeping the carbon copy at home. Rose was being careful to maintain the illusion that these books were entirely her mother's work. She had worked steadily to get the manuscript finished, "not even stopping to sleep." She thanked her mother for having sent along a picture of herself. "I am so glad to have your picture," she wrote, "but I do not think it flatters you at all. Indeed you are much prettier than it." She thought that the camera had made her look too old. "Your eyes are so lively and your expressions change so, and though if one stops to think of it your hair is white, still the effect is really of blonde hair, of light hair that contrasts so with your dark blue eyes and dark lashes, and is always so wavy and pretty."[53]

When this third "Laura and Mary" book—and the fourth overall—appeared at the end of 1937, reviewers praised it in terms similar to the ones that they had used to describe the previous ones. The story was judged to be "fine," "vigorous," "honest," and "magical." Without reverting to sentimentality, it served up "a warm, glowing picture of steadfast family love and devotion," *Horn Book Magazine* commented. The *New York Times's* reviewer welcomed a story in which the characters were allowed to speak

for themselves. Rather than being told by the author what they were like, readers were allowed to observe directly their growth over time and to discover for themselves what kind of people they were. With four books now in circulation, Laura Ingalls Wilder had established a firm reputation for herself as a popular children's author, and her readers were begging for more.[54]

# 8

## Completing the Series

### 1937–1943

જી

*T*he publication of *On the Banks of Plum Creek* toward the end of 1937 further established Laura Ingalls Wilder's stature as one of America's most popular children's authors. By now many of her youthful fans were well acquainted with her characters and wrote letters asking what would happen next to them and when her next book was coming out. Librarians, teachers, and people in the publishing community were also enthusiastic about her work. A teacher in Minneapolis wrote to say that her first two books were being used in every third-grade class in the state.[1]

Further recognition came with an invitation that fall to speak at a Detroit book fair sponsored by the big J. L. Hudson Department Store. Laura's talk was scheduled for October 16. Laura accepted the invitation despite the long distance and her trepidation in front of large audiences. "I have never lost my timidity with total strangers," she wrote Aubrey Sherwood of the *De Smet News*, but this would be a good opportunity to boost book sales, and that helped overcome her initial reluctance. From New York, Rose sent encouraging notes as Laura prepared for the trip. "Everyone who sees or meets you will buy all your books," her daughter wrote, "and every librarian who does will buy a good many copies." She urged her mother not to worry

about spending too much money on the trip. "Whatever it costs, you will make up later simply by meeting people and seeing things and being better known yourself. I do hope to heaven you will not appear only for once and then rush away in order to save a few dollars."[2]

Laura's decision to go was made easier when a young friend of theirs, Silas Seal, agreed to drive them to Detroit. He was familiar with the area, having worked in one of Henry Ford's automobile plants for several years during the 1920s. He and Almanzo had become friendly after he returned to Mansfield in 1928 with his wife, Neta, to open a service station. The young man impressed Almanzo with his friendliness and willingness to work. Silas always washed Almanzo's windshield and checked his oil and tire pressure before even asking whether he wanted to buy any gas. When Almanzo drove Laura into town to shop, he often wiled away his time at the station, striking up conversations with Silas and other loiterers. Laura also enjoyed the Seals' company, and Neta was invited to ride with them on the trip. But unfortunately she got sick and had to stay home. Silas paid a man to take care of his service station for a week, and the threesome headed off to Michigan.[3]

It was a great adventure for Laura and Almanzo. Except for their excursion to South Dakota in 1931, Almanzo had seldom ventured far from home since coming to Missouri in 1894. Laura had been lucky enough to visit the West Coast twice. Silas Seal turned out to be an excellent driver. In Detroit they put two hundred miles on the Chrysler just by driving around the city. Almanzo thought it was a beautiful place. Its parks and streets were neat and clean, and he noted that "if a leaf falls from a tree there is someone to pick it up." He especially enjoyed visiting the Henry Ford Museum and viewing all the exhibits and machinery on display. Besides, the food was great; he figured he could get a better meal in Detroit for forty cents than he could in Springfield at any price.[4]

In a letter from the Grosvenor Hotel in New York, where she was living at the time, Rose was full of reassurance and advice for her mother, who was not used to city life or standing up in front of large audiences. "Remain calm, darling. When in any doubt whatever, always pause and COUNT Ten," she counseled. "Always remember that *you are the one to be served.* Whatever YOU want, that is the right thing." Ida Louise Raymond from Harper and Brothers came for the event, and Rose instructed Laura on how to approach the editor about some publishing ideas that she had been

mulling over, including the possibility of doing a book of poetry. Laura had always enjoyed writing poems, and now she thought that she might be able to publish them. Rose tried to be encouraging, reminding her, "There's a lot you don't know about this whole field of publishing; remember that ignorance is an asset and do not conceal it."[5]

Laura was concerned about giving her speech and the reception it would get, and she solicited Rose's advice in preparing her remarks. She need not have worried. Before leaving home she wrote the entire text on the same kind of lined tablet she used for writing her books. The text added up to sixteen handwritten pages and provided the best explanation she ever gave for how and why she wrote her books. Laura talked a bit about her parents and about the four books she had already finished. She indicated that she was planning three more set in Dakota Territory to complete the series, resulting in a seven-volume novel. She promised that Almanzo, the "Farmer Boy" of book two, would reappear in the fifth volume, the one she was working on at the time. He would go with Laura the rest of the way through the series, which would end happily ("as all good novels should") when the two of them got married. The question that children asked her most, Laura told Rose afterward, was what was going to happen to Laura and Almanzo.[6]

Laura's explanation of why she had begun writing the books—that she wanted to preserve the stories that she and her sisters had loved to hear their father tell—was incomplete. Preservation of family folklore certainly played a role, but equally important factors were her longtime desire to write for publication and her wish to leave something significant behind. She had written *Little House in the Big Woods* to expand the manuscript that Rose had carved out of Laura's autobiography. Probably not sure of what kind of response she would get and not envisioning a long series at the outset, Laura had seen the project grow naturally as time passed. She told her listeners at the book fair that the success of the first volume and letters from children all over the country begging her for more stories had prompted her to reflect further upon her childhood. She realized now that her life encapsulated the several phases of frontier history. She told about her desire to help children understand more about the beginning of things and how they had come to be what they were and how this had led her to conceive of a multivolume "historical novel for children covering every aspect of the American frontier." She failed to point out, however, that she had actually started writing *Farmer Boy* before the release of her first book

and long before delighted readers began asking her for more. It is likely that the formulation of the larger project evolved in her thinking over a period of time. In the end, four more books, not three, would appear, and the entire series would run to eight volumes.[7]

Laura stretched things a bit regarding "On the Banks of Plum Creek," which was being readied for publication at the time, in saying that all of the stories contained in it—all the circumstances and every incident—were true. She and Rose always insisted on the complete historical accuracy of her books, but the two failed to acknowledge that scenes, characters, and dialogue were often modified, embellished, rearranged, or even created when they felt it was necessary. Additionally, Laura's memory was not totally reliable; every year it slipped a little more. Seven years after finishing "Pioneer Girl" she admitted to Rose that her memories of things that had happened many years earlier were no longer nearly as vivid as they had been when she started writing.[8] In addition, the fictional format within which they were operating demanded that they streamline some things, expand upon others, modify chronology, redefine characters, and depart in other ways from strict historical accuracy in order to maximize readability and to obtain what could be called "literary truth." Some things needed to be left out, Laura explained, because they were inappropriate for younger readers. So if her stories were truthful in one sense, they did not always tell the whole truth. The murderous Kate Bender family in Kansas and children freezing to death in a blizzard on Plum Creek—stories like these, Laura said, did not fit into the format that she had adopted.

In her Detroit speech, Laura displayed some of the kind of low-key humor that frequently surprised people. Her husband, she said, still loved horses, but now he drove a Chrysler sedan. At least he held on to the wheel. "Of course I do the driving with my tongue," she laughed. Mainly, though, her intent was serious: to provide people with some idea of how and why she had gone about writing her books and to distill their essence. "The spirit of the frontier," she explained, "was one of humor and cheerfulness no matter what happened and whether the joke was on oneself or the other fellow." People either brought that spirit west with them or acquired it in the process of living there. Her parents had possessed it to a marked degree, she noted. "It shines through all the volumes of my children's novel."[9]

Laura drove home her point more explicitly in a talk to the Sorosis Club of Mountain Grove while she was writing "On the Banks of Plum Creek."

She noted that running "like a golden thread" through all of her stories were certain basic values: "courage, self-reliance, independence, integrity and helpfulness. Cheerfulness and humor were handmaids to courage." Her parents, she observed, had worked diligently, suffered heat and cold, lost their money, endured privation, yet, despite everything, had managed to survive. They had not begged for help and had not expected the government or any person to owe them a living. They had made their own way. "Their old fashioned character values are worth as much today as they ever were to help us over the rough places," Laura noted. The same kinds of virtues were needed in 1937 that had been required sixty years earlier, she asserted. She made it clear that her books were as much about the present as they were about the past. The moral lessons and advice for living that she imparted in them were simply offered up in a different format from what they had been in the biweekly articles that she had written for the *Missouri Ruralist* for more than a decade.[10]

Laura, Almanzo, and Silas Seal returned to Mansfield two days after she gave her talk in Detroit. The trip had been enjoyable, Laura told Rose, promising to send her a copy of her remarks. Rose responded enthusiastically after reading them, "Detroit talk came and it is *fine*. No wonder you made a great hit. Those stories are marvelous." Rose, in fact, was getting heavily into pioneer stories herself. After having once asserted that they held no interest for her, she had written one herself in 1932 and then had tried on and off during the next several years to write something about the hard winter of 1880–1881, largely based on stories that her parents had told her about their own experiences. Somehow the project never jelled, however, and within a short time her mother would be involved in writing her own version of those events.[11]

But now a new story had come into view for Rose to write about, one focusing on her grandparents and the early homesteading experience in Dakota Territory when railroads were pushing into the region, bringing fresh waves of settlers with them. To help visualize the historical context and pinpoint dozens of factual details, Rose had corresponded frequently with her parents during the early months of 1937 while she was still living at the Tiger Hotel in Columbia. They had responded eagerly to her questions, writing long, detailed reports on all of the things that they were able to remember. Not being able to recall the names of many of the plants and wildflowers that had bloomed on the prairie, Laura had written to Grace

to see if she could help. When her sister had reminded her of the crocuses, wild onions, violets, sheep sorrel, yellow buttercups, wild peas, tiger lilies, and wild geraniums that had blanketed the land, Laura had sighed, "To think that I could have forgotten all this which comes back to me now. That's why the sooner I write my stuff the better."[12]

Laura copied down prices and other information from her father's old railroad account book to pass on to her daughter. An entry from June 1879, when the construction camp was at the Big Sioux River, listed:

| | |
|---|---|
| 1 plug Tobaco | $ .10 |
| 1 Rubber Coat | 3.00 |
| 1 Hundred lb. flour | 2.75 |
| 1 lb. Tea | 1.00 |
| 2 Shirts | 1.60 |

Almanzo wrote about what it had been like building the railroad and how homesteaders had turned the sod to get their first crops in. Rose followed up with a long questionnaire, leaving blank spaces between the questions for her father to write his answers. He searched his memory to dredge up information on the cost of lumber, a good horse, and a plow; wages and hours for workers building the railroad; wheat prices; the kinds of trees they had planted; the depth of a well; interest rates, both short-term and long-term; the kinds of newspapers and magazines they had read; song titles; wind velocities; animals that had lived on the plains; the Indians who inhabited the area; and dozens of other things.[13]

In June 1937, Rose finally left the Tiger Hotel in Columbia and moved to New York City. In deciding not to return to Rocky Ridge she made her final break with her parents. Soon she was working full-time on her pioneer story, working fourteen- to twenty-hour days. It was not exactly her grandparents' story, but the setting and the circumstances were similar. The title, "Free Land," was self-consciously ironic and was meant to refute the commonly held notion that homesteads had been obtainable for almost nothing. The idea that "conditions had changed and there wasn't any free land any more" was thoroughly misleading, in her view, since there *never* had been any free land. Nor did she agree with historian Frederick Jackson Turner's thesis about the "end of the frontier," which enjoyed a popular revival during the 1930s among thinkers as disparate as Stuart Chase, Lawrence Dennis, and Franklin D. Roosevelt. Economic opportunity, in

fact, had not been closed off, and people still could make a living for themselves if they were willing to work hard and persevered at the task. Rose and her parents were in total agreement on this point: individuals remained responsible for their own destiny, and the government should stay out of their affairs. Rather than granting the federal government too much credit for its alleged generosity in passing the Homestead Act, praise should be heaped on the farmers and their families who wrested a living from the land by the sweat of their brows and by uncommon perseverance in the face of adversity.[14]

In writing "Free Land," Rose benefited greatly from the stories and information that her parents passed on to her. In an outline that she prepared, she used the name "Cap Gordon" for the protagonist, probably inspired by stories that she had heard her parents tell about Cap Garland. (His name was later changed to David Beaton.) He had come from Almanzo's hometown of Spring Valley, Minnesota. The contractor laying the railroad track was named Stebbins, the same name that her mother used later in writing about the same activity in *By the Shores of Silver Lake*.[15]

The kinds of activities and developments discussed in *Free Land* resembled those her parents had told her about in their stories and those Laura had written about in her autobiography. Rose explicitly stated in a letter to the *New York Times Book Review* that the setting for the story was eastern Dakota Territory between 1879 and 1884. Some of the plot came directly from Laura and Almanzo's recollections (for example, David Beaton's long drive to Yankton to file a land claim). Rose went beyond the stories in extracting a political lesson from the homesteading experience. Historical in one sense, *Free Land* also served as a political tract critical of all government interference with individual freedom. Rose undoubtedly was projecting her own values onto David Beaton: "He did not believe in giving, or getting, something for nothing. He believed in every man's paying his own way. The Beatons had always done it."[16]

Rose sent off the final revised segments of "Free Land" to the *Saturday Evening Post* in November 1937, and the magazine ran the story as an eight-part serial the following March and April. The magazine paid her twenty-five thousand dollars, which was more than twice what she had received for anything else. Coming out in book form in May, it obtained generally favorable reviews and occupied the best-seller lists for several months. The most common criticism leveled against it was that Rose's characters did not

come fully alive. Along with *Let the Hurricane Roar,* which also derived from repeated family stories and from information that her parents had passed on to her, *Free Land* became Rose's most enduring literary legacy. It also turned out to be her last major work of fiction.

Reviewers praised the story as much for its historical references as for its literary merit. Howard Mumford Jones, in the *Saturday Review of Literature,* judged the novel to be "more important as document than as work of art." It was pleasantly written, he said, and it had the effect of restoring one's faith in ordinary people. Many other readers went along with that assessment. A slew of letters poured in to Rose, vouching for the authenticity with which she had depicted events in the 1880s. While some people wrote to quibble about some of the details, others indicated how picture-perfect her descriptions were in capturing their own experiences.[17]

With *Free Land* out of the way, Rose made one last attempt to salvage the work she had done on her Missouri history book. Now she began to envision an entire series of state books designed along the lines of her own, and she would serve as series editor. The books would draw out the essential character of America as it had been manifested in the variety of different state histories and cultures over the course of time. Her concept got a sympathetic hearing from Emporia, Kansas, newspaper publisher William Allen White. She hoped he would volunteer to write the Kansas volume, and she wanted him to help her enlist other writers, such as Zona Gale, Kenneth Roberts, and Stephen Vincent Benet, to work on the other volumes. However, just like the huge ten-volume historical novel that she had dreamed up four years earlier, this idea was far too grandiose and complicated.[18]

Meanwhile, shortly before Christmas in 1937, Rose finally began working on the manuscript that her mother had sent to her about the family's last move, from Walnut Grove to Dakota Territory in 1879. The Great Dakota Boom that picked up speed during the early 1880s was the same theme that Rose had just been working on herself, so she was familiar with the time period. She and both of her parents had been in frequent communication about it for almost a year. As Rose began tackling her mother's "Silver Lake" manuscript, Laura was already thinking about—and perhaps working on—her next volume, about the hard winter of 1880–1881. As she had indicated to her book-fair audience in Detroit, Laura now expected to complete the series with two more volumes, one describing the

hardships of the hard winter and the other (tentatively titled "Prairie Girl") focusing on her schoolgirl days and courtship and marriage to Almanzo. To assist her mother in the process, Rose mailed her the relevant sections from the "Pioneer Girl" manuscript. It was now more than seven years since Laura had written it. She thanked Rose for sending it to her. "All that time is rather dull to me now for some reason," she wrote. "Not nearly so vivid as when I wrote P.G. But maybe I can struggle it out someway." To help Rose see the direction in which she wanted to take the narrative, she sent along synopses of the projected final two volumes. "I hope you like the way I have planned to have all the characters in all the books sort of rounded up in the last one," she wrote.[19]

During the first two months of 1938 a steady stream of letters flowed back and forth between mother and daughter regarding revisions on "Silver Lake." Unfortunately, only a few of the letters that have been preserved were from Rose, but often her ideas can be inferred from the replies that Laura sent back. This cache of letters, extending from early 1937 to August 1938, when the manuscript was essentially completed, provide the best evidence available of the continuing collaboration between mother and daughter in the writing of the books. This was the second time that Rose had to do her editing job at a distance, and she tried both to encourage her mother and to instruct her in the mechanics of novel writing as she understood them. Rose wanted to help Laura become more proficient, partly to reduce her own obligation. She possessed well-thought-out ideas about how to write effectively, and she tried to impress them on her mother in a no-nonsense fashion.[20]

Another possible motive for Rose's heavy commitment to the mentoring role that she had assumed may have been a desire to keep her mother in a position where she could tell her what to do. It allowed her be the expert and superior, while relegating Laura to the position of novice and supplicant. To the degree that Rose felt compelled to exercise mastery and control over people, treating her mother as a student and an inferior in this process may have brought her some measure of satisfaction. She was genuinely trying to help her mother and sincerely wished for her success, but no doubt less noble motives were mixed in, too. Now, at a distance of a thousand miles, mother-daughter love—and conflict, too—operated at a further remove. The collaborative process still sometimes engendered conflict, but in the end it turned out successfully.

Rose's primary concern with her mother's latest manuscript was its opening. Laura had started the narrative at the train depot in Tracy, just down the tracks from Walnut Grove and the end of the line at the time, as Ma and the girls prepared to meet Pa and go back with him to Dakota Territory toward the end of the summer in 1879. Rose wanted to add a brief transition that would link the story to the previous book, explaining the reason for the family's move and filling in what had transpired in the meantime, especially the reason for Mary's going blind. In addition, some of her mother's material seemed to be too adult, one example being Pa's faking of legal papers to assist Mr. Boast in getting back some money that another settler owed him. Rose also underlined the importance of narrating everything from Laura's own point of view. "STAY INSIDE LAURA," she insisted. "If you will read PLUM CREEK, you will see this all the way through. Emotions and sense perceptions . . . are all LAURA'S. Pa, Ma, Mary, Carrie and Jack are all seen from the outside, as Laura saw them." Most important, there was the matter of structure. "Learning how to handle material structurally is a hell of a job," Rose admitted. "I guess it's never done." It was necessary to conceive of the material as a mass and then sort it out into sections and separate the dialogue from the other parts. She suggested that before drafting her next book Laura talk over its structure beforehand with her. Then she could make suggestions before her mother began writing. Nevertheless, Rose emphasized that, despite any criticisms she might make, she really *did* like her mother's prose style. "Most of the writing is perfectly beautiful and I would not change one word of descriptive work," she reassured her. And another time, "Your writing is really lovely. It gets better and better. The only thing I would change at all is some of the structure."[21]

Laura gratefully accepted Rose's input. "I am glad you like my use of words and my descriptions," she wrote in reply, "but without your fine touch, it would be a flop." But she refused to simply accept Rose's advice about the opening without defending her own approach. The two of them went back and forth about it several times, Laura initially insisting on doing it her way before finally capitulating to Rose's view. "Change the beginning of the story if you want," she finally wrote. "Do anything you please with the dam stuff if you will fix it up." Regarding Rose's contention that some of the material was too adult in tone, however, Laura stood her ground. She pointed out that in the late 1800s children had acted more grown-up than was true in the 1930s; they had been given more adult responsibilities, and

this had been reflected in their perspectives. Laura's assignment to take care of her blind sister, Mary, also helped explain her frequently more mature behavior. Moreover, Laura thought that it would not do to make herself appear to be too childish at the age of twelve, since she would be teaching school before she turned sixteen, and that part of the story would have to be believable, too.[22]

In their correspondence back and forth, Rose reemphasized the necessity of establishing a central theme for each volume. She understood the theme of this volume to be railroad and town building, and she wanted to know if she was correct on that score. These subjects were mixed up with homesteading and the family's lonely existence during the winter in the surveyors' house. Rose reminded her mother, "PLUM CREEK didn't fall into a coherent pattern until after a lot of fumbling and waste time and work you wrote me that its theme was the wheat crop. Let's get the theme of this one clear right away." Laura answered that the central theme of her book was clear in her own mind, and that was homesteading. Everything else in the story—railroad building, workers' riots, staying the winter in the surveyors' house, and living in town—were all challenges that the family needed to deal with until they once again were able to live in their own house on the homestead. Laura responded to or took exception to Rose's other suggestions and criticisms. One of her daughter's comments elicited this petulant reply, "From what you wrote, I can't help but think you didn't read my mss. carefully."[23]

Laura was somewhat disappointed that Rose thought so many changes were necessary. Her hope was that she had learned enough from Rose's previous instruction that her copy would require little editing except for "a little pointing up of the highlights." Then she would not be such a burden either. By now Laura had enough confidence in her own skill that she refused to defer automatically to Rose's suggestions. The latter, for her part, was so certain of her own abilities that she believed it necessary to spend considerable chunks of time trying to improve her mother's work. Even while they fiddled with the "Silver Lake" manuscript, Laura pressed ahead on her next volume, which was tentatively titled "The Hard Winter." By mid-February, she had already blocked out the chapters of the book. She thanked Rose for all her helpful suggestions, indicating that she was following her advice on the beginning of this book. She worried about identifying its central theme until she realized that the family's struggle to

survive the physical hardships of the wintry weather constituted theme enough.[24]

Laura and Almanzo had visited De Smet in 1931 and at that time had enjoyed the opportunity to renew old acquaintances, view old haunts, and note how much things had changed since they had left in 1894. Now that Laura had gotten her fictional family to De Smet in "By the Shores of Silver Lake," she and Almanzo decided they could afford to make another trip back as part of a larger excursion that would take them all the way to the West Coast. Laura wanted to take some notes and refresh her memory in preparation for her next two books. Also factoring into their decision to go was Silas Seal's willingness to drive them again. This time his wife, Neta, was feeling fine and was eager to go with them.

The foursome departed on May 11, 1938, with Silas at the wheel, Almanzo sitting on his right, and the two women in back, talking, laughing, and singing as they headed west.[25] Although they were four decades apart in age, the two couples greatly enjoyed each other's company, and the trip was a great adventure for them all. Across Oklahoma, the Texas Panhandle, New Mexico, and Arizona they drove, taking in the Painted Desert, the Grand Canyon, and other exotic sights. They traveled north through Barstow, Hollywood, Beverly Hills, and Santa Barbara. Laura kept notes of the things she saw for part of the trip, describing the miles of vegetable farms and orchards they passed in southern California, the breathtaking view from Mount Diablo, and the ferry across San Francisco Bay.

Crossing the Golden Gate Bridge they caught a glimpse of Alcatraz Island. Farther up the coast they observed Works Progress Administration crews at work. North to Portland and Spokane they traveled, then east to silver-rich Coeur d'Alene, and on across the Continental Divide in Montana. They toured through Deer Lodge National Forest and Yellowstone Park (where they saw Old Faithful), and then they drove through the Crow Indian Reservation and Custer Battlefield on the way to the Black Hills.

At Keystone, in the shadow of Mount Rushmore, they visited with Carrie, and at that point Laura's trip notes ended. Carrie had been living in Keystone since arriving in 1911 to run the newspaper there for E. L. Senn, who owned a string of papers in the state. Her husband, David Swanzey, whom she had married a year after arriving in Keystone, had died in April. From there the two couples drove east across the state, visiting Grace and Nate Dow in Manchester and driving on to De Smet, where Laura and Almanzo

reacquainted themselves with old friends. By the time they returned to Mansfield, they had been on the road for three weeks.[26]

While Laura continued working on her book about the hard winter, Rose fiddled with the "Silver Lake" manuscript, too caught up with other things to get it into final shape for submission to the publisher. Moving into a new house in Danbury, Connecticut, in March and establishing new routines took much of her time and energy. The old malaise returned after the appearance of *Free Land,* and even the praise heaped on the book and the money it brought her could not compensate for her growing intuition that she had run out of ideas for fiction. Gradually it dawned on her that her fiction-writing career was over. "Don't know why I live, or live here," she wrote in her diary. And again: "Should work and can't. What to do with a meaningless life? Am dumb, dull, empty—Blue as hell—Cried all night."[27]

Toward the end of 1938 and into the new year she spent a lot of time campaigning for the Ludlow Amendment, a proposed Constitutional change that would have required a national referendum before the nation could go to war except in the case of an outright attack on American soil. Named after Indiana Democratic congressman Louis Ludlow, the proposed amendment became a rallying cry for isolationists who feared that Roosevelt was leading the country toward war. Rose's personal antipathy to the president reinforced her dislike of his interventionism abroad. Strongly critical of New Deal domestic policy, Rose found the administration's approach to foreign affairs equally repugnant.[28]

In this, as on most political issues, Laura was in full accord with her daughter. To advance the isolationist cause, Laura drafted a letter before the off-year congressional elections addressed simply "To American Mothers" and intended for circulation in newspapers and elsewhere. It encouraged its readers to write their congressional candidates and ask where they stood on the war-referendum issue, and it urged each of them to send copies of the letter to ten friends, who in turn would continue the chain by sending it to their friends. The message concluded, "Your failure to do this may bring disaster to your home and your loved ones and leave the way clear for the War Gods to call your sons to the trenches, to face the hell of shot and shell. Pray that God may save us from another war." Laura told Rose that all of the members of the Athenean Club at Hartville were writing their congressman, urging him to vote in favor of the referendum. Laura planned

to send her letter to people she knew in other states. She was not sure if it would do any good, but in her opinion it could hardly do any harm.[29]

The "Silver Lake" manuscript took longer than usual to get ready for the publisher, not being delivered until May 1939, past the deadline for the fall book list. By now Laura had become so popular that the people at Harper's told her not to worry about it and simply to get the finished copy to them as quickly as possible. Laura told Rose that she was afraid that so much time had elapsed since her last book that her stories would be forgotten. In considering a name for the book, Laura thought that while homesteading was its central theme, using that word in the title would mislead readers since the book discussed so much more than that. *On the Banks of Plum Creek* had gone over so well that using a similar title would be desirable, so they settled on "By the Shores of Silver Lake."[30]

This, her fifth volume, for some reason attracted fewer reviews than the previous ones had. As usual, however, the ones that did appear were generally glowing. "Touching, unsentimental, and real Americana," commented the *New Yorker. Horn Book Magazine* noted, "While all the people are so real that they seem to be next-door neighbors, as it were, Laura is nearest to our hearts."[31]

Laura was already finished with the next volume, tentatively titled "The Hard Winter," by the time "Silver Lake" was sent to the publisher. She wanted to get her new effort into Rose's hands quickly, because she and Almanzo were planning to take another trip to De Smet. "I would rather you had it," Laura wrote her daughter, "so if anything should happen on our trip you could finish it." Unlike their route of the previous year, this one was more direct, and this time Almanzo would do the driving himself. They planned to take it easy on the journey and to stop early when they got tired. And they planned to "not drive at all on Sunday when every crazy loon is drunk and on the road," Laura told Rose. One advantage of going by themselves was the reduced expense and the chance to go at a more leisurely pace. More important from Laura's point of view was the feeling that "if we are by ourselves we will be independent."[32]

The previous year they had arrived in De Smet just before Old Settlers' Day, which was held every year on June 10. This time they planned their visit to coincide with the big celebration. Sixty years had passed since the railroad crews first arrived at Silver Lake, and in 1940 the town itself would celebrate its sixtieth anniversary. Laura and Almanzo drove up from

Missouri through Council Bluffs, Sioux City, and Yankton. In De Smet they again visited with old friends and visited Aubrey Sherwood's newspaper office, where he took a picture of them that ran on the front page the following week. Afterward they visited with Grace and Nate in Manchester, then drove west across the state to see Carrie again in Keystone. From there they traveled through Colorado before returning to Mansfield.[33]

There would be no more long trips like this for Laura and Almanzo, but they did like to make shorter excursions to places around Mansfield. Silas Seal frequently drove them to Springfield, where Laura regularly had her hair cut by a former Mansfield hairdresser. Almanzo often drove them around, too. Once they went to West Plains, sixty-five miles to the southeast, to visit some old friends.[34]

Almanzo was in his eighties now. Never very vigorous since his early bout with diphtheria, he had to take things slowly. The farm was hardly self-supporting; Rose's income supplements had helped enable the two of them to live comfortably during the 1920s and early 1930s, before royalty payments from Laura's books began to build. Laura was grateful to her daughter for what she had done for them and thanked her, "You have contributed to keeping it [Rocky Ridge Farm] up for years." Almanzo no longer had his Morgan horses. But he did keep a donkey and a few goats for milking and planted the garden, growing potatoes, peas, lettuce, radishes, and turnips, among other things. He also liked to make rugs from yarn and old rags. He and Bruce Prock sometimes drove to auction sales.[35]

Almanzo kept the car in running order and liked to loiter around Silas Seal's service station when he drove Laura into town. As their contacts with the Craigs and other friends gradually diminished, their relationship with the Seals grew closer. The couples often ate meals together or took little trips around the countryside. Neta liked to cook Swiss steak for Almanzo when the Wilders came because it was his favorite. She also looked out for Laura, sometimes staying overnight when Laura was not feeling well. The Wilders even loaned the Seals some money when they decided to build a new rooming house in town.[36]

Health problems multiplied as Laura and Almanzo aged. Bouts with the flu were common, and other ailments slowed them down. Almanzo had an ear problem, requiring attention from a specialist, and rheumatism increasingly bothered Laura. She also suffered from asthma and eyestrain. In early 1937 she told Rose that her eyes had "gone on strike," but the

following year she noted that they were doing so well that she had gone back to using a pair of six-year-old eyeglasses.[37]

Laura was conscious of the aging process. She told Rose that she preferred to wear long-sleeved dresses now because her arms were not pretty anymore. She got rid of her laying hens but kept her flower beds. Her frugal ways persisted. Silas Seal observed that Laura was able to get more for her money than anybody else he ever met. She economized by saving scraps of paper to write notes on, and she even had the electricity in the house cut off once in a futile effort to get the power company to reduce its rates.[38]

Laura remained involved, although to a lesser degree, in club activities. The local newspaper made little mention anymore of the Athenians or of Laura attending their meetings. It did note, however, when she was reelected as second vice president of the group in January 1939. From 1937 through 1941 she regularly attended meetings of the Friday Afternoon Book Club. Most of its members were friends from other clubs and organizations. At the March 1938 meeting, Mrs. N. J. Craig gave a review of Rose's *Let the Hurricane Roar.* The book up for discussion when Laura hosted the group at Rocky Ridge in February 1940 was *The Escape,* by Ethel Vance. By 1942, however, Laura's name no longer appeared in reports of those attending the meetings.[39]

Laura also became a regular for a while in a new study club organized in March 1937 at the home of the wife of newspaper publisher O. B. Davis. The names on its roster, once again, were familiar. Laura was chosen, along with two others, to select a suitable name for the club, apparently deciding that nothing more than "Study Club" was necessary. They also developed a program for the first year's meetings, selecting the subject of contemporary American literature. The first book chosen for review was Margaret Mitchell's *Gone with the Wind.* When Laura's turn came to host the club in September 1937, Mrs. Warren Davis gave a review of the twin operas *Cavalleria Rusticana* and *Pagliacci,* by Pietro Mascagni and Ruggiero Leoncavallo, respectively. Laura continued to remain an active member of the club through 1940.[40]

Laura no longer participated much in church or lodge activities, either. The Methodist Ladies Aid Society that she had belonged to reorganized itself as the Women's Society of Christian Service in October 1940. The *Mirror* noted her attendance at some of their meetings in 1942 and 1943. There is little record of her activity in Eastern Star, but the paper did report

her election in January 1939 as chaplain again for the coming year. The newer members of these organizations were a generation or two younger than she, and that made her feel strange. "I can't fit in with the old crowd someway," she wrote Rose. "Never could very well and now I am tired of them more than ever." She indicated that she probably would have to go with "the old church crowd, Burney, Rogers, Hoovers."[41]

Sometimes the Wilders invited guests to Rocky Ridge for a meal or for an evening get-together. On the Saturday after Laura's seventy-third birthday they hosted a Valentine's Day party for five other couples. As reported in the society section of the newspaper, "The rooms were beautifully lighted and a bright gleaming fire in the fire place where wood was piled high, around which guests were seated and elsewhere about the large living room." After some games, cake and coffee were served. In 1943 the Wilders were honored on their fifty-eighth wedding anniversary at a dinner held at the Methodist church.[42]

Despite growing older and having to slow down her pace, Laura did not feel bored or consider herself useless. She kept busy with housework, club activity, and, of course, writing. In December 1937 she told Rose, "The days are so short it takes me all the time to do what work I must to keep a livin'." She still enjoyed crewel work, baking bread, and just puttering around the house. Her sweet tooth craved candy as much as ever, and she especially enjoyed it when Rose sent a box on her birthday, which was just a week before Valentine's Day. "I may wear store teeth," she laughed, "but my old sweet tooth has never been extracted."[43]

As Laura entered her seventies, the world around her continued to change, and she had a growing sense that she was living in the past. While writing her novels, she literally took up residence in her memories. Mansfield's community leaders continued to confront change, encouraging their fellow residents to make the town a better place. Success in this endeavor would be measured by their ability to avoid a major population loss, rather than necessarily making big gains. Fundamental forces—economic, social, and cultural—were accelerating to drive rural residents to larger population centers, and every small town was forced to compete with its neighbors in order to attract business and customers.

Signs of change ranged from an ordinance requiring the licensing of dogs in 1937 to formation of a Lions Club affiliate three years later. The new unit was designed to replace the Business Men's Club, whose purpose,

along with that of several different predecessors, including the Commercial Club and the Mansfield Chamber of Commerce, was to promote the growth and progress of the town and its businesses. Two projects that demanded immediate attention were digging a sewer system and blacktopping the principal streets in town that remained unpaved. The former project had earlier been approved, but then was scrapped when WPA financing was lost. Main Street businessmen also worked, with meager success, to attract new industry into the community. New streetlights, bargain days, band concerts on the square, Santa Claus days, citywide clean-ups: these and a variety of other ideas were implemented in efforts to lure business into town. The *Mansfield Mirror* also observed that getting rid of drunks on the streets would improve the atmosphere of the community. A sign of the times was Mansfield's participation in a 1937 beauty contest to select a Miss Wright County, who would then go on to participate in the state pageant at Sedalia.[44]

If times were changing, reminders of previous ways of life also cast their shadows. In April 1940 the *Mirror* reported the first runaway team of horses in several years in Mansfield. Mansfield poet J. Lon Dennis, whose work appeared from time to time in papers around the area, submitted a poem titled "What Makes Mansfield Grow." In addition to "signs of push and progress," he observed, it was things like "the cow's soft low" and "fruits and berries, cows and chickens" that contributed to a town's growth.[45]

Although many Mansfieldians anticipated their town's population topping a thousand in 1940, the final census tally showed an increase of only 66 since 1930, to 937, amounting to a gain of only 7 percent. Afterward the newspaper editor commented, "The town has grown slightly but not nearly so much as it should have. It is sleeping on the job while other towns are building. It might nap too long."[46]

Time and circumstances led the Wilders to stay more to themselves, cutting them off in significant ways from the wider community. They also now were far removed from their only child, who stayed in contact with them only by mail. Although Rose did not return to Mansfield for more than a decade after finally leaving Missouri in 1937, she was never far from her parents' thoughts. The distance physically separating mother and daughter ironically seemed to draw them closer together in spirit. Resentments and animosities that had sometimes boiled over when they were living close together now dissipated.[47]

Mother and daughter frequently expressed their love for each other in letters sent back and forth as they worked together on the novels. Laura always began her letters "Rose Dearest" and ended them with "much love," "very much love," or "loads and loads of love." Almanzo, the reticent one, addressed his daughter simply as "Dear Rose." In return, Rose wrote back to her "Dear Mama Bess," ending her missives with "much love" or "much, much love." Laura told her, "You are a dear, sweet thing to us all the time. You and your comfort and well being are more to us than anything else. So please take good care of yourself for us." After Laura expressed her love and thanked Rose for sending some birthday candy in 1938, the latter responded humorously, "I love you a lot, too, and hope you are making yourself sick on your birthday candy, you and papa. Isn't that a loving wish?" Laura frequently expressed a sense of humor, too, as in her reply to Rose's flattering comment about a picture taken of her: "Thanks my dear. I am glad you think I am nice to look at, even at this late day in the afternoon. It must be my lovely character showing in my face that people see. And knowing me, I can't see that."[48]

Laura wanted to be certain that Rose was aware of how much both parents appreciated the financial help that she had been giving them. It seemed unbelievable to her how comfortably they were situated now. They had Rose to thank for all of their good fortune, Laura indicated, ticking off the many things they had reason to appreciate: rent money for the house she had built, dividend checks, royalties from her books, furnishings in their house. Laura said that she went to bed thinking "what a wise woman I am to have a daughter like you." Once, after Rose had advised her on how to handle some details with Harper and Brothers, Laura thanked her, saying, "Sometimes I have a suspicion that you are a nice kind of a person."[49]

Another factor that drew mother and daughter closer together was their mutual antipathy toward increased government intervention in people's lives and their common opinion that President Roosevelt and the New Deal had been disastrous for the country. Laura complained about gas taxes they had to pay to run their car and about the scarcity of farm labor, a condition she attributed to FDR's work-relief programs. She referred to first-term Democratic senator Harry Truman as "a liar" and stated her admiration for their district's conservative Republican anti–New Deal congressman, Dewey Short. She "gnashed her teeth" at an article of Eleanor Roosevelt's in *Liberty* on the Ludlow Amendment and was gleeful when a local Democratic

gathering at the Masonic Hall to celebrate the president's birthday failed to sell many tickets. Laura was glad that she had quit the Democratic Party when she did. As war loomed in Europe in 1939, she wrote Rose, "There is no use in trying to say anything about the news. We probably are thinking alike about things."[50]

Laura's sisters were so far away that contacts with them were few. She and Almanzo had visited them on their trips to South Dakota in 1938 and 1939, but her correspondence with them at other times seems to have been sporadic. Laura received a letter from Grace in January 1938, indicating that she had not heard from Carrie for months. Neither had Laura, even at Christmastime. When Laura mentioned anything about her sisters to Rose, it seems often to have been in an unhappy context. In late 1937 she observed that Grace and Nate were on relief, receiving surplus food commodities from the government in addition to conservation checks. It could not have been something she was proud of or approved of, with all her insistence upon self-reliance and keeping government out of people's affairs. Laura also seemed embarrassed in passing on a note from Carrie in May 1939, asking whether Rose had any old clothes that she might be planning to donate to charity. Carrie indicated that she could use them.[51]

Although Laura waited to send Rose her manuscript of "The Hard Winter" until she and Almanzo left to attend the Old Settlers' Day celebration in De Smet in June 1939, she had started working on it a year and a half earlier, during the time that she and Rose were wrangling over the "Silver Lake" manuscript. Both Almanzo and Laura had frequently discussed with Rose the events in De Smet during the storm-filled winter of 1880–1881, and the latter, of course, had read her mother's account of it in her "Pioneer Girl" manuscript, which contained all of the essential features of the book that later was published as *The Long Winter.* No episode in the early history of white settlement in the region inspired more stories or legends than this one. With rail traffic cut off for almost five months and devastating temperatures, along with some of the heaviest snowfall eastern Dakota ever received, people who lived in brand-new railroad towns such as De Smet were literally on the verge of starvation, even though they were situated only a few miles west of more "civilized" places. Whenever old-timers gathered together or wished to impress the uninitiated with the rigors of frontier living, it did not take long for the subject of the hard winter to spring up.

The inherent drama of the way in which the people had twisted hay for fuel, ground wheat in coffee mills, and huddled together to keep warm was so great that Rose had long considered writing the story herself in fictional form just as her parents had told it to her. In 1932, just as her mother's first book was coming out and while she was scrounging for subject matter herself, Rose suggested to her agent, George Bye, a serial for the *Saturday Evening Post* based on stories that her parents had passed on to her. Instead, however, she had written a fictionalized account, using her parents' names and published it as *Let the Hurricane Roar*. But for the next several years she continued to toy with the idea of doing a nonfiction piece about the hard winter in De Smet.[52]

Instead, Laura told the story herself in the one book of hers that consistently emphasized the hardship and meanness of life on the prairie frontier. In this case the major antagonist was the weather itself, although some of the townspeople, too, proved to be villainous or pusillanimous in their behavior. In publishing the book, however, Harper and Brothers demanded a title change, replacing it with the more innocuous "The Long Winter."[53]

In mid-February 1938, Laura wrote Rose indicating that she had blocked out the chapters for "The Hard Winter" much as Rose had suggested. She was still planning to finish the series with just one more volume covering what happened after the winter of 1880–1881. A few days later she indicated that she was going to start the book just as Rose had suggested, with geese flying overhead and strangely not stopping at the lake on their way south for the winter. She had been stumped temporarily in trying to identify a central plot line or "pattern," as Rose liked to refer to it. "There seems to be nothing to it only the struggle to live, through the winter, until spring comes again." Or, she had suggested, she could make Laura's struggle to be a schoolteacher the central story line. In the end, she realized that the struggle against the elements was the obvious, and compelling, central theme for the book.[54]

Most of the letters that Rose sent her mother have been lost, but from reading Laura's letters to her it is clear that Rose had difficulty comprehending the psychology of the townspeople, cooped up and facing starvation during the cold winter blasts. Laura had written about the people's stoicism, causing Rose to wonder about their lack of emotion in the face of such extremity. Laura tried to explain their situation to her: "No! The people in the hard winter were not 'monsters.' I haven't yet been able to get my

meaning across to you." The two went back and forth over several episodes in the story. Most crucial to the narrative development was Laura's decision to leave out entirely the young couple and their baby who had lived with the family in her father's store building throughout the hard winter. To include George and Maggie Masters would ruin the whole impression she was trying to create. As Laura explained it to Rose, "If we put Masters in the story they must be as they were and that would spoil the story. If we make them decent it would spoil the story for we would lose Manly's kindness which I think is worth more than having a baby born." The real-life bravery and generosity of Almanzo and his friend Cap Garland in venturing into the wintry countryside to haul back a load of wheat from a homesteader could be told so long as the Masters remained out the story.[55]

Even as she started working on "The Hard Winter," Laura was already considering what to include in her last volume, which she intended to call "Prairie Girl." By August 1938, she was ready to send Rose a skeletal outline of the plot. Although Laura liked to work from an outline, she frequently departed from it and was continually modifying it. "The only way I can write is to wander along with the story, then rewrite and re-arrange and change it everywhere," she told her daughter.[56]

Laura appreciated Rose's contribution to her books, but she felt bad about the time that it took her away from her own work. She wrote Rose, "I am sorry you still have to work on my books. I would like to have you perfectly free for just your own affairs. But that trouble will soon be over and you will get enough out of it to pay your rent for awhile anyhow." Laura could still feel somewhat hopeful on this score, since Rose had done less work rewriting and rearranging of her draft of "Silver Lake" than she had on the previous four volumes. While in places, especially toward the beginning, Rose had added or changed things considerably, large sections of Laura's manuscript stood mainly intact. When Rose had lived at Rocky Ridge and the two could easily get together or talk on the phone, they had been able to discuss and agree on necessary changes, detail by detail. Working at a distance made such intensive collaboration impossible, and Rose may have found it easier simply to let many things stand as they were, given the difficulty and the time constraints of communicating by mail. Still, more than a year elapsed between the time Rose first looked at the manuscript and its completion, as other activities and writing projects captured her attention most of the time. Much, if not all, of her mother's prose was

capable of standing on its own, and Rose's editorial refashioning of the material, while distinctly improving its overall readability, was in some instances merely a reflection of personal preference. Laura's descriptive powers and lyricism shone through in the following passage, which was altered only slightly in the published text:

> The sun dropped lower and lower still. A ball of pulsing, liquid light, it sank in clouds of crimson and silver. Cold purple shadows rose in the east, crept slowly across the prairie, then gathered in depth on depth of darkness from which the stars swung low and bright.
>
> The wind, which all day long had blown strongly, dropped low with the sun and went whispering among the tall grasses, and the earth seemed to lie breathing softly under the summer night.
>
> Pa drove on and on under the low stars. "Do you know the way Charles, now you can't see the trail?" Ma asked.
>
> "I can see the lights of the camp twinkling ahead," Pa told her. "All I have to do is keep driving toward them. There is nothing between from here to there but smooth prairie and air."[57]

Interestingly, Rose spent more time working on the next manuscript about the legendary hard winter of 1880 and 1881 than she had on "Silver Lake." Her determination to work on this manuscript more thoroughly may have derived from her own extensive knowledge about the subject. Also, since she had stopped writing her own fiction, working on her mother's material may have been, to some extent at least, a way of filling time and being purposeful. As with the previous books, the story and most of the language were Laura's, but Rose went further in rewriting and expanding this draft than she had done in most of the other volumes. For example, she expanded her mother's brief one-page description of storekeeper Daniel Loftus's effort to profit from Almanzo and Cap Garland's brave dash to get the wheat into a much more elaborate five-page scenario.[58]

While Laura worked away on "The Hard Winter," the world edged closer toward military conflict. World War II, when it came, hit the isolationists hard. Pearl Harbor effectively destroyed the influence of isolationism in the United States. Laura, Almanzo, and Rose were forced to accept a larger role for their country in world affairs. Mansfield quickly was caught up in a war boom that brought with it vast changes for the rural small-town way of life.[59]

Long before December 7, 1941, young men were departing regularly for military training camps, the draft having gone into effect a year earlier. Twenty-five hundred Wright County men registered for the first peacetime draft in history at their precinct polling places on October 16, 1940, and signs that the nation was preparing for war multiplied all around. No one could avoid the impact of war mobilization as the process accelerated during 1942. A scrap rubber drive in June netted seven tons of salvage in just four days' time, as mounds of the material piled high at gas stations and garages. A concert given by the high school band in August helped collect twenty-two tons of iron, aluminum, rubber, and other needed materials in another "scrap harvest." During the next four years reminders of the country's wartime footing included stripped-down school athletic schedules, a thirty-five-mile-per-hour speed limit, rationing, blackouts, victory gardens, Red Cross drives, and bond drives. Some events were canceled, such as the Ozark Summit Exposition, but many others went on as usual, including the annual Wright County Singing Convention, Saturday-night band concerts, and Fourth of July celebrations. But no one could forget the centrality of the war.[60]

People in Mansfield slowly woke up to the threat posed to their community, as well as to the opportunities afforded, by the war. For at least two decades small towns had been facing increasing competition from neighboring towns for business. Only fifty miles from Springfield, merchants in Mansfield realized how easy it was becoming for their customers to hop into a car and drive there to do their business. Mail-order warehouses and national chains further eroded their competitive position. Halfway through 1942, the editor of the *Mansfield Mirror* observed, "Business, especially small businesses such as Mansfield is largely made up of, faces one of the toughest periods in history during the next few months—and perhaps a year or more." Some small businesses were already beginning to fold, and others were balanced on the precipice. What at first glance seemed to pose a danger, however, might also contain a golden opportunity, the editor suggested, for "the merchant who is up on his toes has not so much to fear as some of the less aggressive merchants. For in these times, as in many other times, hard work, persistence, and alertness count—count for success." On another occasion he noted that a small town such as Mansfield possessed an opportunity for rebirth as a trading center and might undergo a general renaissance due to wartime conditions. Furthermore, small-town merchants

might be able to regain business that they had been losing. "If they play their cards right, they have the best opportunity in years to stop the huge flow of business away from their towns," he predicted. O. B. Davis's emphasis on the virtues of hard work, persistence, and adaptability mirrored the values that Laura Ingalls Wilder was writing about in her books.[61]

Even before starting work on the sequel to *The Long Winter,* Laura realized that getting the story up to her marriage to Almanzo would take more than the single volume that she had originally projected. It is harder to know about the details of composition and collaboration on the two volumes that finished the series, *Little Town on the Prairie* and *These Happy Golden Years,* because hardly any letters between mother and daughter during this period were preserved, and Rose was not keeping a diary that indicated how she spent her time. It seems probable that the kind of close cooperation that had occurred earlier gave way to sporadic communication and that Rose largely did her work on these manuscripts with little feedback from her mother. In the first of the two, she invoked her editorial prerogative to make major revisions and elaborations of the material on a par with some of her most extensive changes in the previous volumes. Even now, however, the fundamental story line and most of the details of narration were her mother's, and many paragraphs and even whole pages demanded only light editing. Rose did her work on this volume between January and July 1941, and it was published later in the year, receiving, as usual, enthusiastic reviews. The *New Yorker* praised it as "a moving and authentic re-creation of American frontier life." A. T. Eaton in the *New York Times* observed, "Mrs. Wilder writes with ease and charm and a humor that, like the Ingalls family's own attitude toward life in the stories, keeps everything in perspective and refreshingly sane." The *Saturday Review of Literature* called it the best of the "Laura and Mary" books, noting that the entire series was "fresh literature, exciting story, and authentic Americana. Every child should own one."[62]

Interestingly, the final volume in the series, *These Happy Golden Years,* received only relatively cursory attention from Rose, who did her work on it toward the end of 1942, in time for its appearance on the following spring's book list. Not since the first book in the series had Rose done so little to change her mother's manuscript. Perhaps she was simply getting tired of the task. Perhaps Laura had finally achieved her goal of writing better and of being less of a burden to her daughter. Perhaps Rose's new interest in conservative political ideas left her with less time to concentrate

on her mother's work. Whatever the case, no one doubted that this volume, any less than her previous ones, was the authentic work of their admired children's author, Laura Ingalls Wilder. *Library Journal* called the book a "satisfying conclusion to the beloved 'Little House' series." The *Saturday Review* commented, "There is in these books about Laura and her people the freshness and vigor of pioneer America, of the days when there was land to claim beyond the Mississippi. They have a high place in fictionalized United States history."[63]

With the publication of *These Happy Golden Years,* Laura's writing career was finished. She had been working on the series for thirteen years. Now she was seventy-six and ready to retire. The accolades continued to roll in. Although she always modestly told people that her only desire in beginning to write her autobiographical books had been to retell some of the stories she had heard her father relate when she was a little girl, her motives in fact had been more complicated. Always ambitious and possessing a sense of being somewhat elevated from her peers, Laura had carved out a modest writing career for herself in farm newspapers for a decade and a half before turning to children's fiction. She had informed Rose that her goal was prestige more than money, but no doubt both figured in her disciplining herself to sit down and conceptualize her books, outline them and write them, revise them and recopy them once or twice, before finally turning them over to Rose for further editing and collaborative rewriting.

Sometime, probably during the late 1930s, she had written a volume shorter than the rest and intended for adults describing her and Almanzo's first four years of married life. It was a rather spare description, mainly of the hardships and disappointments they suffered before moving temporarily to Almanzo's parents' home in Spring Valley, Minnesota. The manuscript was not discovered and published until much later, after Rose's death, and is generally adjudged to be inferior to the children's novels. There can be no doubt that her real forte was as a children's author. Her daughter's hand in encouraging her and collaborating with her on the preparation of those manuscripts was demonstrably crucial to the success of the books. Ultimately, the genius of the novels lay in their author's powers of perception as a girl, in her detached insight into human nature including her own, and in her ability as a mature woman to sift the memories of her childhood through a dramatic lens that chose what was illuminating and interesting to people and discarded what was dull and uninspiring.

# 9

## *Basking in the Glow of Her Readers' Affection*

### 1943–1957

*ॐ*

With the publication of *These Happy Golden Years,* Laura completed her writing career. She was seventy-six years old and had been working on her children's novels for a dozen years. She was tired. Her work was finished. She did not need more money, as royalties on the first seven books continued to accumulate. Early in the writing process she had decided to carry the story up to her marriage to Almanzo and to stop there.

To have extended the series into her adulthood would have required an entirely different approach, one that she was not sure she was capable of. All of the books had been written from the point of view of a girl the age that Laura had been at the time the action took place. This technique had worked effectively, even though she and Rose had not always seen eye to eye on just what a girl of a certain age was capable of or likely to be thinking about. Book reviewers agreed that her progressively maturing narrative voice had been a useful device for telling her stories. To have carried the story further would have required a new way of telling, a more complex and emotionally richer description of motive and feeling, appropriate to the

lives of adults. It would have required going into setbacks and tragedies that she preferred to forget: their infant son's death, weather disasters, health problems, their house burning down, and their failure to make the farm successful.

To explain why she had stopped when she did, she later told her friend Nava Austin that she preferred to think and talk about pleasant things, not sad ones, implying that her early married years were too painful to think about.[1] Yet, at some point, probably sometime during the late 1930s, she had written a manuscript from an adult point of view about her and Almanzo's first four years of living on the farm. *The First Four Years* was a spare account—shorter than the other books—of their life on the prairie, battling the elements and, in the end, failing. There was no protective family to take care of them then—no father, no mother, no sisters. They all remained peripheral, outside the action of the story. There was no town. De Smet, although only a couple of miles south of their farm, might just as well have been on the moon.

*The First Four Years* revolves almost entirely around the newly married couple's desperate, and ultimately unsuccessful, effort to make the arithmetic of farming work on their behalf. The story was an elemental one of people battling against nature and against the difficult odds that during the late 1880s drove thousands of Dakota farm families off the land or politically radicalized them, converting them into Farmers' Alliance men and then into Populists. But politics, social life, even extended family relations—none of these themes either entered Laura's mind in telling her story or could easily be fitted into her spare account of the struggle that she and Almanzo had endured. Nor were there any hints of conflict or tension between the two of them, except that she recorded her willingness to try the experiment for only three years (later extended to four). After that, if they failed at farming, they would explore other avenues. Laura ended her manuscript on a typical—but rather hollow—note of hopefulness: "The incurable optimism of the farmer who throws his seed on the ground every spring, betting it and his time against the elements, seemed inextricably to blend with the creed of her pioneer forefathers that 'it is better farther on'—only instead of farther on in space, it was farther on in time, over the horizon of the years ahead instead of the far horizon of the west."[2]

It was probably this manuscript that Laura was referring to in a note to agent George Bye in May 1943. "I have thought that 'Golden Years' was

my last," she indicated, "that I would spend what is left of my life living, not writing about it, but a story keeps stirring in my mind and if it pesters me enough I may write it down and send it to you." Whether she had completed her adult novel by this time is uncertain; it is likely that she had. But the incentive to go ahead with it—to expand it and revise it into publishable form—was small. She was old, she was tired, and she had been hugely successful with her children's books. Why bother with more, and why risk her reputation in an area where she had no experience? And with Rose far away in Connecticut, the kind of close collaboration that had been possible when she had started out in the 1930s was no longer feasible. Rose had discouraged her from dissipating her energy in trying an adult novel several years earlier, so Laura probably never even told her that she had gone ahead and drafted one anyway. When the manuscript was discovered with Rose's effects after her death in 1968, she had done nothing with it, and it is doubtful that she would have tried to work on it and get it published even had she lived longer.[3]

Now, with no more writing projects to keep her busy, Laura could relax and enjoy the accolades that came her way. Letters from enthusiastic fans continued to arrive with regularity, the numbers swelling each February around her birthday. Librarians expressed delight at how her books stimulated so many schoolchildren to read. When the Seattle Public Library sponsored a radio dramatization of *On the Banks of Plum Creek,* the committee chair for the program wrote to say how popular the series had been. "I thought you would be interested to know how successful Mary and Laura and the baby have been in the Northwest," she wrote. "We librarians are grateful to you for giving us a series of books so fine and at the same time so appealing to children." Schoolteachers had their classes write Laura letters after reading her books. "I enjoy your books very much," one Los Angeles schoolgirl wrote. "I wish I lived when you did. I would like to live on the prairie because you didn't have to be fenced in a little yard. You had free things to do on the prairie." A boy whose class had already gone through four of the books and was into the middle of the fifth wrote to say that he liked them better than his history text. "I think that your family was an excellent family because you never complained, as when Pa had to walk 200 miles for a job. I tell this because the pioneers had to be tough to start a new country." And a classmate of his wrote, "Your books have helped us

a lot. Your books are more interesting to us to know that the things really happened to real people. Your books are so exciting."[4]

Laura was amazed by all the attention. "The children send me their pictures, Christmas cards and presents, valentines, birthday cards and gifts," she wrote Frances Mason in 1948. "I think I had letters from every state and have always answered them all until recently." Rheumatism in her hands, however, made it increasingly difficult and sometimes painful for her to write, so she became more selective in sending replies. Editor Aubrey Sherwood of the *De Smet News*, whose father had edited the paper back in the 1880s when Laura and Almanzo had lived there, was active in promoting her books and wrote to her from time to time. "Many thanks for the copy of The De Smet News and for your kindness in vouching for the truth of my little books," Laura wrote him. "I appreciate it. Your description of the old prairie road to Lakes Henry and Thompson made both Mr. Wilder and myself very homesick for De Smet. We used to drive that old road on Sunday afternoons in our country days." While she continued to answer many letters personally, Harper and Brothers printed a composite one from her that answered many of the typical questions that readers asked so that she could reduce her writing chores.[5]

People in Mansfield were aware of Laura's success as an author. From time to time a story was published in the *Mansfield Mirror* reminding them of another award or recognition, but they probably underestimated just how well known and highly regarded she was. Her writing career had begun after Rose was already famous. To many people, Rose remained the true celebrity, and her mother's accomplishments somehow remained in her shadow.

Folks saw less and less of the Wilders now. They did not venture off the farm as often. They moved about more slowly, and they were happy just to sit and take things easy. Although some people regarded them as being aloof or even as loners, Laura and Almanzo did go to town now and then to attend church services, to shop, or to visit. He had never been as much of a churchgoer as she, and now even she made it in for Sunday services less frequently. Carlton Knight, the Methodist minister, remembered her coming alone when she did attend. She still managed to go to Friday afternoon meetings of the Women's Society of Christian Service of the Methodist church from time to time. Religious revivalism carried on its strong tradition in the area during the 1940s and into the 1950s, but the

Wilders probably did not attend the revivals anymore or go to the singing conventions in Hartville the first week in July.[6]

For a couple who were in their seventies and eighties, the massive changes unleashed by World War II and its aftermath must have seemed somewhat bewildering. The *Mansfield Mirror* ran stories and pictures depicting the German concentration camps when they were liberated by Allied soldiers in early 1945, and the paper later reported the dropping of the atomic bombs on Japan. The war had been brought home daily to Mansfield's residents by the departure of local young men to the training camps (one of them, the new Fort Leonard Wood, was carved out of the countryside thirty miles northeast of Mansfield in 1941), scrap drives, bond solicitations, V-mail, battlefront news, and many other things. Still it came as a distinct shock to people to discover that human beings could have brutalized their fellow human beings like the Nazis had or that the world was now in danger of being incinerated by the splitting of the atom. The homely optimism and cheerful spirit exuded by the Mary-and-Laura stories may have appeared to some people, at least, to be somehow inadequate to an understanding of such momentous tragedies. Nevertheless, after the war State Department officials distributed Laura's books in occupied Germany and Japan as expressions of America's generous and hopeful spirit, which they hoped would infect people in those countries, too. It would have been interesting to hear Laura's musings on these subjects, in a manner reminiscent of the columns that she had written for the *Missouri Ruralist* during and after World War I. Whatever thoughts she might have had, they were not written and preserved.[7]

Like the rest of the country, Mansfield became caught up in the throes of change after the war. In a manner similar to small towns like it all around the country, Mansfield faced daunting challenges, as more highly populated places enticed job seekers wanting to advance themselves economically. Fewer and fewer young people seemed willing to live the kinds of lives their parents and grandparents had been content with on the farm and in rural communities. Economic opportunities were limited in rural areas. Mansfield's civic leaders, increasingly aware of this fact, sought energetically to remedy the situation by boosting the town's prospects and by extending invitations to industries to relocate there.

Recognizing that the war had intensified Mansfield's perennial housing shortage, Main Street businessmen and professionals sought to encourage

investment and low-interest loans. But the problem was difficult to deal with, and only modest progress occurred. More was accomplished in beefing up city services and amenities. During the postwar years, higher tax levies and bond issues funded the hard-surfacing of city streets that remained graveled and made possible the installation of new water and sewer systems. Bright lights creating a "white way" around the business district were installed, and a seventy-five-thousand-dollar clinic and hospital were built. In the countryside, power lines financed by the federal Rural Electrification Administration brought electricity into many farm homes for the first time by the start of the 1950s. In 1957 a new dial telephone system rendered obsolete most of the operators who had handled calls until then.[8]

At the center of town, the park on the square had grown more and more ill-kempt until efforts to spruce it up were launched. The decrepit octagonal bandstand, which had witnessed countless concerts since its appearance in 1911, was finally replaced. New benches and plantings beautified the park, which continued to draw large crowds of listeners for Saturday night band concerts in the summertime. The intersection of U.S. Highway 60, which ran along the north side of the square, and State Highway 5 in the middle of town was considered a significant business asset to the community, drawing in traffic and shoppers from miles around. Many store owners worried when rumors spread that one or both highways were going to be routed around the town to speed up traffic. The bypasses were eventually constructed, but not until the late 1950s.[9]

Town boosters realized that efforts to keep traffic flowing through the community, improve its appearance, and expand services to its residents were insufficient in and of themselves to maintain and possibly bring about an increase in population. The 1950 census figures augured poorly for the future. While Mansfield's count of 963 was up by 41 over 1940—giving it a better record than that of most nearby towns—the county's population dipped by 2,133 during the decade and seemed likely to continue downward unless some kind of dramatic economic turnaround occurred. Wartime exigencies had accelerated the process of mechanization on the farm, and during the postwar years agriculture in Wright County underwent the same kind of transformation that affected farmers all around the country: increased dependence upon labor-saving machinery, the widespread use of productivity-enhancing chemicals and fertilizers, and modernized methods of production that left fewer farm families on

the land—and smaller families at that. Small-town storekeepers, who were in business to serve them, saw demand for their products and services dwindle, squeezing their profits and forcing many of them out of business.[10]

The only way out of their dilemma, many Mansfield businessmen believed, was to attract new industry that would provide jobs that could keep local residents and farm families from having to move elsewhere to find employment. Industry had come and gone over the years. The tomato factory and cheese plant had shut down. The brief enthusiasm for lead and zinc mining had died, revived, and died again, although talk resurfaced of possibly making the activity profitable once more. A new lime mill and a frozen-food locker plant started operations soon after the war, but not until the early 1950s did concerted efforts begin to attract industry to Mansfield.

In April 1952 the Lions Club formed an industrial committee to conduct a survey and to figure out methods of advertising the community to prospective employers. Three years later a Mansfield Industrial Development Corporation was set up for the purpose of wooing industry and raising funds to facilitate the construction of factories in town. Although selling stock in the corporation proceeded more slowly than desired, within a short time the Tobin-Hamilton Shoe Company of St. Louis decided to relocate its operations to Mansfield. Starting with about a hundred employees, within two years' time it had built an addition onto its factory and more than doubled its workforce. By 1959 there were 375 employees working for the company. Other industries were slower to develop in Mansfield (later, a major steel factory would locate there). In the 1960 census Mansfield's population dropped slightly from 963 to 949.[11]

For Laura and Almanzo, the transformations that they had witnessed during their lifetimes were immense. "Times have changed within my memory and I am sure we have all changed too," she marveled in February 1947. "As I remembered the things of which I told in my stories I could hardly believe I was the same person as the Laura of whom I wrote."[12] Laura's and Almanzo's childhoods had been ones of log cabins, dugouts and sod houses, candlelight illumination, horse-and-buggy transportation, backbreaking labor on the farm, home entertainment, confrontations with Indians on the frontier, grinding wheat in coffee mills, shooting rabbits and geese for dinner, and walking miles across the prairie to get from one place to another. During their lifetime they had witnessed the coming of the railroad and, in its wake, the emergence of the automobile, moving

pictures, radio, television, air travel, X-rays, radar, and other technological marvels. By the time Almanzo died, atomic bombs had been detonated, and in the year Laura died the first earth satellite was launched. Many of these developments they welcomed and enjoyed. Driving to Detroit and California in an automobile had been great adventures for them, and Almanzo appreciated the mobility his car afforded him. They had a radio too, but there never was a television set in the house. Occasionally when Rose had lived with them they had gone to the movies, but they never became great movie fans.

Life at Rocky Ridge, while affected to a degree by modern developments and technologies, remained something of a throwback to an earlier era. Almanzo still liked to putter around in his shop. He enjoyed working with wood and built some beautiful furniture. He possessed a bevy of canes made from different kinds of wood that he had picked up on the farm or that people had given to him. One of them was quite unique, containing a variety of different kinds of wood, each piece being only about an inch long. He also kept some goats and trained them to put their front legs up on a little stool, making it easier for him to milk them because of his bad leg, which prevented him from stooping. He used a bunch of white handkerchiefs to clean their udders. Laura could not stand the handkerchiefs, so he took them to a woman in town to get them laundered.[13]

Sometimes when he went to town he would wander over to the pool hall next door to the old theater on the west side of the square and watch the games going on there. He never took part himself; he just sat and visited with the other men. Everybody knew that he had an injured foot, causing him to limp and requiring a special shoe. He would make a cut in the toe of the shoe and stitch around it so that it would fit his foot better. He walked with a cane, and he wore suspenders. He was the quiet type, not very talkative around most people. His big white moustache could give him a stern appearance, and to some people he seemed grouchy and unapproachable. But others said that once you got to know him, he could be quite outgoing and even playful. Peggy Dennis, a young woman in her early twenties who waited on him when he came into the Pennington grocery store, considered him a cutup because he always liked to clown around with her mother. Anna Gutschke, who knew the Wilders for almost a half century, liked him a lot. She recalled, "He had great humor, he enjoyed entertaining. He was absolutely the greatest. He had lots of fun, he was a

joy." Whether people thought of him as a cutup or a grouch, however, he was, in their minds, different, someone a little bit out of the ordinary.[14]

Laura was different in her own way. Although as a child and adolescent she had disliked snobbery and social distinctions, as an adult she sometimes gave people the impression that she was a little snooty herself. This reflected less haughtiness and arrogance on her part than certain ingrained habits, a strong sense of propriety, and a measure of shyness that she never fully overcame. No doubt also it mirrored some attitudes that she had learned from her mother about distinctions separating people on the basis of proper behavior and social bearing.[15]

Although she had always done her part of the heavy labor—both inside and out—on the farm, Laura always dressed up when she went to town, usually taking care to wear some (cheap) jewelry, a ladylike hat, and sometimes gloves. To town women and farmers' wives who did not mind being seen in calico dresses, such behavior was certainly different and, to some, slightly pretentious. She liked the color blue, but she must have worn frequently her red velvet dress, because many people remembered seeing her wearing it.[16]

Talkative in private, Laura tended to get nervous in crowds. If this sometimes made her seem distant or even haughty, people who knew Laura better generally described her as being friendly and likable, sweet and gracious. Roscoe Jones, who as a kid did odd jobs for her, remembered her as "a very, very kind person and a real sweet lady." She had a wonderful disposition, said Neta Seal, who got to know her about as well as anybody.[17]

During the 1940s, before Almanzo died, the two of them frequently joined Neta and Silas Seal for dinner at their rooming house. The younger couple reciprocated by coming for meals at Rocky Ridge. Sometimes all of them would go out to eat at a restaurant, maybe down to Branson or Hollister or some other place in the area. Laura loved chicken and dumplings. Neta made a delicious Swiss steak. Almanzo always requested it when she asked him to choose the menu, and he would praise her extravagantly afterward. Once, upon arriving at their apartment, he announced, "Now, Neta, I can't brag on your Swiss steak. Bessie don't want me to, ha ha." Had Laura become a bit jealous because of his effusive appreciation of her cooking? Perhaps. In any case, there is a hint here of Laura's ability—or at least of her continuing effort—to keep "the man of the place" under strict control. For a while Almanzo believed that he would like to move into town

to live in one of the Seals' apartments, but Laura squelched the notion. One day she told him, "Now, Manly, you go out to your workshop; we can't take that with us, you know. You'll have to sort it out and sell it. Now you go out there and make a list of anything you're going to sell before we move in." Almanzo could not bear to part with his tools and workshop. That ended his talk about moving into town.[18]

Both of them probably would have felt uncomfortable living in town anyway. Although the eastern edge of Mansfield was only about a mile from their farmhouse, they were country folks through and through, and that fact was not likely to change this late in life. Almanzo, Laura's "Farmer Boy," still liked having animals around, and Laura enjoyed living in natural surroundings. Her living-room windows remained her picture frames for looking out into the great outdoors. Although they had lived in town for a few years four decades earlier, moving back now would require a change in their entire outlook. They felt comfortable on Rocky Ridge, and that is where they would stay.

They were no longer physically able to keep the place up, however. In October 1948 they sold the farm to H. L. Shorter and his wife, Gireda, on an installment plan for eight thousand dollars. The Shorters agreed to pay two thousand dollars as a down payment and the balance in fifty-dollar monthly payments. Indicating why he preferred that to a lump sum, Almanzo explained, "I want some income. I'll let him pay it out in payments each month and then I'll have some money." The Shorters had previously purchased part of the land from them in 1943. Now they agreed to let Laura and Almanzo continue living in the house and use the outbuildings around it throughout their lifetimes.[19]

For someone whose health had been supposedly poor since his bout of diphtheria when he was in his late twenties, Almanzo lived a long time. In 1947, when he turned ninety and Laura turned eighty, they were invited to a birthday celebration in her honor sponsored by Chicago's large Carson, Pirie Scott Department Store, but they excused themselves because of Almanzo's failing health. Later that year, however, when the illustrator Garth Williams drove to Mansfield to talk to Laura about the illustrations that he had been commissioned to do for a new edition of her books, he was impressed to see Almanzo still doing chores in the barn. His health became her excuse for staying home again later that spring when the Detroit Public Library opened a new branch in her name. In lieu of her own appearance

there, she sent a message to be read at the ceremony and gave them the original manuscripts, handwritten in pencil, of *The Long Winter* and *These Happy Golden Years.*[20]

Despite his growing feebleness, Almanzo put in a garden in the spring of 1949, but a serious heart attack in July left him nearly helpless. Afterward, Neta and Silas Seal dropped by the farmhouse often to help out or to drive Laura to town for groceries. Sensing that the end was near, Almanzo began disposing of his goats, the car, and other items that Laura would not need or be able to take care of. Then, surprisingly, he began improving. When death finally came, early on Sunday morning, October 23, it was unexpected. After Almanzo suffered another heart attack, Laura telephoned the Seals, who hurried over. By the time they arrived, he was dead and Laura was clutching him in a big, wide-armed chair. She did not seem to want to let him go. For a while after the funeral, Neta came to the farmhouse regularly to stay with Laura. She was surprised to discover that the two of them had been sleeping in twin beds, his next to her writing nook, hers by the bathroom. The first evening Neta stayed with her, Laura asked, "Neta, do you care if I sleep in Almanzo's bed and you sleep in mine?" Neta guessed that she felt closer to him sleeping in his bed.[21]

After sixty-four years of married life, Laura was now alone. "I am very lonely," she wrote in a letter, saying that her plans were uncertain. "My heart is too sore to write more."[22] He had been her "Farmer Boy," the hero of her second novel, the young gallant who had won her affection, though he was a decade older. He was the doting husband who had brought her bouquets of wildflowers. But they also were capable of quarreling and bickering with each other, enough that it frequently drove Rose upstairs to escape their flare-ups while she was living in the same house with them during the 1920s.

It is difficult, if not impossible, to penetrate the veil of privacy that obscured the relationship between husband and wife. Evidence contained in Laura's writings and letters, reminiscences of friends and neighbors, and Rose's journals and diaries remains scant. In the triangular relationship among husband, wife, and only child, Almanzo sometimes appeared to be the odd man out. The intense feelings of affection and resentment, pride and irritation that existed between mother and daughter can be documented, mainly through traces left by Rose. But Almanzo seldom was mentioned in her journals and diaries, and when he was, it was usually in a secondary role.

Letters between husband and wife written the few times they were apart indicate that while he exceeded her in years, she was the dominant figure in the relationship. She watched over him like a mother hen, careful to make sure that he was able to get along without her by his side. The romantic descriptions of their courtship in *These Happy Golden Years* suggest that they possessed feelings for each other expected of every prospectively married couple at the time. More telling, however, was Laura's insistence that she not be required to use the word *obey* in their marriage vows. Hardly a feminist then or later, she was an individualist whose commitment to freedom and autonomy was a personal rather than a social or political stance. Almanzo's failing health necessitated her heavy participation in physical labor on the farm and reinforced what was probably well established by the time he suffered his stroke: he was more dependent on her than she was on him. It was a partnership that they lived out for sixty-four years, but few people who were acquainted with them more than casually doubted who was the dominant partner.

When Rose returned for her father's funeral, it was her first time home in Mansfield since she had left Missouri in 1937. Having tormented herself for years by believing that her parents needed her on the premises and that she could not honorably abandon them, once she made her escape she did not find it necessary or important enough to visit them even once before Almanzo died. Obviously, the ties that had bound her to the place and to her parents as well as the antipathies and differences that had driven them apart were profound. No one had forced Rose to live with or near them; no one had made her stay away after she left. The volatile relationship generating so much emotional force was that between mother and daughter; in many ways they were two of a kind. For her father Rose harbored affection, admiration, even pride. But there never could be the same kind of intensity in their interactions that existed between her and her mother because they were so unalike. Almanzo was a farmer, a husband, a father, a neighbor, and an individualist. He was essentially an ordinary fellow with the same kinds of goals and expectations that characterized most of his friends. He lived his life with dignity and stoical restraint. He never expected too much from life, and thus he was largely content. Disappointments had frequently visited him, but all in all he was cheerful and satisfied with his lot. His daughter seldom mentioned him in her diaries and journals. He was a constant presence in her life but not a distinctly important one.

Rose's mother, on the other hand, could drive her to distraction. The two were alike in so many ways: intelligent, self-disciplined, perfectionist, critical of other people's foibles and shortcomings, capable of bursts of energy, and highly ambitious to achieve something significant. Each was an individualist, and each opposed governmental intrusions. Each one saw herself as being set apart from the ordinary run of people, and each let no one else do her thinking for her. Rose, the precocious child, demonstrated a brilliance of intellect not evident in her mother. But Laura proved her competence over and over as a housewife, farm manager, loan officer, and author. In her own special way, she was as remarkable a person as Rose. Yet, their differences outweighed their similarities. One was devout, the other a skeptic. One was traditional, the other avant-garde. One was ruled by convention, the other ridiculed it. One enjoyed rural ways, the other escaped to the city as soon as she could. One settled down and lived with a man for two-thirds of a century, the other found it impossible to accommodate herself to any other person for any length of time. One was content, the other restless. One found meaning and satisfaction in simple ways and simple people, the other remained at heart an elitist.

Where did Rose acquire all of her resentments, rebelliousness, ambitiousness, tenacity, creativity, passions, and commitments? Somewhere inside a household that was poverty stricken, worried by illness, beset by disappointment, but inspired by hopes and dreams, sustained by talent and ambition and resourcefulness—somewhere among these hopes, fears, and disappointments Rose developed a personality that distinguished her from her playmates and schoolmates and always set her apart as an adult. The relationship that shaped her was not that between her and her father but rather the one with her mother. With only one child to raise, nurture, and mold, Laura had approached the task with the same kind of tenacity she applied to all of her major activities. To a little girl, her mother's all-encompassing, overprotective watchfulness must have been as much of a burden as the grinding poverty her family endured most of the time that she was growing up.

Central to the relationship between mother and daughter was the struggle for control that persisted far beyond the time that it should have. The mother's efforts to control her daughter's behavior and to attempt to control the environment in which she grew up must have often seemed stifling to Rose. The resentments that flared up frequently and were recorded in her

journal entries during the 1930s probably went unrecognized by Laura most of the time. The desire to control also entailed self-control, and both mother and daughter were masters of it, seldom betraying to others their true feelings. But if they constantly got on each other's nerves, they still harbored real love and commitment beneath it all.

During the 1940s, for the first time, Rose finally discovered a commitment that she considered worthy of her full devotion and effort. No place could hold her forever. No man was able to, either. Her desire to write great literature waned, and no other party or organization captured her unqualified loyalty. But finally during World War II she seemed to have found her true calling, in whose direction she had been drifting for a long time. Writing a column, "Rose Lane Says," for a small weekly newspaper, the *Pittsburgh Courier,* provided her with an outlet for her radically individualist viewpoint. Then she made national news by writing an antigovernment diatribe in pamphlet form titled *What Is This—the Gestapo?* after FBI agents came inquiring about criticisms that she had written about Social Security. She found a real intellectual home in taking over the job of book editor of the National Economic Council's monthly *Review of Books* in 1945. It gave her the opportunity to read political theory and conservative ideology and provided her with a chance to work out more systematically her ideas about the role of government and the place of the individual in modern mass society. Her 1943 book, *The Discovery of Freedom,* contained the most highly developed example of her conservative philosophy.[23]

Now that her mother was alone, Rose came to Mansfield periodically to stay with her, usually during the winter months. In March 1953 she stopped for several days with Mr. and Mrs. Alfred M. Morgan, friends from Danbury, after spending the winter in the South. Rose was the only family Laura had left now. The previous year she had bequested to her daughter all of her possessions, providing that upon Rose's death the copyrights to her books would be transferred to the library in Mansfield. Grace had died of heart disease in Manchester in November 1941. Her husband, Nate Dow, had succumbed two years later. Both were buried in the De Smet cemetery.[24]

Carrie had traveled to Mansfield by train in 1944 to visit Laura and Almanzo. She had sold the family's Third Street house in De Smet that year, but since she was living across the state in Keystone, a pile of old junk and keepsakes were left in storage in one of the rooms, waiting to be disposed of. Among them were pictures, dishes, bedding, some of Mary's

old braille books, and other items. After Carrie died in June 1946, the owners hauled most of the stuff to the dump, but they did save two large portraits of the parents, which were shipped to Laura in Mansfield, since she was now the only surviving member of the family. Having no room—or not wanting to make room—on the walls of the farmhouse to hang the pictures, Laura donated them to the State Historical Society in Pierre, where she and her sisters (none of whom had children of their own) earlier had sent their father's fiddle to be displayed.[25]

The days at Rocky Ridge went by slowly now. Laura emerged from the house only infrequently. Almanzo was gone, and month by month lifelong friends and acquaintances were dying, too. M. A. Freeman, the banker, succumbed at eighty-two in January 1948. Dr. John Fuson, who had practiced medicine in Mansfield for forty-four years, died the following year. In 1951 it was longtime friend Mrs. N. J. Craig. Now and then people dropped by to visit. Berta and Elmer Hader from Nyack, New York, stopped on their way to California in May 1950. Laura had not seen them again since first meeting them in San Francisco in 1915. More often than not it was younger friends, like the Seals, who looked out for her. They invited her to their place for dinner from time to time, and Neta stopped by to visit or to run errands for her or to drive her around.[26]

As Laura's life grew quieter, Mansfield itself became busier and busier, if only temporarily, although she was no longer part of that activity. Thursdays and Saturdays witnessed the heaviest traffic in town. Thursday was sale day. Large crowds gathered at the sale barn, where farmers brought their cattle and other animals to market. Saturdays, when people came to shop and buy their groceries and to sell their eggs, chickens, and produce, the sidewalks were so full of people that they sometimes had to step into the street to get around each other. Women sat and visited in front of the stores, and the men moved into the park or headed to the pool hall. In the evening in the summertime, the band played in the park, while kids ran around and the adults sat in their cars and listened, honking their horns in appreciation after the songs. Stores stayed open late, and there were the movie theater, pool hall, bowling alley, and skating rink to liven things up.[27]

Softball became a big attraction during the late 1940s and into the 1950s. With help from the chamber of commerce and the school board, funds were raised to put up lights in 1947, and hundreds of people sometimes showed up to watch the action. A thousand people, the largest crowd

ever to witness a match in town, came for a game soon after the lights were installed. Even more came for the annual rodeo sponsored by the Mansfield Round-Up Club several years later. Hunting and fishing were also big attractions in the Ozarks, drawing many from out of town. Main Street businessmen did their part to keep shoppers coming into town by sponsoring sale days, Miss Merry Christmas parades, local talent shows, and other special events. A Boy Scout troop was organized, languished, reorganized, languished, and reorganized again. Organizational activities ebbed and flowed as townspeople tried to keep Mansfield on the upward swing, competitive with its rivals in the surrounding region.[28]

Laura, meanwhile, had become Mansfield's most famous citizen, surpassing baseball pitcher Carl Mays. The latter's sidearm delivery had hit a Cleveland batter in 1920 when he was playing for the New York Yankees, gaining him notoriety as the only major leaguer ever to kill another player in a game. Even Rose, who for three decades had reigned as Mansfield's most famous literary product, now began to fall under the shadow of her mother's reputation. People seldom saw Laura anymore, but they were aware of her presence in the farmhouse at Rocky Ridge, and from time to time they could read about some new award or recognition that she had received.

A feature story in the *Kansas City Star* in 1949 and reprinted in the *Mansfield Mirror* observed that her books about American pioneer life were being read around the world as well as by millions of Americans. "By all standards Mrs. Wilder is a famous author," the story indicated. "Nevertheless, she is unaffected and as unassuming as in her earlier days here when she helped 'pull a crosscut saw' on Ozark timber." In August 1950 the Athenian Club sponsored a tea for her at the Wright County Library in Hartville, proclaiming it Laura Ingalls Wilder Day. About 135 people attended the event. The *Missouri Blue Book*, the official manual of the state, recognized her that year in a section devoted to famous Missourians.[29]

When the Pomona, California, public library renamed its children's reading room the "Laura Ingalls Wilder Room" in May 1950, Laura sent the original manuscript of *Little Town on the Prairie*. The following year the Mansfield branch of the Wright County Library system moved into new quarters in a former office building on east Commercial Avenue and named it the Laura Ingalls Wilder Library. A dedication ceremony was held on September 28, 1951, in the Mansfield High School gymnasium. Laura

wore her favorite red velvet dress for the occasion and an orchid, a gift from the library. State librarian Paxton Price was the principal speaker of the day, and a violinist played some of the songs that her father had once played and that she had mentioned in her books. The local newspaper took pictures of her standing in front of the library and inside by a shelf containing her books and also a batch of birthday cards that she had received from school children the previous February. "She appeared far younger than her 84 years as she graciously responded to the tribute paid her," the story in the *Mirror* reported. Laura later gave the library a set of her books and various heirlooms and mementos to display. They included the trowel that had been used to build the farmhouse in New York where Almanzo had grown up and used later to build their first farm home in Dakota Territory and then their house at Rocky Ridge, a set of dolls that had been given to Laura depicting her family's members, some of Almanzo's walking canes, pictures, and other items.[30]

During Children's Book Week in November 1952, Laura agreed to attend an autograph party at Brown's Book Store in Springfield, which declared the day "Laura Ingalls Wilder Day." As usual, she wore her red velvet dress, and she smiled radiantly for the photographer as children gathered around her to get their autographs and a word of greeting. The following year, in December, *The Horn Book,* a magazine devoted to children's literature, published a special Laura Ingalls Wilder issue. Harper's also published in October 1953 a new edition of her books, illustrated by Garth Williams, one of America's premier illustrators. He had spent time over several years researching and making the drawings, visiting the sites where the action in the novels took place, and driving to Mansfield to talk to Laura. Laura sent her publisher a statement to use for advertising purposes, "Laura and Mary and their folks live again in these illustrations."[31]

Laura now spent most of her time at Rocky Ridge reading, sewing, playing solitaire, and puttering around the house. The parlor usually remained dark, since she lived mostly in the kitchen, the dining room, and her bedroom. She still did some sewing, crocheting, and embroidering, but as she grew feebler, she was able to work at them less and less. Her little kitchen was always neat, but then there was not much to untidy it. She told Nava Austin, the librarian, that reading and playing solitaire were her livelihood. She liked to have the radio on, but she never owned a television set. She enjoyed reading detective stories and other light fare,

but her preferred form of fiction was westerns. Luke Short and Zane Grey were favorites of hers. As she explained to Nava Austin, "People probably wonder why this is my type of reading, but they are easy to hold, and I just enjoy them."[32]

Every Wednesday she dressed up and rode into town to do her grocery shopping and stop by the library to pick up some new books. She and Nava would chat for a while, and sometimes Laura told her stories about what things had been like in the old days. She especially enjoyed talking about Mary. Afterward, she would drop by the newspaper office for a chat with the editor or by the bank if she had any business to do there and then walk to Daisy Freeman's or perhaps go for tea with an elderly friend. Then she would have lunch at Owens Cafe or some other restaurant. Once, when she received an unexpected five-hundred-dollar royalty check in the mail, she invited Nava to come along and have lunch with her at the café. When the librarian replied that she probably should stay and tend to the books since the library did not close during the lunch hour, Laura volunteered to order shrimp dinners for the two of them and have them ready and waiting so that Nava would not have to take too much time off from her job.[33]

Laura's driver on these weekly excursions was Jim Hartley, who ran a taxi service in town. After finishing her lunch, Laura asked him to drive her through the countryside or perhaps to some nearby town. She especially enjoyed taking the picturesque road down to Ava. On Sundays she frequently had Hartley drive her to Mountain Grove to a restaurant called Frederick's on the east side of town. He would join her for dinner and then drive her home. In 1954 she bought a new Oldsmobile, which she had him keep in his garage since she could not drive it herself. Once when Rose was back for a visit, she took a series of pictures of her mother getting in and out of the car and being driven around in it. When Jim Hartley died in 1954, Laura was distraught. Virginia Hartley, his daughter-in-law, went to comfort Laura, took over as Laura's driver, and became someone on whom Laura could depend when she needed help. The two of them drove to Mountain Grove on Sundays or maybe to Cabool or some other town for dinner.[34]

The year that Laura celebrated her eighty-seventh birthday, there were two parties for her in Mansfield, and cards and letters poured in from all over. She was not able to answer all of her letters anymore and usually preferred not to talk to enthusiastic fans who sometimes stopped by the

house to catch a glimpse of her. She did appreciate the accolades and honors heaped upon her, however. In 1954 the American Library Association inaugurated the Laura Ingalls Wilder Award, honoring authors who had made lasting and important contributions to children's literature. Fittingly, she was designated the first recipient of the award, which was a medal designed by Garth Williams. Explaining why she would be unable to attend the ceremonies in Minneapolis, she noted, "Being 87 years old with a tired heart I have to avoid excitement even if pleasant."[35]

Even as her body grew weaker, her mind remained engaged. Almanzo had lived past ninety, and she said she wanted to, too. But realizing that she could not live forever, she began giving some of her mementos to people who were close to her. To Nava Austin she gave her family Bible, which she had received from her father and mother at the time of her marriage. In it were some clippings and obituaries, including one of her and Almanzo's infant son, who had died in 1889 soon after birth. It was a surprise to Nava to read about it, because Laura had never talked to her about him. Laura explained her purpose in disposing of some of her keepsakes, "I'm giving things to people that I think they will enjoy and take care of."[36]

Even now she retained a sense of adventure. Rose, who generally came back yearly to spend several months at Rocky Ridge with her mother, invited her to return with her to Danbury to visit there for a while. It was Laura's first plane ride, but she was willing to try it for a chance to see the place where Rose had been living for the past two decades. The girl her father had called his little "flutterbudget" had observed transportation evolve from the horse and buggy to jet airplanes.[37]

On February 10, 1957, just three days after her ninetieth birthday, Laura died. When Rose had arrived the previous Thanksgiving to visit, she immediately realized that Laura's health had taken a drastic turn for the worse since the last time she had seen her. Soon it became necessary to transfer her to a hospital in Springfield, where doctors diagnosed the problem as diabetes. Then, for a while, her condition improved. Within a few weeks' time Rose was reporting to friends, "She looks and feels better than she has for years." The day after Christmas she took her mother back home to Rocky Ridge.[38]

Rose's earlier report proved overoptimistic, however, and Laura's condition again began to deteriorate. The daughter said later that these were "the most harrowing and exhausting weeks of my life." Two local women

volunteered to take turns staying up at night with her at the farmhouse so that one of them could be there to help, if she was needed. On Sunday, February 10, the night Laura died, it was Virginia Hartley's turn to be on duty. When the end came, it was with a mixture of dread and relief that Rose responded to it. The mother who had brought her into the world, who had loved her, smothered and controlled her, and who had depended heavily upon her had caused both pain and joy. Now she was gone. It was like a heavy burden had been lifted from her.[39]

Laura was a prominent enough personage to rate an article in the *New York Times,* on page 27, on her death, but the compositors somehow substituted Mansfield, Ohio, for Mansfield, Missouri, in the Associated Press wire story's dateline. The headline, "LAURA I. WILDER, AUTHOR, DIES AT 90," may have been the only instance when she was ever referred to as "Laura I.," but otherwise the story did get things right: she *was* an author. Prairie girl, student, schoolteacher, wife, mother, farmer, club member, churchgoer, farm-loan officer, failed political candidate, moralist—she was all of these. But most of all, Laura Ingalls Wilder, as she came affectionately to be known after the publication of her first book in 1932, was a writer. "Writer of the 'Little House' Series for Children Was an Ex-Newspaper Editor," noted the *Times* in its subheadline.[40]

From the age of forty-four, mainly in articles for the *Missouri Ruralist,* Wilder discovered her true vocation: writing commentaries and stories that had a point or a moral to them. Whether in nonfictional form or as autobiographical fiction, the words that she wrote were purposeful. Not always did she herself live up to the elevated standards that she upheld; she even admitted her imperfections and her nonconformist nature in her writings. For her, the ideal was as important as—even more important than—the real. In creating a persona for herself—as a beloved children's book author—she came to realize the wisdom of the saying that a person should be careful with regard to what she pretends to be, for ultimately she becomes that person. The Laura Ingalls Wilder that the world came to know was both better and worse than the image conjured up by many of her readers and celebrators over the years. Not nearly the perfect "nice old lady" who wrote those "wonderful books" that won so much acclaim, she could be selfish, mean-spirited, and narrow-minded, like anybody. In that sense, she was not as good as her image suggested. But by the same token, she was well aware of the frailties of human nature and realized that in her own

life she partook of them, too. Her observations about people and her keen psychological insights were supplemented by an abiding religious faith that trusted God to make ultimate judgments and issue his just rewards. Combined, these provided her with the tools that made her stories more than mere recountings of hardship and adventure. They provided her with the basis for genuine insight and wisdom. Reflected first in her *Missouri Ruralist* articles, these insights later came garbed in fictional form in her novels. In that sense, her writings were more profound than they are often given credit for. With the help of her daughter, Rose, who took already good writing and added luster to it, she became one of America's greatest children's authors.

Her success was not without a cost, though. The tangled relationship between mother and daughter was clearly crucial to the success of Laura Ingalls Wilder as a published author. Without Rose's help and encouragement, there would have been no "Laura Ingalls Wilder" as we know her today, only a sprightly, energetic Ozarks farm woman and sometime farm-newspaper writer known as "Mrs. A. J. Wilder." But then without her mother and the attentions that she lavished upon her daughter, there would have been no "Rose Wilder Lane," either. Both—in the end—found it hard to live with each other, but both also depended heavily upon each other. It was a symbiotic relationship of personalities extremely different in some senses but profoundly similar in others. Both achieved degrees of success far above the ordinary; both encountered disappointments, too.

With their lives so integrally intertwined, it was no wonder that Rose responded to her mother's death with a sense of relief. Funeral arrangements quickly were made. Final rites were conducted at the Mansfield Methodist church on Wednesday, February 13, at two o'clock. Rev. Walter Brunner conducted the service, and six men from town served as pallbearers. Rose afterward appeared as if a great burden had been lifted from her shoulders. Rather than seeming to be devastated by her mother's death, the psychological release it brought with it left her almost buoyant. Her only wish seemed to be to get away from Mansfield as quickly as possible.[41]

Her mother's estate, when it was inventoried in county probate court by her friend and executor N. J. Craig, totaled $77,814.42, including $9,866 in corporate stocks, $36,000 in U.S. Savings Bonds, and an attributed value of $30,000 in the copyrights of her eight novels. In addition to her will, Laura had left a letter, written on July 30, 1952, for Rose to read upon her

death. "Rose Dearest," she had written, "when you read this letter I will be gone and you will have inherited all I have." It went on to instruct her on how to dispose of her books, jewelry, china, and some of her other things. "My love will be with you always," Laura finished, signing the note, "Mama Bess (Laura Ingalls Wilder)."[42]

# Notes

ﾞꕤ

The following abbreviations are used in the notes:

| | |
|---|---|
| LIW | Laura Ingalls Wilder |
| AJW | Almanzo J. Wilder |
| RWL | Rose Wilder Lane |
| Lane Papers | Rose Wilder Lane Papers, Herbert Hoover Presidential Library, West Branch, Iowa |
| "Pioneer Girl" | Wilder's handwritten draft of her unpublished autobiography, written in 1930 (microfilm copy at State Historical Society of Missouri, Columbia) |

Wilder's handwritten drafts of her eight novels are located in the following places:

State Historical Society of Missouri, Columbia (microfilm; originals are located at the Laura Ingalls Wilder Memorial Association, Mansfield, Missouri):

> "Little House in the Big Woods"
> "Farmer Boy"
> "Little House on the Prairie"
> "On the Banks of Plum Creek"
> "By the Shores of Silver Lake"

Detroit Public Library, Rare Book Room:

> "The Long Winter"
> "These Happy Golden Years"

Pomona, California, Public Library:

> "Little Town on the Prairie"

All of the books were published in New York by Harper and Brothers and Harper and Row. References in the notes are to the revised editions, illustrated by Garth Williams, published in 1953. Original publication dates for the books were:

> *Little House in the Big Woods*, 1932
> *Farmer Boy*, 1933
> *Little House on the Prairie*, 1935
> *On the Banks of Plum Creek*, 1937
> *By the Shores of Silver Lake*, 1939
> *The Long Winter*, 1940
> *Little Town on the Prairie*, 1941
> *These Happy Golden Years*, 1943
> *The First Four Years*, 1971

## Introduction

1. William Holtz, *The Ghost in the Little House: A Life of Rose Wilder Lane* (Columbia: University of Missouri Press, 1993), 230, 302, 313, 375, 379–85; see also William Holtz, "The Ghost in the Little House Books," *Liberty* 5 (March 1992): 51–54, and William Holtz, "Ghost and Host in the Little House Books," *Studies in the Literary Imagination* 29 (fall 1996): 41–51.

2. Rosa Ann Moore, "Laura Ingalls Wilder's Orange Notebooks and the Art of the Little House Books," in *Children's Literature* (Philadelphia: Temple University Press, 1975), 4:105–19; Rosa Ann Moore, "Laura Ingalls Wilder and Rose Wilder Lane: The Chemistry of Collaboration," *Children's Literature in Education* 2 (autumn 1980): 101–9; William T. Anderson, "The Literary Apprenticeship of Laura Ingalls Wilder," *South Dakota History* 13 (winter 1983): 285–331; William T. Anderson, "Laura Ingalls Wilder and Rose Wilder Lane: The Continuing Collaboration," *South Dakota History* 16 (summer 1986): 89–143; Caroline Fraser, "The Prairie Queen," *New York Review of Books* 41 (December 22, 1994): 38–45.

## 1. Pioneer Girl, 1867–1879

1. *New York Times,* February 8, 1867.

2. Robert H. Wiebe, *The Search for Order, 1877–1920* (New York: Hill and Wang, 1967); Samuel P. Hays, *The Response to Industrialism, 1885–1914* (Chicago: University of Chicago Press, 1957); John F. Stover, *The Life and Decline of the American Railroad* (New York: Oxford University Press, 1970), chap. 3.

3. *Pepin County Press,* June 2, 1860, March 1, 1862.

4. LIW, *Little House in the Big Woods,* 1–2; *Durand Times,* December 12, 1865.

5. Robert F. Fries, *Empire in Pine: The Story of Lumbering in Wisconsin, 1830–1900* (Madison: State Historical Society of Wisconsin, 1951), 7–8, 20–23, 78–82; Charles E. Twining, *Downriver: Orrin H. Ingram and the Empire Lumber Company* (Madison: State Historical Society of Wisconsin, 1975), 28–29, 105–6; Malcolm Rosholt, *Lumbermen on the Chippewa* (Rosholt, Wis.: Rosholt House, 1982); John N. Vogel, *Great Lakes Lumber on the Great Plains: The Laird, Norton Lumber Company in South Dakota* (Iowa City: University of Iowa Press, 1992), esp. chaps. 5–6.

6. Everett N. Dick, *The Sod-House Frontier, 1854–1890* (New York: D. Appleton-Century, 1937); Robert V. Hine, *Community on the American Frontier: Separate but Not Alone* (Norman: University of Oklahoma Press, 1980); Richard A. Bartlett, *The New Country: A Social History of the American Frontier, 1776–1890* (New York: Oxford University Press, 1974).

7. Donald Zochert, *Laura: The Life of Laura Ingalls Wilder* (New York: Avon, 1977), 12–14; John C. Hudson, "Two Dakota Homestead Frontiers," *Annals of the Association of American Geographers* 63 (December 1973): 448; Gerald W. McFarland, *A Scattered People: An American Family Moves West* (New York: Pantheon Books, 1985), 49.

8. On the Yankee migration, see John C. Hudson, "Yankeeland in the Middle West," *Journal of Geography* 85 (September–October 1986): 195–200; Carleton Beals, *Our Yankee Heritage: New England's Contribution to American Civilization* (New York: David McKay, 1955); Stewart Holbrook, *The Yankee Exodus: An Account of Migration from New England* (New York: Macmillan, 1950); and Lois K. Mathews, *The Expansion of New England* (New York: Russell and Russell, 1909).

9. Ruth Bunker Christiansen, *American and Royal Ancestors of Laura Ingalls Wilder* (Frederic, Wis.: Sally Gustafson, 1984), 5–6; *Notes from Laura Ingalls Wilder Memorial Society, Inc., Pepin, Wis.* 3 (December 1978): 3; Zochert, *Laura*, 2.

10. Zochert, *Laura*, 3–5, 10; Elisha Keyes, "Early Days in Jefferson County," *Collections of the State Historical Society of Wisconsin* 11 (1888): 416–34; John Henry Ott, ed., *Jefferson County, Wisconsin, and Its People* (Chicago: S. J. Clarke, 1917), 1:36–69.

11. Zochert, *Laura*, 6–8.

12. Ibid., 8–9; William T. Anderson, *Laura Ingalls Wilder: A Biography* (New York: HarperCollins, 1992), 21–22.

13. Zochert, *Laura*, 11–12; Anderson, *Laura Ingalls Wilder*, 23–24.

14. Zochert, *Laura*, 12–14; Anderson, *Laura Ingalls Wilder*, 24.

15. Robert C. Nesbit, *Wisconsin: A History* (Madison: University of Wisconsin Press, 1973), 248; Richard N. Current, *The History of Wisconsin*, vol. 2, *The Civil War Era, 1848–1873* (Madison: State Historical Society of Wisconsin, 1976), 335; *Notes from Laura Ingalls Wilder Memorial Society (Pepin)* 3 (June 1978): 3 and 4 (June 1979): 3; Zochert, *Laura*, 18. The enlistment files and muster rolls of Hiram and James Ingalls in Co. E, 1st Minnesota Heavy Artillery (Nos. 1149 and 1150) are located in the National Archives.

16. Zochert, *Laura,* 15; Pepin County History Book Committee, *Pepin County History* (Dallas: Taylor, 1985), 29; Franklyn Curtiss-Wedge, comp., *History of Buffalo and Pepin Counties, Wisconsin* (Winona, Minn.: H. C. Cooper Jr., 1919), 959; *Durand Times,* December 12, 1865.

17. Curtiss-Wedge, comp., *History of Buffalo and Pepin Counties,* 960, 1005–7; Pepin County History Book Committee, *Pepin County History,* 28–29; *Pepin County Press,* June 2, September 8, 1860, August 3, 1861; *Pepin Independent,* June 11, 1858.

18. *Durand Times,* September 26, 1871. Long litigation preceded a court decision in 1867, which confirmed the removal. Curtiss-Wedge, comp., *History of Buffalo and Pepin Counties,* 962.

19. Curtiss-Wedge, comp., *History of Buffalo and Pepin Counties,* 1007–8.

20. The legal description of the 160 acres was SW 1/4 of Section 27, Township 24 North, Range 15 West. The transaction was recorded in *Deed Book F,* 488, and *Mortgage Record Book A,* 545–46, Pepin County Courthouse, Durand, Wis. See also Zochert, *Laura,* 15–17.

21. LIW, *Little House in the Big Woods,* 6–7, 12, 31, 45, 102, 119, 186, 194, 212, 216. See also LIW, "Pioneer Girl."

22. Richard N. Current, *Civil War Era,* 452–54; Zochert, *Laura,* 20; Anderson, *Laura Ingalls Wilder,* 31–32. The transactions were recorded in *Deed Book F,* 410, 490, *Deed Book G,* 162, 164, and *Mortgage Record Book C,* 67, Pepin County Courthouse, Durand, Wis.

23. Zochert, *Laura,* 23; *Warranty Deed Book D,* 121–22, Montgomery County Courthouse, Independence, Kans.

24. *Warranty Deed Book 11,* 381, Montgomery County Courthouse, Independence, Kans. But also see Zochert, *Laura,* 38.

25. James R. Shortridge, *Peopling the Plains: Who Settled Where in Frontier Kansas* (Lawrence: University Press of Kansas, 1995), 46–49; William F. Zornow, *Kansas: A History of the Jayhawk State* (Norman: University of Oklahoma Press, 1957), 161–63.

26. L. Wallace Duncan, *History of Montgomery County, Kansas* (Iola, Kans.: Press of Iola Register, 1903), 43, 79.

27. In *Little House on the Prairie,* Laura wrote that they were forty miles from town, which may explain why she and Rose were looking around in Oklahoma and never found the place when they drove out in the 1930s to do research for the book (76). The actual location was the SW 1/4 of Section 36-33-14; Zochert, *Laura,* 39, 43; *1870 Manuscript Census.*

28. *1870 Manuscript Census.*

29. Ibid.; Shortridge, *Peopling the Plains,* 49.

30. Willard H. Rollings, *The Osage: An Ethnocultural Study of Hegemony on the Prairie-Plains* (Columbia: University of Missouri Press, 1992); John J. Mathews, *The Osages: Children of the Middle Waters* (Norman: University of Oklahoma Press, 1961), 650–92.

31. H. Craig Miner and William E. Unrau, *The End of Indian Kansas: A Study of Cultural Revolution, 1854–1871* (Lawrence: Regents Press of Kansas, 1978), 107–8.

32. Ibid., 117.

33. Ibid., 121–23; Paul W. Gates, *Fifty Million Acres: Conflicts over Kansas Land Policy, 1854–1890* (Ithaca: Cornell University Press, 1954), 194–206.

34. Gates, *Fifty Million Acres,* 221–22.

35. Ibid., 222; Miner and Unrau, *End of Indian Kansas,* 125, 138.

36. LIW, *Little House on the Prairie,* 52–65, 149–71, 185–98. In telling about their Kansas adventures, Laura said that Carrie had come with them from Wisconsin, although she was not actually born until the family arrived in Kansas.

37. Anderson, *Laura Ingalls Wilder,* 41–43; Zochert, *Laura,* 46–51. Later, Laura would suggest that her father had been part of a posse that dispatched the bloody Bender family, who robbed and killed passing travelers who visited their store in nearby Labette County on the road between Fort Scott and Independence. She said that she had avoiding writing about it in her novels because the story was inappropriate for young readers. She was no doubt mistaken in this, however, since the Benders did not arrive until 1871, after the Ingallses had left Kansas and returned to Wisconsin (LIW and RWL, *A Little House Sampler,* ed. William T. Anderson [Lincoln: University of Nebraska Press, 1988], 220–22; Edith Connelley Ross, "The Bloody Benders," *Kansas Historical Collections* 17 [1926–1928], 464–79).

38. In *Little House in the Big Woods* Wilder spelled the family's name "Huleatt" (180); the *1870 Manuscript Census* gave it as "Hewlet."

39. LIW, *Little House in the Big Woods,* 178; *1870 Manuscript Census.*

40. LIW, *Little House in the Big Woods,* 12–13, 199–202; *Durand Times,* October 10, 1871.

41. LIW, "Pioneer Girl."

42. Ibid.; *Notes from Laura Ingalls Wilder Memorial Society (Pepin)* 6 (May 1981): 2; LIW, *Little House in the Big Woods,* 64, 131–55; Anderson, *Laura Ingalls Wilder,* 42–43.

43. Zochert, *Laura,* 52–53; *Notes from Laura Ingalls Wilder Memorial Society (Pepin)* 16 (May 1991): 3.

44. Zochert, *Laura,* 52–55.

45. LIW, *Little House in the Big Woods,* 84–85; *Laura Ingalls Wilder Lore* 2 (fall 1976): 7. The book was 761 pages long and published in 1871.

46. *Notes from Laura Ingalls Wilder Memorial Society (Pepin)* 7 (May 1982): 2, 4; *A Pathway through Pepin's History* (Pepin, Wis.: Pepin Commercial Club, n.d.), 7. A high degree of social democracy and community involvement is suggested by the presence of those traits in nearby Trempeleau County, as described in Merle Curti, *The Making of an American Community: A Case Study of Democracy in a Frontier County* (Stanford: Stanford University Press, 1959), 112–15, 139.

47. LIW, *Little House in the Big Woods,* 33–36, 39.

48. Ibid., 28–33, 38. On the limited alternatives available to frontier women, see Julie Roy Jeffrey, *Frontier Women: The Trans-Mississippi West, 1840–1880* (New

York: Hill and Wang, 1979), xvi, 10, 62, 190; Glenda Riley, *The Female Frontier: A Comparative View of Women on the Prairie and the Plains* (Lawrence: University Press of Kansas, 1988), 3–4, 76; and Deborah Fink, *Agrarian Women: Wives and Mothers in Rural Nebraska, 1880–1940* (Chapel Hill: University of North Carolina Press, 1992), 65–67. Elizabeth Jameson, however, notes the creativity and assertiveness demonstrated by many western women in playing out their prescribed roles in "Women as Workers, Women as Civilizers: True Womanhood in the American West," in *The Women's West*, ed. Susan Armitage and Elizabeth Jameson, 148–64 (Norman: University of Oklahoma Press, 1987).

49. LIW, "Pioneer Girl"; LIW, *Little House in Big Woods*, 44, 238.

50. *Deed Book J*, 150, Pepin County Courthouse, Durand, Wis.; Henry and Polly Quiner also received one thousand dollars for their half, from Oscar Anderson. *Deed Book J*, 160, Pepin County Courthouse, Durand, Wis.; Anderson, *Laura Ingalls Wilder*, 46–49; Zochert, *Laura*, 63–67.

51. Zochert, *Laura*, 72.

52. Charles W. Howe, ed., *A Half Century of Progress: Walnut Grove, Minnesota and Vicinity, from 1866 to 1916* (Walnut Grove, Minn.: Walnut Grove Tribune, 1916), 3–4, 39–40; William T. Anderson, *The Walnut Grove Story of Laura Ingalls Wilder* (Walnut Grove, Minn.: Laura Ingalls Wilder Museum, 1987), 13, 15.

53. Webb and Swedberg, *Redwood: The Story of a County*, 134–36.

54. Quoted in ibid., 133.

55. Anderson, *Walnut Grove Story*, 13. The farm was located on the northwest corner of Section 18, Township 109, Range 38. Charles Ingalls made final payment on the farm on July 7, 1876 (*Redwood County Deed Record No. 5*, 411–13, Redwood County Courthouse, Redwood Falls, Minn.).

56. Webb and Swedberg, *Redwood*, 155; Franklyn Curtiss-Wedge, *The History of Redwood County, Minnesota* (Chicago: H. C. Cooper Jr., 1916), 1:266; Annette Atkins, *Harvest of Grief: Grasshopper Plagues and Public Assistance in Minnesota, 1873–1878* (St. Paul: Minnesota Historical Society Press, 1984), 13–29.

57. Zochert, *Laura*, 73–78; Anderson, *Walnut Grove Story*, 15; *Laura Ingalls Wilder Lore* 6 (fall–winter 1980): 5.

58. Zochert, *Laura*, 81–83; LIW, *On the Banks of Plum Creek*, 172–76.

59. LIW, "Prairie Girl."

60. The transaction was recorded in *Redwood County Deed Record No. 5*, 412.

61. Edwin C. Bailey, *Past and Present of Winneshiek County, Iowa* (Chicago: S. J. Clarke, 1913), 1:102–4; W. E. Alexander, *History of Winneshiek and Allamakee Counties, Iowa* (Sioux City: Western, 1882), 120, 180–81.

62. Bailey, *Past and Present*, 1:7–9, 55–59, 65–66.

63. Zochert, *Laura*, 98; Anderson, *Laura Ingalls Wilder*, 65; Charles H. Sparks, *History of Winneshiek County with Biographical Sketches of Its Eminent Men* (Decorah, Iowa: J. A. Leonard, 1877), 71–72.

64. LIW, "Pioneer Girl"; Zochert, *Laura*, 99–100.

65. LIW, "Pioneer Girl"; Zochert, *Laura*, 101, 107.

66. Zochert, *Laura,* 106, 110; *Decorah Republican,* February 11, 1876, March 1, 15, June 7, 1878.

67. Wilder's "Pioneer Girl" manuscript is invaluable for this entire chapter, but this paragraph and the several following ones are especially dependent upon it.

68. Ibid.

69. Ibid.; Zochert, *Laura,* 112.

70. Zochert, *Laura,* 117–19.

71. LIW, "Pioneer Girl."

72. Ibid.

73. Ibid.

74. Ibid.; Howe, *Half Century of Progress,* 4; display with election results at LIW Museum, Walnut Grove, Minn.

75. LIW, "Pioneer Girl."

## 2. Schoolgirl and Courting Days, 1879–1885

1. LIW, "Pioneer Girl"; Zochert, *Laura,* 129–30.

2. LIW, "Pioneer Girl"; Zochert, *Laura,* 130–31.

3. Herbert S. Schell, *History of South Dakota,* 3rd. ed. (Lincoln: University of Nebraska Press, 1975), 158–74.

4. "Alexander Mitchell," *Dictionary of American Biography* (New York: Charles Scribner's Sons, 1934), 8:39–40; Robert J. Casey and W. A. S. Douglas, *Pioneer Railroad: The Story of the Chicago and North Western System* (New York: McGraw-Hill, 1948), 135–38.

5. Casey and Douglas, *Pioneer Railroad,* 161–65; James F. Hamburg, *The Influence of Railroads upon the Processes and Patterns of Settlement in South Dakota* (New York: Arno Press, 1981), 82–116.

6. Kenneth Hammer, "Dakota Railroads" (Ph.D. diss., South Dakota State University, 1966), 183–201. On the Dakota, or Sioux, Indians, see Royal B. Hassrick, et al., *The Sioux: Life and Customs of a Warrior Society* (Norman: University of Oklahoma Press, 1964); James H. Howard, *The Dakota or Sioux Indians: A Study in Human Ecology* (Vermillion: Dakota Museum, 1966); Robert M. Utley, *The Last Days of the Sioux Nation* (New Haven: Yale University Press, 1963).

7. George W. Kingsbury, *History of Dakota Territory* (Chicago: S. J. Clarke, 1915), 2:1053–59.

8. LIW, *By the Shores of Silver Lake,* 61–62.

9. *Brookings County Press,* March 27, July 10, 24, August 21, 1879; Brookings County History Book Committee, *Brookings County History Book* (Freeman, S.Dak.: Pine Hill Press, 1989), 45.

10. *Brookings County Press,* May 15, August 21, September 11, October 9, 23, 30, November 6, 1879 (quotation from September 25).

11. LIW, *By the Shores of Silver Lake,* 41, 57.

12. Ibid., 58–59; John U. Terrell, *Black Robe: The Life of Pierre-Jean De Smet, Missionary, Explorer and Pioneer* (Garden City, N.Y.: Doubleday, 1964).

13. LIW, *By the Shores of Silver Lake,* 158–61, 168–71, 209–13.

14. Ibid., 183–86; *De Smet News,* June 6, 1930 (fiftieth anniversary issue).

15. Charles Ingalls, Homestead Application No. 4091 (Final Certificate No. 2708), May 11, 1886, National Archives; LIW, *By the Shores of Silver Lake,* 233–37.

16. LIW, *By the Shores of Silver Lake,* 240–42; LIW, "Pioneer Girl."

17. LIW, *By the Shores of Silver Lake,* 241–42.

18. Hamburg, *Influence of Railroads,* 90; On T-towns, see John C. Hudson, *Plains Country Towns* (Minneapolis: University of Minnesota Press, 1985), chap. 7; *Town Lot Record Book No. 1,* 3–4, Kingsbury County Courthouse, De Smet, S.Dak.

19. A map published in the *De Smet Leader* on September 22, 1883, identified the locations of all the businesses in town and several of the residences.

20. LIW, *By the Shores of Silver Lake,* 247–48, 272–73.

21. Ibid., 267–75; LIW, *The Long Winter,* 28–31. Although Wilder made it sound as if her mother had been averse to fieldwork in *The Long Winter* (4), in her "Pioneer Girl" manuscript she indicated that her mother, in fact, did help in the field if it was necessary. That women's fieldwork was not uncommon is made clear by Riley, *Female Frontier,* 53, 117–18, 132–33; Fink, *Agrarian Women,* 68–69; Janet M. Labrie, "The Depiction of Women's Field Work in Rural Fiction," *Agricultural History* 67 (spring 1993): 123–27.

22. Schell, *History of South Dakota,* 180–88; LIW, "Pioneer Girl"; LIW, *The Long Winter,* 74.

23. LIW, *The Long Winter,* 77–80; John E. Miller, *Laura Ingalls Wilder's Little Town: Where History and Literature Meet* (Lawrence: University Press of Kansas, 1994), 58–59.

24. LIW, "Pioneer Girl."

25. LIW, *The Long Winter,* 288.

26. LIW, "Pioneer Girl"; LIW to RWL, March 7, 1938, Box 13, Lane Papers.

27. LIW, *The Long Winter,* 127, 133–35, 140, 143–44, 147, 157, 169; LIW, "Pioneer Girl."

28. In *The Long Winter,* Wilder and Lane told the story somewhat differently and at much greater length from the way Wilder had originally related it in "Pioneer Girl" (262–85, 295–308).

29. In *Little Town on the Prairie,* Wilder changed Clayson's name to Clancy (35–46, 56).

30. Ibid., 28, 37, 48–49, 111–12, 307.

31. LIW, *The Long Winter,* 65, 129, 175; LIW, *On the Banks of Plum Creek,* 55–60, 105, 173–76; LIW, *Little Town on the Prairie,* 8, 11–13.

32. LIW, *Little Town on the Prairie,* 93–94, 184, 228.

33. Ibid., 41–46, 56.

34. LIW, "Pioneer Girl."

35. Ibid.

36. Ibid.; LIW, *Little Town on the Prairie,* 127–36, 145–84.

37. LIW, "Pioneer Girl."

38. Ibid.; LIW, *Little Town on the Prairie,* 239–51.

39. LIW, "Pioneer Girl."

40. Miller, *Laura Ingalls Wilder's Little Town,* 117–21.

41. Ibid., 118–20.

42. *1880 Manuscript Census.*

43. Miller, *Laura Ingalls Wilder's Little Town,* 122–23, 140.

44. *De Smet Leader,* August 9, 1884; *Laura Ingalls Wilder Lore* 6 (fall–winter 1980): 6; LIW, *Little Town on the Prairie,* 277.

45. Grade ten was added in 1893, eleven in 1899, and twelve in 1908. John E. Miller, "End of an Era: De Smet High School Class of 1912," *South Dakota History* 20 (fall 1990): 201.

46. Miller, *Laura Ingalls Wilder's Little Town,* chap. 4.

47. Ibid., 60–61; LIW, "Pioneer Girl"; LIW to RWL, March 7, 1938, Box 13, Lane Papers.

48. *1880 Manuscript Census.*

49. LIW, "Pioneer Girl"; LIW, *Little Town on the Prairie,* 197–99.

50. LIW, "Pioneer Girl"; LIW, *These Happy Golden Years,* 100, 114–22, 130, 133–34.

51. Gilbert C. Fite, *The Farmers' Frontier, 1865–1900* (New York: Holt, Rinehart and Winston, 1966), 44, 104–5; Ray A. Billington and Martin Ridge, *Westward Expansion: A History of the American Frontier,* 5th ed. (New York: Macmillan, 1982), 634–36.

52. LIW, "Pioneer Girl"; LIW, *These Happy Golden Years,* 96–98.

53. LIW, "Pioneer Girl"; Miller, *Laura Ingalls Wilder's Little Town,* chap. 7.

54. LIW, "Pioneer Girl." Contract on display at the Laura Ingalls Wilder Museum in Mansfield, Mo.

55. LIW, "Pioneer Girl."

56. Ibid. In *These Happy Golden Years,* Wilder melded Stella into the character of Nellie Oleson (171–81).

57. LIW, "Pioneer Girl"; LIW, *These Happy Golden Years,* 185–99.

58. LIW, "Pioneer Girl"; LIW, *These Happy Golden Years,* 214–16.

59. LIW, "Pioneer Girl."

60. Ibid.; Kingsbury, *History of Dakota Territory,* 2:1363–70. Several De Smetites went to New Orleans (*De Smet Leader,* February 14, March 7, 1885).

61. Contract on display at Laura Ingalls Wilder Museum, Mansfield, Mo.; LIW, "Pioneer Girl."

62. Ibid.; AJW, Homestead Application No. 3610 (Final Certificate No. 1490), September 16, 1884, National Archives.

63. LIW, "Pioneer Girl"; Anderson, *Laura Ingalls Wilder,* 127–28.

64. LIW, "Pioneer Girl."

65. Ibid.

## 3. The Joys and Sorrows of Early Married Life, 1885–1894

1. LIW, *The First Four Years,* 3–6.

2. William T. Anderson, *The Story of the Wilders* (by the author, 1973), 2–5; Dorothy Smith, *The Wilder Family Story* (Malone, N.Y.: Industrial Press, 1972), 7–8.

3. Anderson, *Story of the Wilders,* 5–6; Smith, *Wilder Family Story,* 15–18, 21.

4. William T. Anderson, ed., *A Wilder in the West: The Story of Eliza Jane Wilder* (De Smet, S.Dak.: Laura Ingalls Wilder Memorial Society, 1985).

5. Ibid., 5; AJW, Homestead Application No. 3610 (Final Certificate No. 1490), September 16, 1884, AJW, Cash Entry No. 10979, August 6, 1891, National Archives.

6. "I wrote Free Land," Rose told the *Saturday Evening Post,* "because I could no longer bear hearing people say, 'But everything is so changed now; there's no more free land.' Everything certainly is changed now, but as to really 'free' land, there never was any" (*Saturday Evening Post* 210 [March 5, 1938]: 34).

7. Royal's and Eliza's claims are also on file at the National Archives. They are also recorded in *Tract Book 22* for South Dakota, Township 111 North, Range 56 West.

8. See *Tract Book 22* referred to in previous note.

9. For Almanzo's homestead's file, see footnote 5, above.

10. LIW, *The First Four Years,* 23, 49, 50, 52.

11. Ibid., 11–14, 22, 24, 29, 45; LIW and RWL, *Little House Sampler,* ed. Anderson, 9.

12. Ibid., 131–32; LIW, *The First Four Years,* 22.

13. *De Smet Leader,* July 7, 28, August 11, September 15, October 27, November 10, December 8, 15, 1883, August 30, 1884.

14. Ibid., August 11, 1883, June 5, 12, 26, 1886, May 7, 21, 1887.

15. Ibid., November 13, 1886.

16. Ibid., November 7, 1885, August 7, 28, November 6, December 11, 1886.

17. Ibid., February 17, April 7, 1883, February 6, August 15, September 18, 1886, February 26, 1887.

18. Ibid., July 11, December 26, 1885, January 9, April 17, September 11, December 25, 1886, January 15, March 26, April 16, August 6, 1887.

19. LIW, *The First Four Years,* 48.

20. Ibid., 43–44, 52, 54; *De Smet Leader,* July 3, August 7, 1886.

21. LIW, *The First Four Years,* 62–63.

22. Ibid., 70–72.

23. Grace Ingalls Diary, January 12, March 20, 1887, March 5, 1888, Box 17, Lane Papers.

24. LIW, *The First Four Years,* 102–3, 116.

25. Ibid., 72–73; *De Smet Leader,* July 30, August 6, September 3, 1887.

26. LIW, *The First Four Years,* 82–83; *De Smet Leader,* July 30, 1887.

27. *De Smet Leader,* September 26, October 3, 1885, May 14, 1887; LIW, *The First Four Years,* 87–88.

28. Anderson, *Laura Ingalls Wilder,* 134; LIW, *The First Four Years,* 88; Grace Ingalls Diary, March 5, April 18, 1888, Box 17, Lane Papers.

29. LIW, *The First Four Years,* 89.

30. Ibid., 89–90. Almanzo's sworn affidavit for purchasing the land later as a preemption claim said that they were back at the tree claim by April 1888 (AJW, Cash Entry No. 10979, August 6, 1891, National Archives).

31. LIW, *The First Four Years,* 87, 93–95 (quotation on 95).

32. Ibid., 121–22; John E. Miller, "More than Statehood on Their Minds: South Dakota Joins the Union, 1889," *Great Plains Quarterly* 10 (fall 1990), 214–15.

33. *De Smet Leader,* January 24, 1885, March 13, September 18, 1886, July 23, 1887, June 7–July 12, 1890; *Dakota Huronite,* December 25, 1884; Schell, *History of South Dakota,* 223–27.

34. Grace Ingalls Diary, August 27, 1889, Box 17, Lane Papers; LIW, *The First Four Years,* 125–27.

35. Quoted in William T. Anderson, *Laura's Rose: The Story of Rose Wilder Lane* (De Smet, S.Dak.: Laura Ingalls Wilder Memorial Society, 1976), 4.

36. LIW, *The First Four Years,* 128–31.

37. Ibid., 131–32; Grace Ingalls Diary, November 17, 1889, Box 17, Lane Papers.

38. Grace Ingalls Diary, November 17, 1889, May 18, 1890, Box 17, Lane Papers; Anderson, *Story of the Wilders,* 9–10; Mary Jo Dathe, *Spring Valley: The Laura Ingalls Wilder "Connection," 1890* (by the author, 1990), 14; Anderson, *Laura Ingalls Wilder,* 138; AJW, Cash Entry No. 10979, August 6, 1891, National Archives.

39. AJW, Cash Entry No. 10979, August 6, 1891, National Archives.

40. *De Smet Leader,* February 1, March 22, April 5, July 12, 1890; Grace Ingalls Diary, May 18, 1890, Box 17, Lane Papers.

41. Dathe, *Spring Valley,* 14–16, 20–21.

42. Ibid., 19–20.

43. Ibid., 22–23, 25; Alene M. Warnock, *Laura Ingalls Wilder: The Westville, Florida, Years* (by the author, 1979), 7; Anderson, *Laura Ingalls Wilder,* 139.

44. Warnock, *Westville, Florida, Years,* 8; quotation in LIW and RWL, *Little House Sampler,* ed. Anderson, 40.

45. RWL, "Innocence," *Harper's* (April 1922), reprinted in LIW and RWL, *Little House Sampler,* ed. Anderson, 44.

46. Ibid., 46, 48–49; RWL, "Grandpa's Fiddle," in LIW and RWL, *Little House Sampler,* ed. Anderson, 65.

47. Zochert, *Laura,* 194.

48. Smith, *Wilder Family Story,* 25–26; Anderson, *Story of the Wilders,* 6–7, 10–13; Anderson, *Wilder in the West,* 31.

49. LIW and RWL, *Little House Sampler,* ed. Anderson, 56–58; William T. Anderson, *The Story of the Ingalls* (by the author, 1971), 15.

50. LIW and RWL, *Little House Sampler,* ed. Anderson, 60–64.

51. Ibid., 55–56.

52. Ibid., 65–66.

## 4. In the Land of the Big Red Apple, 1894–1911

1. *Missouri Ruralist,* December 1, 1923.

2. Kansas City, Fort Scott, and Memphis Railway Company, "Among the Ozarks: The Land of 'Big Red Apples,'" 2nd ed. (Kansas City: Hudson-Kimberly, 1892), 17 (copy on file at State Historical Society of Missouri, Columbia).

3. Ray Ginger, *Age of Excess: The United States from 1877 to 1914* (New York: Macmillan, 1975), chap. 8; Nell Irvin Painter, *Standing at Armageddon: The United States, 1877–1919* (New York: W. W. Norton, 1987), chap. 4.

4. Anderson, *Laura Ingalls Wilder,* 144–45; RWL, introduction to *On the Way Home: The Diary of a Trip from South Dakota to Mansfield, Missouri, in 1894,* by LIW (New York: Harper and Row, 1962), 6–12.

5. LIW, *On the Way Home,* 15–21.

6. Ibid., 25, 27n.

7. Ibid., 28–59 (quotation on 59).

8. Anderson, *Laura Ingalls Wilder,* 148–49; LIW, *On the Way Home,* 62–65 (quotation on 65).

9. LIW, *On the Way Home,* 67–71.

10. Ibid., 71, 74.

11. RWL, afterword to ibid., 75–76.

12. *Missouri Ruralist,* July 22, 1911; Anderson, *Laura Ingalls Wilder,* 150–51.

13. *Warranty Deed Record Book No. 28,* 178, Wright County Courthouse, Hartville, Mo.; RWL, afterword to *On the Way Home,* by LIW, 77–83.

14. *Missouri Ruralist,* July 22, 1911, June 1, 1912, February 20, 1918.

15. Ibid., July 22, 1911, February 20, 1918; Anderson, *Laura Ingalls Wilder,* 152–53.

16. Vearl Rowe, *Sketches of Wright County, Part III: Schools and Education* (by the author, n.d.), 68–69; *Mansfield Mirror,* March 25, 1948; RWL to Jasper Crane, December 13, 1961, Box 4, Lane Papers; William Holtz, *Ghost in the Little House,* 32–33; LIW, *On the Way Home,* 95; Anderson, *Laura Ingalls Wilder,* 153–54.

17. Anderson, *Laura Ingalls Wilder,* 155–56.

18. Ibid., 157–58.

19. RWL, *Old Home Town* (1935; reprint, Lincoln: University of Nebraska Press, 1985), 8–9.

20. Charles Ingalls, in a biographical sketch about him published in Ogle's *Compendium of Biography* (1898), identified himself as a Populist. *Laura Ingalls*

*Wilder Lore* 6 (fall–winter 1980): 6. In July 1948, as the national party conventions were approaching, Rose wrote in the *Economic Council Review of Books,* "At the age of three, prone on the rag carpet in a Dakota claim-shanty, I licked a pencil-point thoroughly and with anxious care cast my first vote, for Cleveland, on a sample ballot. (My father had previously given me my first political instruction)" (4). Allowing for some faulty recollection on her part (she would have been still a month short of two years old in November 1888, and may rather have been thinking of 1892, when Cleveland ran a third time for the presidency), Rose's memory would support the notion that her father had been a Democrat at that time. On the Republican tenor of Mansfield and the surrounding region, see *Mansfield Mirror,* April 8, 1948 (fortieth anniversary issue); *History of Laclede, Camden, Dallas, Webster, Wright, Texas, Pulaski, Phelps and Dent Counties, Missouri* (Chicago: Goodspeed, 1889), 379; and election voting returns.

21. *Warranty Deed Record Book No. 39,* 489, Wright County Courthouse, Hartville, Mo.

22. Anderson, *Laura Ingalls Wilder,* 162–63.

23. *Warranty Deed Record Book No. 36,* 317–18, Wright County Courthouse, Hartville, Mo.; Anderson, *Laura Ingalls Wilder,* 165–66.

24. RWL, afterword to *On the Way Home,* by LIW, 83–84.

25. *Mansfield Mail,* January 22, May 6, 27, 1904, December 22, 1906; *Mansfield Press,* October 9, 1908, April 23, May 21, 1909; Larry Dennis and Debbie Arnall, *Mansfield, Missouri: The First Hundred Years, 1882–1982* (Mansfield, Mo.: Centennial Book Committee, 1983), 185.

26. Clyde A. Rowan, ed., *History and Families: Wright County, Missouri* (Hartville, Mo.: Wright County Historical Society, 1993), 12, 14, 160; *Mansfield Mirror,* April 8, 1948; *History of Laclede,* 413–23. Milton D. Rafferty notes the crucial importance of the coming of the railroad in transforming the economic and cultural geography of the Ozarks region (*The Ozarks: Land and Life* [Norman: University of Oklahoma Press, 1980], 98).

27. Vearl Rowe, *Sketches of Wright County, Part I: General History* (Mountain Grove, Mo.: by the author, 1984), 13.

28. Rafferty, *Ozarks,* 47–48; Russel Gerlach, *Settlement Patterns in Missouri: A Study of Population Origins with a Wall Map* (Columbia: University of Missouri Press, 1986), 21–22; Russel Gerlach, "The Ozark Scotch-Irish," in *Cultural Geography of Missouri,* ed. Michael O. Roark, 11–29 (Cape Girardeau: Southeast Missouri State University, 1983); Floyd C. Shoemaker, "Missouri's Tennessee Heritage," *Missouri Historical Review* 49 (January 1955): 127–42; Vearl Rowe, *Sketches of Wright County, Part IV: Churches* (Mountain Grove, Mo.: by the author, n.d.), 33–39; Dennis and Arnall, *Mansfield, Missouri,* 177–80.

29. Robert K. Gilmore, *Ozark Baptizings, Hangings, and Other Diversions: Theatrical Folkways of Rural Missouri, 1885–1910* (Norman: University of Oklahoma Press,

1984); Douglas Mahnkey, *Bright Glowed My Hills* (Point Lookout, Mo.: School of the Ozarks Press, 1968), 2, 35.

30. David Thelen, *Paths of Resistance: Tradition and Dignity in Industrializing Missouri* (New York: Oxford University Press, 1986). While the language of the introduction to *Old Home Town* as published blurs the identity of the town and implies that her comments were relevant to small towns everywhere, the original drafts of the manuscript at the Hoover Presidential Library make clear that Lane had Mansfield in mind in writing this piece (see drafts, Box 40, Lane Papers). For an analysis of this collection of short stories, see William Holtz, "Rose Wilder Lane's *Old Home Town*," *Studies in Short Fiction* 26 (fall 1989): 479–87.

31. RWL, *Old Home Town*, 23.

32. Ibid., 23–24.

33. RWL, postscript to *On the Way Home*, by LIW, 77.

34. RWL, "I, Rose Wilder Lane . . . ," *Cosmopolitan* 80 (June 1926): 42.

35. RWL, Journal, April 10, 1933, Box 23, Lane Papers.

36. Quoted in Holtz, *Ghost in the Little House*, 33.

37. RWL, "I, Rose Wilder Lane . . . ," 42.

38. RWL, *Economic Council Review of Books* (September 1947), 2; RWL, "Rose Wilder Lane, by Herself," *Sunset, the Pacific Monthly* 41 (November 1918): 26; RWL, "We Women Are Not Good Citizens," *Woman's Day* (March 1939), 4.

39. RWL to Norma Lee Browning Ogg, May 17, 1964, Box 10, RWL to Jasper Crane, December 13, 1961, Box 4, Lane Papers.

40. Rowe, *Sketches of Wright County, Part III*, 68; RWL to Jasper Crane, December 13, 1961, Box 4, Lane Papers.

41. Holtz, *Ghost in the Little House*, 41–48; Anderson, *Laura Ingalls Wilder*, 168–69.

42. Anderson, *Laura Ingalls Wilder*, 169, 171; *Warranty Deed Record Book No. 42*, 483, *No. 53*, 112, *No. 55*, 452, 511, and *No. 63*, 496, Wright County Courthouse, Hartville, Mo.

43. *History of Laclede*, 355; Rowe, *Sketches of Wright County, Part I*, 29.

44. State of Missouri, *Twenty-Fourth Annual Report of the Bureau of Labor Statistics and Inspection* (1902), 64.

45. *Missouri Yearbook of Agriculture* (1915), 301, 304, 307–8; *Forty-Third Annual Report of the Missouri State Board of Agriculture* (1910), 474–79.

46. *Mansfield Mail*, October 28, 1905, September 7, 1906; *Mansfield Press*, October 9, 16, 1908, April 2, 1909.

47. *De Smet News*, September 11, October 16, 1903; Anderson, *Laura Ingalls Wilder*, 166–67.

48. See fragment beginning, "In the days of old when black magic was practiced," in folder titled "Laura's 'Ideas for Work,' 1903+," Box 14, Lane Papers.

49. Holtz, *Ghost in the Little House*, 48–53. Rose may have later had a child that lived only a short time or may have suffered a miscarriage that left her unable to have any more children.

50. Peggy Dennis interview, by the author, Mansfield, Mo., June 18, 1993; Anderson, *Laura Ingalls Wilder,* 173.

51. Anderson, *Laura Ingalls Wilder,* 171–75.

## 5. Building a Writing Career, 1911–1923

1. Anderson, *Laura Ingalls Wilder,* 176.

2. *Missouri Ruralist,* February 18, 1911.

3. Ibid., July 22, 1911.

4. Ibid., June 1, 1912, February 5, April 20, June 20, 1914, November 20, December 5, 1915.

5. *Mansfield Mirror,* October 2, 1913.

6. Ibid.

7. Ibid., March 20, July 24, 31, August 7, 1913.

8. Ibid., July 10, 1913, May 6, 1915.

9. Ibid., July 24, December 4, 1913, October 8, 1914, May 27, 1915, May 4, December 21, 1916 (the quotation is from the July 1, 1915, issue).

10. *Mansfield Mirror,* January 23, December 26, 1912, March 13, 1913.

11. Ibid., February 13, March 27, November 27, December 4, 1913, June 4, 1914, February 11, May 13, 1915, March 16, May 18, November 9, 23, December 14, 1916, December 13, 1917, February 7, 1918. The contradictory relationship between the movies of the time and traditional culture is noted by Robert Sklar in *Movie-Made America: A Social History of American Movies* (New York: Random House, 1975), 139–40.

12. *Mansfield Mirror,* September 25, October 2, 1913, October 22, 1914, August 16, 1917.

13. RWL to LIW, undated [December —] (begins "I am sending you some drapery samples"), Box 13, Lane Papers.

14. RWL to LIW, undated (page 4 begins "How would it be, with your organizing ability"), Box 13, Lane Papers.

15. RWL to LIW, undated (begins "The Star Farmer looks quite nifty"), undated (begins "I open this letter to suggest"), Box 13, Lane Papers.

16. LIW, *West from Home: Letters of Laura Ingalls Wilder to Almanzo Wilder, San Francisco 1915,* ed. Roger Lea MacBride, 3–5 (New York: HarperTrophy, 1976).

17. Ibid., 8–9, 12–14, 17, 20.

18. Ibid., 30, 35, 38–39, 41.

19. *Missouri Ruralist,* March 5, 1916.

20. LIW, *West from Home,* 43–46, 71–73, 78–79, 98. See also original letter, LIW to AJW, September 23, 1915, Box 13, Lane Papers, whose statement "Rose hoots at that idea" was edited out of the published letters.

21. LIW, *West from Home,* 67, 92–93.

22. Ibid., 95.

23. Ibid., 110–11, 113; *Missouri Ruralist,* December 5, 1915.

24. LIW, *West from Home,* 109.

25. RWL to LIW, undated (begins "I open this letter to suggest"), Box 13, Lane Papers.

26. John E. Miller, "Laura Ingalls Wilder's Apprenticeship as a Farm Author," *Papers of the Twenty-Sixth Annual Dakota History Conference,* comp. Arthur R. Huseboe and Harry F. Thompson, 481–88 (Sioux Falls, S.Dak.: Augustana College, 1994).

27. *Missouri Ruralist,* July 22, 1911, July 20, 1916, February 20, 1919, March 20, 1920.

28. Ibid., February 5, 1920.

29. Ibid., August 20, 1916, April 20, 1918, December 5, 1919; LIW, *The Long Winter,* 65.

30. *Missouri Ruralist,* February 18, 1911, July 20, 1917, November 20, 1919, June 15, 1922, January 1, 1924.

31. Ibid., October 5, 20, 1916, January 5, February 20, 1917, September 5, October 20, November 5, 1918.

32. Ibid., May 20, 1918, March 5, 1919, October 20, 1920, June 15, 1921.

33. Ibid., February 1, 1924, April 5, June 20, 1916.

34. Ibid., May 5, 1917.

35. Lawrence O. Christensen, "Popular Reaction to World War I in Missouri," *Missouri Historical Review* 86 (July 1992): 386–95; John C. Crighton, *Missouri and the World War, 1914–1917: A Study in Public Opinion* (Columbia: University of Missouri Studies, 1947); *Mansfield Mirror,* June 10, 17, August 9, 1917; *Missouri Ruralist,* August 5, 1917.

36. *Mansfield Mirror,* May 17, July 5, August 2, 9, 1917, April 18, 1918.

37. Ibid., January 3, March 21, April 25, August 15, 22, September 19, October 24, 1918.

38. *Mansfield Mirror,* April 4, 25, May 2, 9, 1918; *Missouri Ruralist,* January 5, 1918.

39. *Missouri Ruralist,* February 20, July 5, 1918.

40. *Mansfield Mirror,* November 7, 14, 1918, February 6, May 8, 1919.

41. *Missouri Ruralist,* August 5, 1919.

42. Ibid., October 5, 1916.

43. Ibid., November 5, 1917.

44. Ibid., October 5, 1917, February 20, 1918, April 1, 1924.

45. Ibid., November 1, 1922.

46. LIW, "Whom Will You Marry?" *McCall's* 49 (June 1919): 8, 62.

47. RWL to LIW, April 11, 1919, Box 13, Lane Papers.

48. Ibid.

49. *San Francisco Bulletin,* February 10, March 19, April 24, 1915.

50. Holtz, *Ghost in the Little House,* 93–136, 184.

51. Ibid., 136–41.

## 6. Turning to Autobiography, 1923–1932

1. RWL to "Dear Comrades" [Berta and Elmer Hader], [December 1924], Box 5, Lane Papers; Holtz, *Ghost in the Little House,* 141.

2. RWL to Guy Moyston, December 24, 1923, Box 9, Lane Papers.

3. RWL to Guy Moyston, undated, January 19, 1924, May 4, 1925, Box 9, Lane Papers.

4. RWL to Guy Moyston, February 9, 1924, July 27, 1925, Box 9, Lane Papers.

5. RWL to Guy Moyston, February 9, 1924, August 30, [1925], Box 9, Lane Papers.

6. RWL to Guy Moyston, [late 1924], May 7, December 1, 1925, Box 9, Lane Papers; Holtz, *Ghost in the Little House,* 142.

7. *Mansfield Mirror,* April 3, 1924; Holtz, *Ghost in the Little House,* 144–45, 151–52.

8. RWL to Guy Moyston, July 9, 1924, Box 9, Lane Papers; *Mansfield Mirror,* July 10, 1924, July 7, 1927, July 12, 1928, June 13, 1929, June 23, 1932; RWL, "Prairie Hollow Singing," *Country Gentleman* 91 (February 1926): 15–16, 135–36, 139. The county singing conventions continued into the 1960s.

9. *Mansfield Mirror,* January 10, June 12, 1924; RWL, Diary, January 3, 1924, Box 21, Lane Papers.

10. RWL to Guy Moyston, July 9, 1924, Box 9, Lane Papers.

11. *Mansfield Mirror,* February 5, April 23, 1925, January 21, June 17, December 23, 1926, January 5, 1928, January 24, 1929.

12. Ibid., March 5, July 16, 1925, April 29, July 29, 1926, April 7, May 5, 1927, February 2, 1928.

13. Rose mentioned her fox-hunting expeditions and her efforts to get a fox-hunting article published in her diary on March 7, June 1, 7, and July 21, 1930, Box 21, Lane Papers. Amon Short recalled how when he was a young boy his father took Rose fox hunting (interview by the author, Mansfield, Mo., August 19, 1995).

14. LIW, "My Ozark Kitchen," *Country Gentleman* 90 (January 17, 1925): 19, 22; LIW, "The Farm Dining Room," *Country Gentleman* 90 (June 13, 1925): 21–22; LIW and RWL, *Little House Sampler,* ed. Anderson, 137; Holtz, *Ghost in the Little House,* 148; RWL to LIW, [November 1924], Box 13, Lane Papers.

15. Ibid.

16. Ibid., RWL to LIW, November 12, 1924, Box 13, Lane Papers.

17. RWL to Guy Moyston, February 17, March 31, 1925, Box 9, Lane Papers.

18. *Mansfield Mirror,* February 26, 1925.

19. RWL to Guy Moyston, March 9, 22, 1925, Box 9, Lane Papers.

20. *Mansfield Mirror,* March 19, April 2, 1925; RWL to Guy Moyston, April 1, 1925, Box 9, Lane Papers.

21. *De Smet News,* April 25, May 2, 1924; LIW to Martha Carpenter, June 22, 1925, Box 17, Lane Papers.

22. LIW to Martha Carpenter, June 22, September 2, October 9, 1925, Box 17, Lane Papers.

23. RWL to Guy Moyston, July 27, 1925, Box 9, Lane Papers.

24. Ibid., May 7, 1925.

25. Ibid., June 9, August 10, 1925.

26. Ibid., July 27, 1925.

27. Ibid. On the relationship between mother and daughter, see Holtz, *Ghost in the Little House*, 31–34, 142–44, 155, 194–96, 220–25, 230–32, 237–39, 243–45, 264–65, 273–76, 293–94, 334–35, 373–76; and Anita Clair Fellman, "Laura Ingalls Wilder and Rose Wilder Lane: The Politics of a Mother-Daughter Relationship," *Signs: Journal of Women in Culture and Society* 15 (spring 1990), 535–61.

28. RWL to Guy Moyston, September 12, 1925, Box 9, Lane Papers.

29. Ibid., January 14, [1925].

30. Ibid., February 17, [ca. April 20], 1925; Holtz, *Ghost in the Little House*, 153–54.

31. RWL to Guy Moyston, March 19, 1925, Box 9, Lane Papers.

32. *Mansfield Mirror*, June 25, July 23, 1925, April 4, 25, 1929, November 20, 1930, April 30, June 25, 1931.

33. *Ninth Biennial Report of the State Highway Commission of Missouri* (1934), 37, 45; *Mansfield Mirror*, January 29, 1931, June 30, July 28, 1927, July 19, 1928; RWL, "Thirty-Mile Neighbors," *Country Gentleman* 90 (May 16, 1925), 33.

34. LIW to AJW, September 18, 1925, Box 13, Lane Papers.

35. Holtz, *Ghost in the Little House*, 157–58; RWL to Guy Moyston, October 31, 1925, Box 9, Lane Papers.

36. Holtz, *Ghost in the Little House*, 162.

37. RWL to Guy Moyston, December 17, 1925, LIW to Guy Moyston, June 28, 1926, Box 9, Lane Papers; *Mansfield Mirror*, June 17, July 22, September 30, November 4, 1926, March 10, November 10, 24, 1927.

38. LIW to Guy Moyston, June 28, 1926, Box 9, Lane Papers; *Mansfield Mirror*, January 3, February 21, 1924, August 6, October 15, 22, November 19, 1925, May 13, 1926, January 13, May 5, June 9, 1927, January 23, 1930.

39. RWL to LIW and AJW, September 25, October 7, 1926, Box 13, Lane Papers.

40. Ibid., RWL to Guy Moyston, January 20, 1925; *Mansfield Mirror*, May 20, July 8, August 19, 1926, February 17, April 21, July 21, October 20, 1927, March 15, 1928.

41. *Mansfield Mirror*, November 26, 1925, July 28, September 1, 1927, March 8, April 5, June 21, 1928.

42. Ibid., December 30, 1926, February 17, April 28, July 21, 28, 1927, March 29, June 14, July 5, 1928, October 10, 1929.

43. Ibid., May 1, 1924, April 1, September 9, 23, November 18, 1926, March 3, April 7, June 30, August 11, December 22, 1927, January 5, 1928, April 4, 1929, October 2, 1930, February 19, 1931.

44. Ibid., January 13, February 24, 1927.

45. RWL to Clarence Day, September 3, 1927, Box 1, Lane Papers.

46. Holtz, *Ghost in the Little House,* 184–85; RWL to Guy Moyston, March 6, 1928, Box 9, Lane Papers.

47. RWL to Fremont Older, April 20, 1928, Box 10, Lane Papers.

48. RWL to Guy Moyston, August 1, 1926, Box 9, RWL to Clarence Day, June 26, 1928, Box 10, Lane Papers.

49. RWL to Carl Brandt, April 24, 1928, Box 1, RWL to Clarence Day, June 26, 1928, Box 5, Lane Papers.

50. RWL, Diary, July 31 and memorandum at end of year, 1928, Box 21, RWL to Fremont Older, October 31, 1928, Box 10, Lane Papers; Holtz, *Ghost in the Little House,* 194–96.

51. RWL, Diary, December 22, 1928, Box 21, RWL to Fremont Older, October 31, 1928, January 23, 1929, Box 10, Lane Papers.

52. RWL to Fremont Older, June 27, 1928, Box 10, Lane Papers.

53. RWL to Clarence Day, April 8, 1928, Box 5, Lane Papers; *Mansfield Mirror,* August 11, 1927, April 26, 1928, March 7, July 25, October 10, 31, 1929, January 16, February 27, March 6, 20, May 15, July 17, August 21, September 25, October 30, November 13, 1930, May 7, October 8, 1931; RWL, Diary, April 19, 1928, September 27, October 9, 17, 1929, March 19, 1930, Box 21, Lane Papers.

54. RWL, Diary, January–February 1929, Box 21, RWL to Fremont Older, April 12, 1929, Box 10, Lane Papers.

55. Holtz, *Ghost in the Little House,* 197; RWL, Journal, May 28, 1929, Box 20, RWL to Fremont Older, July 28, 1929, Box 10, Lane Papers.

56. RWL to Clarence Day, April 8, 1928, Box 5, Lane Papers.

57. RWL to Fremont Older, October 7, November 3, 1929, Box 10, Lane Papers.

58. RWL, Diary, May 23–29, June 15–21, 1930, Box 21, RWL to Rexh Meta, June 7, 28, 1930, Box 8, Lane Papers.

59. RWL, Diary, January 30, 1930, May 7–17, July 31–August 5, August 15–22, August 28–September 2, 1930, Box 21, Lane Papers; Holtz, *Ghost in the Little House,* 220.

60. RWL, Diary, July 31, 1930, Box 21, Lane Papers.

61. Anderson, "Literary Apprenticeship," 319, 324; RWL to LIW, [November 12, 1930], Box 13, Lane Papers.

62. Holtz, *Ghost in the Little House,* 225; list of authors is attached to George T. Bye to RWL, February 30, 1935, Box 1, Lane Papers; quotation is from Bye to RWL, April 6, 1931, Box 13, Lane Papers.

63. Marion Fiery to LIW, February 12, 1931, Box 13, Lane Papers.

64. Ibid., RWL to LIW, February 16, 1931.

65. Ibid.

66. Anderson, "Literary Apprenticeship," 324; Marion Fiery to LIW, March 3, 1931, Box 13, RWL, Diary, May 8, 18, 20, 1931, Box 22, Lane Papers.

67. RWL, Diary, May 21–27, 1931, Box 22, Lane Papers.

68. RWL to Marion Fiery, May 27, 1931, Fiery to RWL, September 17, 1931, Box 13, RWL, Diary, June 6, 1931, Box 22, Lane Papers; *De Smet News,* June 19, 1931; Anderson, "Literary Apprenticeship," 326.

69. RWL to George T. Bye, September 25, October 5, 1931, Box 13, Lane Papers. Further indication of Rose's low estimate of the importance of her mother's book came in an undated letter to Marion Fiery written sometime in early November 1931: "I don't feel like asking [George Bye] to take on, as a favor to me, a lot of petty detail work on my mother's stuff; his time's too valuable" (ibid.).

70. Marion Fiery to RWL, November 3, December 4, 1931, Box 13, RWL, Diary, November 26, 1931, Box 22, Lane Papers; Virginia Kirkus, "The Discovery of Laura Ingalls Wilder," *Horn Book Magazine* 29 (December 1953): 428–29; Anderson, "Literary Apprenticeship," 328.

71. Virginia Kirkus to LIW, December 8, 1931, Box 13, Lane Papers; Anderson, "Literary Apprenticeship," 328–29.

72. Virginia Kirkus to LIW, December 18, 1931, Box 13, RWL, Diary, January 20, March 28, 1932, Box 22, Lane Papers.

## 7. Becoming a Celebrated Author, 1932–1937

1. *Book Review Digest* (1932), 1021.

2. RWL, Diary, June 6, August 24, September 11, 12, 19, 1931, November 9, 26, 1931, January 1, 1932, Box 22, Lane Papers.

3. Ibid., September 9, October 15, 26, November 4, 19, December 3, 5, 1931, end of year memorandum, February 6, 7, 12, 29, March 3, 1932.

4. Ibid., end of October memorandum, November 3, 1931.

5. Ibid., March 6–11, May 9–22, 28, June 2–15, 21, August 12–16, 1932.

6. *De Smet News,* June 20, 1930.

7. RWL, Diary, June 6, 1931, Box 22, Lane Papers; Anderson, *Laura Ingalls Wilder,* 196–97.

8. Anderson, *Laura Ingalls Wilder,* 197–98.

9. RWL, Diary, June 15, 29, 1931, Box 22, Lane Papers.

10. Ibid., June 26–July 1, 13, 15, August 1, 6–7, 1932, February 2, 1933.

11. RWL, Journal, May 29, 31, June 8, 1932, Box 22, RWL to Guy Moyston, May 30, 1925, Box 9, Lane Papers.

12. Ibid., January 25, 1933; LIW and RWL, *Little House Sampler,* ed. Anderson, 200–215.

13. RWL to Jasper Crane, April 18, 1955, Box 3, Lane Papers; RWL to Eleanor Garst, reprinted in *Better Homes and Gardens* 12 (December 1933): 19.

14. RWL, Diary, August 12–15, September 22, 1932, Box 22, Lane Papers.

15. Richard S. Kirkendall, *A History of Missouri: Volume V, 1919 to 1953* (Columbia: University of Missouri Press, 1986), 131, 133, 165; *Mansfield Mirror,* August 15, 1935.

16. *Mansfield Mirror,* September 6, 27, 1934, August 20, 1936; RWL, Diary, July 19, 22, 1934, Box 22, RWL to Adelaide Neall, July 20, 1934, Box 10, Lane Papers; Kirkendall, *History of Missouri,* 131.

17. *Mansfield Mirror,* November 17, 1932, November 15, 1934, November 5, 12, 1936; *Official Manual of the State of Missouri* (1933–1934), 214, 374; *Official Manual of the State of Missouri* (1937–1938), 227, 332; Robert S. Wiley, *Dewey Short: Orator of the Ozarks* (Cassville, Mo.: Litho Printers, 1985).

18. *Mansfield Mirror,* November 30, 1933, January 9, March 12, May 14, September 17, December 3, 1936.

19. Ibid., September 28, October 5, 26, November 2, 30, 1933, April 5, August 16, September 20, 1934; Kirkendall, *History of Missouri,* 164.

20. RWL to Mark Sullivan, August 16, 1938, Box 11, Lane Papers.

21. RWL, Journal, March 24, 1933, Box 23, Lane Papers.

22. Ibid., January 24, 1933.

23. Ibid., January 24, 27, 1933; RWL, Diary, January 13–March 2, 1933, Box 22, Lane Papers.

24. RWL, Journal, January 25, 27, 1933, Box 23, Lane Papers.

25. Ibid., February 11, 18, March 25, April 29, 1933, RWL, Diary, end of March 1933 memorandum, Box 22, Lane Papers.

26. RWL, Journal, April 10, 1933, Box 23, Lane Papers.

27. Ibid., May 20, 1933.

28. George Bye to RWL, March 24, 1933, RWL to Bye, April 2, 1933, Box 13, RWL, Diary, June 1, 1933, Box 22, Lane Papers.

29. *Book Review Digest* (1933), 1016–17.

30. Anderson, *Laura Ingalls Wilder,* 201; Holtz, *Ghost in the Little House,* 253; Grant Foreman to RWL, March 26, 27, 1933, R. B. Selvidge to LIW, July 5, 1933, Helen McFarland to LIW, June 19, 1933, Box 14, RWL, Journal, March 17, April 8, June 26, 1933, Box 23, George Bye to RWL, August 9, 1932, Box 1, RWL to Adelaide Neall, June 23, 1934, Box 10, RWL, Diary, June 25, 1933, March 19, June 27, 1934, Box 22, Lane Papers; John E. Miller, "Rose Wilder Lane and Thomas Hart Benton: A Turn toward History during the 1930s," *American Studies* 37 (fall 1996): 83–101.

31. *Mansfield Mirror,* September 6, October 4, 1934, September 5, 1935.

32. RWL, Diary, April 23, September 11, 1932, January 16, February 5, 1933, September 10, 1934, February, 25, 1935, Box 22, Lane Papers.

33. Ibid., December 24, 1932, March 12, June 9, December 5, 1933, January 7, February 15, June 10, October 7, December 24, 1934, January 4, February 10, May 18, 1935.

34. RWL, Journal, December 16, 1933, Box 23, Lane Papers; Holtz, *Ghost in the Little House,* 108–9, 184, 198, 248–49, 253–54.

35. RWL, Journal, December 29, 1933, Box 23, Lane Papers.

36. RWL, Diary, February 1, 1934, Box 22, Lane Papers.

37. *Mansfield Mirror,* July 14, 1927, August 2, 1928.

38. RWL, Diary, May 19–21, 27–28, 30–31, June 10, 25, 1934, Box 22, Lane Papers.

39. Ibid., July 13, 17, 20, August 27, 1934, February 26, 1935 (in memoranda section at end of year).

40. George Bye to RWL, April 26, 1935, Box 1, Lane Papers.

41. Ibid., February 19, 1936.

42. Ida Louise Raymond to LIW, July 13, August 27, 1934, Box 13, Lane Papers; *Mansfield Mirror,* October 3, 1935; *Book Review Digest* (1935), 1068–69.

43. RWL, Diary, March 29, May 10, 1936, Box 23, Lane Papers; see income tax returns, "Miss Rose Wilder Lane—Statement for Calendar Year 1936," in George Bye file, Box 1, Lane Papers; Holtz, *Ghost in the Little House,* 264, 268–69.

44. LIW to RWL, August 6, 1936, attached to manuscript of LIW, *On the Banks of Plum Creek,* folder 19, Missouri State Historical Society, Columbia.

45. This and the next several notes come from mainly undated notes and correspondence between Rose and Laura as they collaborated on the writing of *On the Banks of Plum Creek* in June, July, and August 1936. The letters are attached to the manuscript in folder 19, Missouri State Historical Society, Columbia.

46. Ibid.

47. Ibid.

48. Ibid.

49. Ibid.; LIW, *On the Banks of Plum Creek,* 299–312.

50. LIW to RWL, July 3, 1936, attached to manuscript of LIW, *On the Banks of Plum Creek,* folder 19, Missouri Historical Society, Columbia.

51. LIW to RWL, June 25, 1936, ibid.; Holtz, *Ghost in the Little House,* 264.

52. RWL, Diary, August 10, 1940, Box 23, Lane Papers.

53. RWL to LIW, September 21, 1936, Box 13, Lane Papers.

54. *Book Review Digest* (1937), 1049.

## 8. Completing the Series, 1937–1943

1. LIW and RWL, *Little House Sampler,* ed. Anderson, 179.

2. Ibid., 215; RWL to LIW, October 11, 1937, Box 13, Lane Papers.

3. Neta Seal interview, by the author, Mansfield, Mo., June 18, 1993; Helen Burkhiser, *Neta, Laura's Friend* (by the author, 1989), 8–11.

4. AJW to RWL, December 19, 1937, Box 13, Lane Papers.

5. Ibid., RWL to LIW, October 11, 1937.

6. Ibid., LIW to RWL, January 26, [1938].

7. LIW and RWL, *Little House Sampler,* ed. Anderson, 216–17.

8. LIW to RWL, March 22, 1937, Box 13, Lane Papers.

9. LIW and RWL, *Little House Sampler,* ed. Anderson, 219, 222–23.

10. Ibid., 180.

11. RWL to LIW, [late October 1937], Box 13, Lane Papers.

12. Ibid., LIW to RWL, February 5, 1937.

13. Ibid., AJW to RWL, March 12, 1937; LIW and RWL, *Little House Sampler,* ed. Anderson, 200–215.

14. Holtz, *Ghost in the Little House,* 272; Steven Kesselman, "The Frontier Thesis and the Great Depression," *Journal of the History of Ideas* 29 (April–June 1968): 253–68. On the political assumptions that lay behind *Free Land,* see Holtz, "Rose Wilder Lane's *Free Land:* The Political Background," *South Dakota Review* 30 (spring 1992): 46–60.

15. RWL, *Free Land:* Outline of Manuscript and Fragments, Box 33, Lane Papers.

16. *New York Times Book Review,* June 5, 1938, 24. Compare the story in RWL, *Free Land* (1938; reprint, Lincoln: University of Nebraska Press, 1966), 18–33, with the letter from AJW to RWL, March 20, 1937, Box 13, Lane Papers; the quotation is from *Free Land,* 7.

17. *Saturday Review of Literature* 18 (May 7, 1938): 5; letters in file titled "Saturday Evening Post Pioneer Stories," Box 11, Lane Papers.

18. RWL to LIW, December 20, 1937, Box 13, RWL to William Allen White, January 28, February 1, 13, 1938, White to RWL, February 8, 1938, Box 12, Lane Papers.

19. LIW to RWL, [March 20, 22, 1937], Box 13, Lane Papers.

20. Miller, *Laura Ingalls Wilder's Little Town,* chap. 6.

21. RWL to LIW, December 19, 1937, Box 13, Lane Papers.

22. LIW, undated response to RWL's letter of December 19, 1937, LIW, undated notes on "Silver Lake," [ca. February 1938], LIW to RWL, January 26, [1938], Box 13, Lane Papers.

23. Ibid., RWL to LIW, January 21, 1938, LIW to RWL, January 25, 1938.

24. Ibid., LIW to RWL, January 28, February 15, 19, 1938.

25. The *Mansfield Mirror* reported their departure and return (May 12, June 2, 1938). The story of their trip and the places they visited is recounted in Burkhiser, *Neta, Laura's Friend,* 11–18; see also *De Smet News,* June 3, 1938.

26. Burkhiser, *Neta, Laura's Friend,* 18; AJW to RWL, January 15, 1939, Box 13, Lane Papers; Anderson, *Story of the Ingalls,* 26–29.

27. RWL, Diary, August 9, 12, 1938, Box 23, Lane Papers.

28. Holtz, *Ghost in the Little House,* 287–88.

29. LIW, "To American Mothers," [1938], LIW to RWL, September 26, 1938, Box 13, Lane Papers.

30. Ibid., LIW to RWL, April 2, 10, May 23, 1939, Ida Louise Raymond to LIW, April 6, 1939.

31. *Book Review Digest* (1939), 1044.

32. LIW to RWL, May 23, 1939, Box 13, Lane Papers.

33. Ibid., June 3, 1939; *Mansfield Mirror,* June 22, 29, 1939; *De Smet News,* June 8, 15, 29, 1939; *Laura Ingalls Wilder Lore* 15 (spring–summer 1989): 1, 5.

34. LIW to RWL, January 6, February 15, 1938, March 17, 1939, Box 13, Lane Papers.

35. Ibid., March 12, 1937, January 12, 1938; Burkhiser, *Neta, Laura's Friend,* 18.

36. Burkhiser, *Neta, Laura's Friend,* 18–19.

37. LIW to RWL, February 5, March 22, 1937, May 4, 1938, April 2, 10, 1939, Box 13, Lane Papers.

38. Ibid., February 5, 1937, March 17, 1939, AJW to RWL, January 15, 1939; Burkhiser, *Neta, Laura's Friend,* 18.

39. *Mansfield Mirror,* December 16, 1937, March 17, 1938, January 19, 1939, February 15, 1940.

40. Ibid., March 25, September 16, 1937.

41. Ibid., January 26, 1939, October 10, 1940, December 24, 1942, March 4, 1943; LIW to RWL, January 27, 1939, [March 17, 1939], Box 13, Lane Papers.

42. *Mansfield Mirror,* February 15, 1940, August 26, 1943.

43. LIW to RWL, response to latter's letter of December 19, 1937, Box 13, Lane Papers. See also LIW to RWL, [ca. February 1937], August 19, 1937, May 4, 1938, February 20, 1939, Box 13, Lane Papers.

44. *Mansfield Mirror,* April 15, June 3, July 8, 1937, April 25, 1940, September 18, 1941.

45. Ibid., January 14, 1937, April 25, 1940.

46. Ibid., May 16, 1940.

47. Holtz, *Ghost in the Little House,* 308.

48. LIW to RWL, [early February 1938], February 19, March 15, 1938, Box 13, Lane Papers.

49. Ibid., January 27, May 23, 1939.

50. Ibid., February 5, March 12, 1937, February 20, March 17, April 2, 1939.

51. Ibid., [December 29, 1937, on back of recipe for dandelion wine], January 6, 1938, Carrie Ingalls Swanzey to LIW, attached to letter from LIW to RWL, May 24, 1939.

52. *Laura Ingalls Wilder Lore* 16 (spring–summer 1990): 3.

53. Holtz, *Ghost in the Little House,* 302.

54. LIW to RWL, February 15, 19, 1938, Box 13, Lane Papers.

55. Ibid., March 7, 1938.

56. Ibid., March 15, August 17, 1938.

57. Ibid., March 17, 1939; Holtz, *Ghost in the Little House,* 275, 279, 292; LIW, Draft No. 2 of *By the Shores of Silver Lake,* Missouri Historical Society, Columbia; compare this draft with the published text of the book on page 67.

58. LIW, Draft of *The Long Winter,* Missouri Historical Society, Columbia; compare LIW, *The Long Winter,* 302–7.

59. On the social history of the United States during World War II, see Geoffrey Perrett, *Days of Sadness, Years of Triumph: The American People, 1939–1945* (New York: Coward, McCann and Geohagan, 1973); William L. O'Neill, *A Democracy at War: America's Fight at Home and Abroad in World War II* (New York: Free Press,

1993); John M. Blum, *V Was for Victory: Politics and American Culture during World War II* (New York: Harcourt Brace Jovanovich, 1976).

60. *Mansfield Mirror,* October 10, 1940, June 18, July 9, August 20, November 12, December 10, 17, 1942, February 18, March 11, June 24, July 8, August 12, 1943, May 25, July 6, 1944.

61. Ibid., January 22, June 11, 1942.

62. *Book Review Digest* (1941), 958.

63. Ibid. (1943), 869.

## 9. Basking in the Glow of Her Readers' Affection, 1943–1957

1. Nava Austin interview, by the author, Mansfield, Mo., August 19, 1995; Stephen W. Hines, *I Remember Laura* (Nashville: Thomas Nelson, 1994), 121–22.

2. LIW, *The First Four Years,* 133–34.

3. Holtz, *Ghost in the Little House,* 313–14.

4. Grace Stevenson to LIW, May 27, 1942, Katherine Afonin to LIW, May 28, 1949, Robert Neuman to LIW, May 13, 1948, Dorothy Allen to LIW, May 13, 1948, Box 14, Lane Papers.

5. Ibid., LIW to Frances Mason, October 1, 1948; LIW to Aubrey Sherwood, July 29, 1942, reprinted in *De Smet News,* August 6, 1942; LIW, Composite Letter, LIW File, Missouri State Historical Society, Columbia.

6. Hines, *I Remember Laura,* 223–24, 238; Society club reports in the *Mansfield Mirror* recorded Laura's presence at a number of meetings in 1945 and 1946. See issues for January 1, October 25, 1945, January 31, July 4, October 31, 1946. On religious revivals, see the *Mirror* for July 5, 1945, July 4, 1946, June 23, 1949, July 6, 1950, July 10, 1952, June 17, 1954.

7. *Mansfield Mirror,* May 10, July 5, 12, August 9, 1945; Caroline Fraser, "The Prairie Queen," 38.

8. *Mansfield Mirror,* November 11, 1945, March 21, 1946, January 30, May 8, November 27, 1947, January 8, 1948, June 29, July 13, 1950, January 29, September 17, 1953, January 7, 1954, August 16, 1956, January 24, 1957.

9. Ibid., July 5, 1945, August 14, 1947, May 26, 1949, April 10, 1952, July 19, 1956, May 22, 1958.

10. Ibid., May 25, June 8, 1950; Richard S. Kirkendall, *History of Missouri,* chaps. 9–10.

11. *Mansfield Mirror,* January 31, July 25, August 1, 1946, May 5, 1952, January 20, 27, March 3, 1955, September 26, 1957, April 9, 1959.

12. LIW to D. L. Blocher, February 21, 1947, on display at LIW Museum, Walnut Grove, Minn.

13. Hines, *I Remember Laura,* 110–11; Nava Austin interview.

14. Clifford Cooper interview, by the author, Mansfield Mo., August 18, 1995;

Peggy Dennis interview; Dan L. White and Robert F. White, *Laura's Friends Remember* (Hartville, Mo.: Ashley-Preston, 1992), 14, 34.

15. These comments are based on conversations that the author had with people in Mansfield in August 1995.

16. Hines, *I Remember Laura*, 128, 135, 144, 224.

17. Ibid., 134, 144, 220, 224; Peggy Dennis interview; Neta Seal interview.

18. Neta Seal interview; Peggy Dennis interview; Hines, *I Remember Laura*, 110–11.

19. *Warranty Deed Record Book No. 126*, 107–8, *No. 113*, 422, 618, *No. 118*, 273, *No. 125*, 466–67; Hines, *I Remember Laura*, 111.

20. Anderson, *Story of the Wilders*, 31; Anderson, *Laura Ingalls Wilder*, 221; *Mansfield Mirror*, December 23, 1948.

21. Anderson, *Story of the Wilders*, 32; White and White, *Laura's Friends Remember*, 30–31; *Mansfield Mirror*, October 27, 1949.

22. LIW to "Dear Friend," November 19, 1949, displayed at LIW Museum, Mansfield, Mo.

23. Holtz, *Ghost in the Little House*, 315–18, 325–27.

24. Ibid., 335–37; Anderson, *Laura Ingalls Wilder*, 230; *Mansfield Mirror*, April 2, 1953; LIW, Last Will and Testament, February 6, 1952, on file at Wright County Courthouse, Hartville, Mo.; Anderson, *Story of the Ingalls*, 31.

25. Anderson, *Laura Ingalls Wilder*, 214–15; *Laura Ingalls Wilder Lore* 12 (spring–summer 1986): 3.

26. *Mansfield Mirror*, January 22, 1948, November 17, 1949, May 18, 1950, May 3, 1951. Two "Local Newsette" items in the *Mirror* noted such dinner visits, January 14, 1952, and February 12, 1953. Such local paragraphs about Laura and Almanzo were rare during the 1940s and 1950s.

27. Clifford Cooper interview; Amon Short interview; Carl Hartley interview, by the author, Mansfield, Mo., June 19, 1993; Peggy Dennis interview.

28. Clifford Cooper interview; *Mansfield Mirror*, June 6, 1940, January 9, June 12, 1947, December 28, 1948, July 19, 1951, October 30, 1952, February 10, 1955.

29. *Kansas City Star*, April 10, 1949, reprinted in *Mansfield Mirror*, May 5, 1949; see also *Mirror* issues of March 16 and August 10, 1950.

30. *Kansas City Star*, September 20, 1951; *Mansfield Mirror*, September 20, October 4, 1951, November 5, 1953, September 29, 1954.

31. *Mansfield Mirror*, November 13, 1952, October 15, November 19, 1953; see articles reprinted in William T. Anderson, ed., *The "Horn Book's" Laura Ingalls Wilder* (Horn Book, 1987); *Laura Ingalls Wilder Lore* 13 (spring–summer, 1987): 4–5 and 13 (fall–winter 1987–1988): 10.

32. Hines, *I Remember Laura*, 111–12, 120, 127, 141; Anderson, *Laura Ingalls Wilder*, 225–26.

33. Nava Austin interview; Anderson, *Laura Ingalls Wilder*, 228; Hines, *I Remember Laura*, 116, 229.

34. Carl Hartley interview; Virginia Hartley interview, by the author, Mansfield, Mo., August 19, 1995; Hines, *I Remember Laura,* 145; *Laura Ingalls Wilder Lore* 17 (spring–summer 1991): 1.

35. Cornelia Meigs et al., *A Critical History of Children's Literature* (New York: Macmillan, 1969), 414; Anderson, *Laura Ingalls Wilder,* 229–30.

36. Anderson, *Laura Ingalls Wilder,* 228; Hines, *I Remember Laura,* 117–18.

37. Anderson, *Laura Ingalls Wilder,* 230–31.

38. Ibid., 231.

39. RWL to Jasper Crane, January 5, 1957, Box 3, Lane Papers; Holtz, *Ghost in the Little House,* 337; Virginia Hartley interview.

40. *New York Times,* February 12, 1957, p. 27.

41. *Mansfield Mirror,* February 14, 1957; Virginia Hartley interview.

42. Probate Court Records in the Estate of Laura Ingalls Wilder, No. 2498, February 27, 1957, Wright County Courthouse, Hartville, Mo.; LIW to RWL, July 30, 1952, Box 14, Lane Papers.

# Index

✣

197–98, 275n20; town square, 100,
118–19, 133, 173, 246; lodges, 101;
history, 101; population, 101, 117, 173,
231, 232, 246, 247; as basis for RWL's
fiction, 103, 122; agriculture, 109–10;
as subject for LIW's writing, 117; town
boosters, 117, 118–19, 173, 231–32;
social activities, 119–20, 255–56; in
World War I, 132–35; patiarchal society,
137; automobiles, 169; recreation,
173; economic development of, 171,
174, 245–47, 255–56; during Great
Depression, 196–97; attitudes of people
toward LIW, 189, 244, 256; in World
War II, 238
Mansfield Agricultural and Stock Show,
120–21
Mansfield Grays, 173
Mansfield High School, 108, 205, 256
Mansfield Industrial Development
Corporation, 247
*Mansfield Mail*, 111
*Mansfield Mirror*, 117, 118, 119, 133, 134,
159, 163, 169, 171, 172, 174, 179,
189, 203, 208, 230, 232, 238, 244,
245, 256, 257
Mansfield, Ohio, 260
Mansfield Post Office, 213
*Mansfield Press*, 111
Mansfield Public Library, 254
Mansfield Round-Up Club, 256
Marshall, Minn., 31
"Mary and Laura" books. *See* "Laura and
Mary" books
Maryland, 23, 24, 27
Mason, Ed, 23
Mason, Frances, 244
Mason-Dixon Line, 99
Masonic Hall, 134, 234
Masonic Lodge, 19, 77, 101, 164
Massachusetts, 16, 27
Masters, Emeline, 41
Masters, Genevieve, 54, 59, 60, 68, 78
Masters, George, 55–56, 59, 236
Masters, Gussie, 68
Masters, Maggie, 55–56, 236
Masters, Sam, 55, 59
Masters, William, 37, 41, 44
Masters Hotel, 37
Mays, Carl, 256

Medary, Dakota Territory, 48
Mellette, Arthur C., 82
Memphis, Tenn., 174
Mennonites, 93
Meta, Rexh, 140, 190
Methodists, 19, 29, 42, 63, 86, 95, 102,
135, 160, 230, 244, 261
Michigan, 24
Midwest, 15, 17, 28, 61, 82
*Millbank*, 29
Miller, Bertha, 134
Milwaukee, Wis., 16, 17
Minneapolis, Minn., 215, 259
Minnesota: migration to, 16, 61; home
of Ingalls family, 30–36, 40–42; home
of Wilder family, 72, 85; as fictional
subject, 209, 210; mentioned, 18, 19,
20, 39, 46, 48, 51, 60, 62, 69, 73
Minnesota River, 31, 32
Mississippi River: sawmills on, 15; travel
on, 19, 21; mentioned, 13, 14, 18, 20,
31, 86, 240
Missouri: land purchased by Charles
Ingalls, 22; LIW and AJW move
to, 91; in Depression of 1890s, 98;
at the Panama-Pacific International
Exposition, 127; highway improvement
program, 168; automobiles, 170;
in Great Depression, 180, 196–97;
politics, 197; subject of RWL history
book, 203, 207–8, 222
*Missouri Blue Book*, 256
Missouri Development Association, 173
Missouri River, 22, 45, 46, 50, 51, 93
*Missouri Ruralist*: 4–5, 11–12, 47, 96,
115–16, 123, 124, 127, 128–32, 135,
136, 137, 138, 140, 161, 165, 170,
178, 181, 219, 245, 260, 261
Missouri State Agricultural College, 133
Missouri State Historical Society, 208
Mitchell, Alexander, 45, 46
Mitchell, Margaret, 230
Montana, 46, 226
Monterey, Calif., 170
Montgomery County, Kan., 22
Montgomery, Kan., 23
Moore, Rosa Ann, 5
Morgan, Alfred M., 254
Morgan horses, 67, 199, 229
Mountain Grove, Mo.: history, 101;